Why the Church?

D0732626

Other Books in the Reframing New Testament Theology Series
Why Salvation? by Joel B. Green
Why the Cross? by Donald Senior

Praise for *Why the Church?*

"Atheists ask, 'Why the church?' with scorn and derision. Spiritual-but-not-religious folks ask the same question with indifference. Robert Wall, an ordained Christian scholar, poses the query with both theological sympathy and acumen. Beginning with the conviction that all the New Testament is ecclesiology and using the ancient creedal description of the church as 'one, holy, catholic, and apostolic,' Wall constructs a biblical theology of the church from the groupings of the canonical writings. He tackles the pluriform witness of scripture and produces a coherent, if complex, portrait of the followers of Jesus. The result is a work of theological interpretation and canonical criticism that is impressive in its own right and also a model of how such thematic study can be done. Biblical theology, like Jonathan Swift's Gulliver, has too often been tied down by a thousand higher-critical quibbles and qualifications, like so many Lilliputian cords. In this volume—without any *sacrificium intellectus*—Gulliver breaks free."

—N. Clayton Croy, Professor of New Testament, Trinity Lutheran Seminary, Columbus, OH

"Greater clarity and emphasis on a doctrine of the church is an urgent task for Protestant churches, and Rob Wall has provided a cogent and powerful analysis of New Testament resources for such a doctrine."

—Scott J. Jones, Bishop, Great Plains Area, The United Methodist Church

"In this fascinating monograph, Rob Wall brings his skills as theologian, interpreter, and minister to bear, producing a most helpful volume on the church. Reading the New Testament documents through a canonical lens, Wall traces the themes of the church as one, holy, catholic, and apostolic. Through his superb engagement with the biblical text, he demonstrates that these themes are not superimposed upon the New Testament writings but arise rather naturally from them. Reflecting on these and related themes by means of the energetic embrace of scripture for which he is known, Wall provides the reader with a relevant, thoughtful, and at times prophetic study of the church in its contemporary postmodern context. This book by a leading Wesleyan New Testament scholar is a welcome gift for all those interested in exploring this topic academically and pastorally."

—John Christopher Thomas, Clarence J. Abbott Professor of Biblical Studies, Pentecostal Theological Seminary, Cleveland, TN

Reframing New Testament Theology
Edited by Joel B. Green

Why the Church?

ROBERT W. WALL

Abingdon Press™

Nashville

WHY THE CHURCH?

Copyright © 2015 by Abingdon Press

All rights reserved.

No part of this work may be reproduced or transmitted in any form or by any means, electronic or mechanical, including photocopying and recording, or by any information storage or retrieval system, except as may be expressly permitted by the 1976 Copyright Act or in writing from the publisher. Requests for permission should be addressed to Permissions, Abingdon Press, 2222 Rosa L. Parks Blvd., PO Box 280988, Nashville, TN 37228-0988 or permissions@umpublishing.org.

This book is printed on acid-free paper.

Library of Congress Cataloging-in-Publication Data has been requested.

ISBN 978-1-4267-5938-3

All scripture quotations unless noted otherwise are from the Common English Bible. Copyright © 2011 by the Common English Bible. All rights reserved. Used by permission. www.CommonEnglishBible.com.

Scripture quotations marked (NRSV) are taken from the New Revised Standard Version of the Bible, copyright 1989, Division of Christian Education of the National Council of the Churches of Christ in the United States of America. Used by permission. All rights reserved.

Scripture quoted by permission. Quotations designated (NET) are from the NET Bible" copyright ©1996-2006 by Biblical Studies Press, L.L.C. http://netbible.com All rights reserved.

Scripture quotations marked (NASB) are taken from the New American Standard Bible", Copyright © 1960, 1962, 1963, 1968, 1971, 1972, 1973, 1975, 1977, 1995 by The Lockman Foundation. Used by permission. (www.Lockman.org)

Scripture quotations marked (AT) are the author's own translation.

15 16 17 18 19 20 21 22 23 24—10 9 8 7 6 5 4 3 2 1

MANUFACTURED IN THE UNITED STATES OF AMERICA

Contents

Foreword

At first glance, the phrase "New Testament theology" seems clear enough. However, attempts to explain it immediately expose some speed bumps. Do we want to describe the theology we find in the New Testament? Construct a theology on a New Testament foundation? Or perhaps sketch an account of early Christian beliefs and practices from the New Testament era? This series of books frames the question in a different way: How do we take seriously that, together with the Old Testament, the New Testament has in the past and ought in the present inform, form, and transform the church's faith and life?

Almost everyone will agree that the New Testament books concern themselves with *theology*. This truism is supported on almost every page as New Testament writers speak of God, the significance of Jesus of Nazareth for God's agenda for the world, the character of God's people, faithful life before God, and God's coming to set the world right.

How does the New Testament witness relate to the church's life today? This is less clear and therefore more controversial. The church affirms its allegiance to the God of whom scripture speaks and, therefore, ties itself, its faith and witness, to the Old and New Testaments. How the church's affirmations work themselves out in terms of engagement with the New Testament materials—this is the question.

Reframing New Testament Theology gets at this question by encouraging active, theological engagement with the New Testament itself. Readers will find among the books in this series an awareness of the obstacles we face—obstacles like the following:

- New Testament texts were written in another time and another place. In what sense, then, can we say that they were written *to* us or *for* us? After all, those first readers of Matthew's Gospel or the Letter of James would be dumbstruck by the idea of streaming video in a church service, just as most of us lack any firsthand experience with anything analogous to the challenges of peasant farmers and fisherfolk in ancient Galilee.

- What of the sheer variety of voices we hear among the New Testament books? If we want the New Testament to help orient our thinking about mission or salvation, how do we make sense of the different perspectives we sometimes encounter? Do we accord privilege to some voices over others? Do we try to synthesize various viewpoints?

- New Testament writers raise issues that may seem foreign to us today and overlook some of our contemporary concerns. Our educational systems, political structures, immigration policies, knowledge of the universe, modes of transportation, and the countless other day-to-day realities that we take for granted separate us from the equally countless assumptions, beliefs, and behaviors that characterized people living in the ancient Mediterranean world. Faced with these differences, how do we work with scripture?

Additionally, our readers will find an awareness of a range of questions about how best to think about "New Testament theology"—questions like these:

- Since the "new" in "New Testament" presumes an "Old Testament," what status should our New Testament theological explorations assign to the Old Testament? How do we understand the theological witness of the New Testament in relation to the Old?

- Are we concerned primarily with what the New Testament writers *taught* (past tense) their first readers theologically, or do we want to know what the New Testament *teaches* (present tense) us? Is "New Testament theology" a descriptive task or a prescriptive one?

- Do we learn from the New Testament writers the "stuff" of Christian theology, or do we apprentice ourselves to them so that we might learn how to engage in the theological task ourselves? Does the New Testament provide the raw material for contemporary theology, or does it invite us into ongoing reflection with it about God and God's ways?

If contributions to this series demonstrate an awareness of obstacles and issues like these, this does not mean that they address them in a uniform manner. Nor are these books concerned primarily with showing how to navigate or resolve conundrums like these. What holds this series together is not a particular set of methodological commitments but a keen sense that scripture has in the past and should in the present instruct and shape the church's faith and life. What does it mean to engage the New Testament from within the church and for the church?

One further consideration: The church turns to the scriptures believing that the Bible is authoritative for what we believe and what we do, but it does so while recognizing that the church's theology is shaped in other ways, too—by God's self-disclosure in God's "book of nature," for example—and in relation to the ecumenical creeds with which the church has identified itself: the Apostles' Creed, the Nicene Creed, and the Athanasian Creed. Not surprisingly, New Testament "theology" invites reflecting on, interacting with, learning from, and sometimes struggling with the scriptures, and doing so in relation to human understanding more generally as well as in the context of our common Christian confessions.

Intended for people interested in studying the New Testament and the nature of the Christian message and the Christian life, for classrooms, group interaction, and personal study, these volumes invite readers into a conversation with New Testament theology.

Joel B. Green
General Editor

Acknowledgments

I am indebted to many congregations of different communions whose fellowship, instruction, and worship over many years have shaped my deep love for God's church. My sensibility as a scholar of and for God's people is founded in that holy and happy experience. In particular, I mention First Free Methodist Church of Seattle, a beloved family of believers with whom I currently serve on the pastoral staff as scholar-in-residence. My work on the faculty of Seattle Pacific University and Seminary is another rich source of constant delights and illuminations. I thank especially those undergraduate students who gathered with me during fall quarter, 2012, to work our way through the New Testament's teaching about the church. The raw materials of this book were mined in conversation with them. Thanks, friends! And to the wonderful band of colleagues who teach scripture, theology, and ministry alongside me at the university and at the seminary, I admit my dependence upon your brilliance, your daily wisdom, and especially your faithful friendship. In particular, I thank Daniel Castelo and Rick Steele (theology), Bob Drovdahl (ministry), Dave Nienhuis (New Testament), and Doug Strong (dean) for their friendship and intellectual hospitality.

To Hope McPherson and Kelsey Rorem, for their careful reading of the manuscript and indispensable help in crafting the chapter summaries. To my research assistants, Nathan Sosnovske and C. Adam Baker, for helping me track down answers to all kinds of questions that sometimes led us on wild-goose chases and down rabbit trails. But what fun we had! Thank you all again and again.

To my beloved companion and remarkable conversation partner during our forty-five years together: Carla, I thank God for all of the precious gifts you bring into the lives of so many people, especially into mine. But now, let me simply express my thanks to you, once again, for your help commenting on and editing early drafts of this book.

Words fail to express the sheer delight our granddaughter, Aria, brings into our lives. Daily! What constant fun she is and what renewed hope she inspires in us. Our prayer is that the church, which has baptized her into God's saving grace, will continue to nurture her faith and to guide her life as God's daughter. This book is dedicated to you, Aria Michel Scheffler, with my love and thanksgiving.

Chapter One

Why the Church?

T he title of this book raises a common but hard question: Why the church? Many have attempted to answer it. Even a cursory review of their various responses notes that this question is typically prompted and shaped by a range of different intellectual postures forged in various social worlds. Each response may suggest a different approach to a study of the New Testament's response to this question.

For example, the question "why the church?" may well be asked by those believers who are disaffected with the institutional church. Some sociologists have even pegged this group as an entire generation that has migrated into a post-Christian era with a firm perception of the church's cultural irrelevance or naiveté. "Why the church?" is a typical question asked, then, by believers of a certain age with a shrug of their shoulders, whose observations of the church's declining public role or role in their own lives have left them spiritually unfulfilled and intellectually indifferent.

Similar to other seminarians, in a poll we took of our incoming students, more than 80 percent expressed no interest in becoming members of the clergy. Most came from "nondenominational" congregations without any connection to other congregations held together in formal institutional structures, a common discipline, and confession of faith. These students are more entrepreneurial, interested in start-ups and ad hoc ministries of one kind or another. It has become increasingly difficult to speak of scripture as the "church's book" or of an approach to its interpretation as "for and of" the church to students so rootless and restless.

Familiar reasons are sometimes given to explain why this disaffection with the institutional or denominational church has happened. In a recent study of current trends within the religious world, George Barna observes that the decline in church attendance, especially noticeable among educated young adults, is due to a perceived disconnect between the social patterns and intellectual interests of the church culture they have experienced growing up and the nonreligious world in which they now work and live. Surveys tell us that they still believe in God and even in the Bible's characterization of God. Many claim to practice prayer and believe in life after death, even if they do so only to the extent that it doesn't cross the line into superstition; mystery is fine but magic is not. Despite the evident influence of new and functional atheisms about the way in which Christians think about their faith, these surveys suggest that the reasons are less intellectual than they are existential. Their growing disaffection is for a particular kind of faith community, not for the community's faith.[1]

Barna's survey includes "nomadic" Christians who are no longer attending church. This book aims to put their dis-ease to rights. For example, the failure of the church to speak into the "real world" in which most live and work may be challenged by the biblical vision of a missional church. At the same time, the church sometimes presents and even demonizes the social world as corrupt, making it at odds with the everyday experience of most people. The result is the impression of a "straw man" gospel that is largely irrelevant to the real questions most Christians ask: So "why the church" when one's churchly experience is thought optional or a waste of time? A more careful description of the workplace and neighborhood may help guide the application of scripture's teaching about the church to the church. This is also true when people are surveyed about their theological education. Studies reveal that most Christians come to church only to find that God has gone missing from the pulpit or from educational programming. In a word, the church, by and large, has failed to catechize its membership in the theological goods of the faith. So first, the problem of the church is not its material presence—it's not unhip architecture or even the church's presumed civil role within the public square. The problem is not edificial but spiritual: for many, the church is not a place where they go to find God.

The so-called new atheism is a mostly political movement whose press releases by famous pundits and entertainers have far outstripped its now wan-

---

1. This observation is thematic of several studies recently published by the Barna Group, but perhaps none is more fully developed and nuanced than George Barna, *Grow Your Church from the Outside: Understanding the Unchurched and How to Reach Them* (Ventura, CA: Regal Books, 2009).

ing influence. But the hard question remains: What do these skeptics tell us about the status of today's church, since their rejection of God is rarely for purely intellectual reasons and is more typically rooted in an experience of church or its membership? Perhaps it is a general apprehension of the public church that allows the movement's intellectual leaders (e.g., Richard Dawkins and Daniel Dennett) to get away with uncritical, inaccurate caricatures of theism, as though it is the source of all that is wrong with modern culture. They ask "why the church?" with scorn and ridicule. Unfortunately, many educated believers have found that the church is unable to explain adequately the relationship between faith and science/reason, at least in a thoughtful way that would help them negotiate their Christian faith in a secular workplace or public classroom where the veracity of a strictly secular worldview is assumed. Naturalism or materialism, to some disaffected believers, seems to be a better intellectual explanation of the real world than the kingdom of God.

The popular definition of true religion has less to do with theological beliefs and more to do with lifestyle issues. In part, this is due to the investment of social media as brokers of religious discourse in the economy; the central topics of social media concern the ethics of human relationships. The perceived problem is not only the inability of many communions to speak in decisively biblical ways into the many hot-button social issues that confront the membership of any public institution (e.g., war on terror, homosexual marriage, immigration reform, or gun violence) but also the inherently discriminating effect that applying the Christian gospel will surely have. While the global church is "catholic" by every meaningful index, it is also exclusive in its core beliefs and traditional practices. Precisely as a public institution, the church's life in the world is distinguishable from other institutions. For a growing number of young believers, shaped by an ethos of tolerance and inclusivity, then, their conflict with the exclusive character of their faith has turned some against the institution itself.

The liberal ethos of modernity, of course, is naturally suspicious of traditional authorities, especially when they may derail or shortchange the individual's freedom to make his or her own choices. The canons and creeds of Christian faith draw boundaries in a way that place any transgressor outside its embrace. Indeed, scripture's objection to those who doubt God does not play well in a modern world where this very thing is celebrated as a growing-up experience. The purpose of this book does not include some heady prognosis for this dis-ease, but it will seek to construct a NT conception of God's people that will help address, if only implicitly, the practical concerns of disaffected Christians.

The second problem is theological, mostly Protestant, and concerns the lack of an ecclesiology to underwrite the community's grammar of faith. For all of the interest recently vested by professional theologians in a dogmatic explanation of "church," especially to explain new global phenomena such as Pentecostal/charismatic movements or ecumenical/interfaith dialogue, there is noticeable inattention given to it in ancillary, often contentious, discussions of Christian beliefs. The question "why the church?" may therefore be asked by puzzled students with a scratch of their heads, who wonder how ecclesiology might contribute to discussions about the authority of the church's scripture, the economy of God's salvation, or God's mission in the world to establish God's kingdom on earth as it now is in heaven.

If God's people formed the NT in order to help form itself into the church, then it follows that, in a sense, all of the NT is ecclesiology; its study implicates readers in a range of discussions that concern what it means to belong to God's people and to believe and behave as they ought. The crisis is not only that the lack of a robust ecclesiology in these various theological discussions impoverishes them intellectually; the crisis is also existential, since the failure to treat scripture's address, which is ecclesial, subverts its formative role in shaping a community who continues to experience the risen One and to proclaim him in word and deed for the world.

This book responds to the neglect of this topic for those students in search of a biblical understanding of the church, and perhaps then on this basis to lead them in the spiritual renewal of their congregations. What scripture animates is a vision of God's people, not a blueprint of congregational renewal or clergy reform but an inspiring witness of God's providential sojourn with God's people that cultivates in its readers the wisdom necessary to think and respond to the demanding vocation of being the church in and for our own day.

Does God Need the Church?

As important as it is to consider different reasons why people might question or defend their need for the church, more pertinent is the *theological* question as to whether God needs the church, especially one whose failures are notorious! Isn't even the suggestion that our omni-God should need anything outrageous? Still more ludicrous is that God should require the services of a stumbling, bumbling church that only gets in God's way! And yet any student who prepares to study scripture's conception of the church must face this challenging question: Why does God elect and bring a particular people into existence to love and treasure and to commission and call? After all, God, being an omni-God, doesn't act without good reason. Why the church?

Three broad lines of argument may be useful in sketching an answer to this question: the church provides a home for a covenant-making God, the church actively participates with God in a shared mission to save the world, and the church bears passive witness to the gracious operations of a saving God.

Church as God's Home

We should agree that the persona of the triune God is sociable. We observe this in the intimate, familial manner of the Son's address of the Father according to the Gospels: Jesus calls God "Father" and God calls Jesus "beloved Son." They enjoy each other's company and seek to work together in common projects. Not surprisingly, then, we gladly observe that God needs a home in which to dwell with God's adopted children; the church provides God with such a home. Ephesians 2:22 stands as a stunning witness to this belief. An interpersonal God needs a home and a family with whom to fellowship and love and from whom to receive worship and love. Moreover, especially John's apostolic tradition speaks of believers as God's birth children (not adopted) in whom God abides forever. It strikes me that the more active roles in which the church engages on God's behalf are deeply rooted in this primary idea: the church provides God a place to dwell in full deity and doxological praise.

Church as God's Partner

The book of Acts begins with a succession story that moves the ministry of the risen Jesus, who is soon to depart into the heavens, into the apostles-led, Spirit-filled messianic community that he leaves behind. What is clear from this opening story in Acts is that God does not intend to end salvation's history with the risen messiah's ascension; the Lord's departure, rather, marks the beginning of "the last days" (cf. Acts 2:17) leading up to God's final victory over death. In fact, the Spirit's promised baptism, soon to arrive with light and sound effects at Pentecost, purposes to empower the community's membership to continue what the departed Jesus had begun to do and say (Acts 1:1, 8). While God's reign was brought near and established by Jesus's messianic mission, its future is heralded and even anticipated by the church's ongoing mission in his absence. The narrative of Acts cultivates the sense that the church is a necessary feature of the economy of God's salvation, not merely the human agent of God's saving grace in the world. The church provides public testimony of the real results of God's grace to herald its final triumph in a new creation. The reader may allow, then, that the church as the earthly body of the departed Christ is presently needed as both agent and witness of God's saving grace until Christ returns.

However, the question of whether the church's existence is necessary to the *missio Dei* is rarely benign, asked by the naïve but serious student interested in tracking down a topic of evident theological importance in the NT. In an increasingly post-Christian world, this question is asked with deep suspicion even by thoughtful Christians: Why is the church necessary? Certainly God, being God, doesn't need anyone or anything to do what God has promised to do according to scripture. But if the believer responds that God doesn't need the church to accomplish the work of salvation, then one is allowed to cast suspicion on the continuing relevance of scripture, the sacraments, or any ecclesial practice that we might otherwise consider providential in the economy of God. Christianity would devolve into a spectator sport, awaiting God's magical performances and nothing more.

Church as God's Witness

In his important book, Gerhard Lohfink famously asks, "Does God need the church?"—an evocative question asked rhetorically and firmly, assuming an affirmative response.[2] Lohfink admits that it is not self-evident that God should require anything from anyone—that a sovereign God should *need* the church is nothing short of miraculous because, he argues, participation with God is both consistent with the nature of who God is and aligns with scripture's witness to God's saving activities in the world.

I would note that Lohfink's argument doesn't turn on the missional church's agency as a broker of God's salvation during the absence of the ascended Christ, even if the portrait of God's people in Acts may allow for this; rather, the church is needed precisely because God needs a people to freely choose God's grace in order to demonstrate (or "proclaim") the way of salvation in healing creation with integrity (cf. Eph 3:8-13). Indeed, there are alternate ways of dealing with creation's brokenness, and these are evident in the biblical story of creation. Stories of deception, violence, mob rule, and

---

2. Gerhard Lohfink, *Does God Need the Church? Toward a Theology of the People of God* (Collegeville, MN: Liturgical Press, 1999), esp. 1–50, 203–310.

Babel, all found in the opening chapters of Genesis, indicate different political approaches in ordering a broken creation. Apart from God's grace, however, the world would still be populated by those who are "not a people," still shrouded in darkness outside of God's "amazing light" (1 Pet 2:9-10). But enabled by and reliant upon grace, God's own people are preserved through time as the instantiation of "God's life-giving and enduring word" (1 Pet 1:23-25).

The narratives of two mighty acts of creation in making the world (Gen 1) and electing Israel (Gen 12; Exod 19–20) explain why God needs the church's partnership in sustaining the economy of grace. The plotline of God's creation, introduced in Genesis 1, follows a week of mighty acts beginning with a formless and darkened earth and ending with a hallowed earth filled with a surplus of "very good" creatures. As such, the biblical story of creation is a narrative of grace-filled redemption that depicts the material transformation of a real place. Of course, the reader may well imagine that God, being God, could have executed this creative act in any number of ways and for any number of different ends. But this biblical narrative of creation testifies that the creator-savior of the universe did so by commanding the earth to participate in the creative process, and so the earth did (Gen 1:11-12); and then by making humankind in God's likeness to fill and steward it to the ends of the earth (Gen 1:26-28), and so humankind did so, although with limited success.

Two elements of scripture's opening narrative introduce nonnegotiable beliefs about the nature of God that may help explain why one might allow that God "needs" the church. Not only does a wholly gracious God exist prior to all things, whose word is necessary not only to their creaturely existence but also to their redemption as active participants in a "very good" world, but also God chooses to collaborate with those creatures so that they participate in God's creative, redemptive work. Christians also believe that in creating humankind in God's own image, God made humans free to make similar choices. For us to participate with God in the economy of grace requires a decision to do so, and people are made "very good" but hardly "perfect"! The risk of God's doing so is quickly made clear, since the earth God once observed as very good is soon filled with evil (Gen 6:11-12). The motion of history and the movement of redemption within it is an exercise of risk management, since the freedom God grants humankind at creation is never withdrawn. God's intuition to redeem what is formless and lifeless and to choose to do so in partnership with creatures that are free to choose to remain formless and lifeless is a central feature of the history of salvation according to scripture.

In this sense, then, God already knows the risk of covenanting with humankind for the work of stewarding creation, especially following Babel's misplaced hubris. God's election of Abraham and Sarah's progeny for the work of grace in blessing the families of earth is surely a case study in risk management! But the aesthetic of salvation follows the order of creation. Even as God creates people on the sixth day to steward the land God had created on the third day, which reflects the symmetry of a well-designed, life-producing earth, so also God elects a particular people to occupy a particular land as stewards of the salvation God promises to all the families of earth. God calls out this couple to freely choose to trust God's way of ordering life. The biblical narrative of Abraham and Sarah's struggle to do so suggests that their decision to trust God is counterintuitive. Freedom is necessary to the providential operations of divine grace and divine grace is necessary to the experience of salvation. That is, God chooses a particular family in the fullness of time with whom to covenant for the work of salvation, but God needs members of that family to obey the mandate God has given them for the sake of the other families of the earth.

There is nothing inherently special about the elected people; they are special precisely because God has given them a task to perform, although mostly passive, of providing nations with a creaturely witness to the nature of God's salvation. This includes humanity's freedom to receive and to use God's gift of salvation while not under duress to do so. Moreover, the result of grace, freely used, is transformed existence as promised. That is, the promise of God's grace is for a real change and not one cast in mere forensic terms at heaven's door.

Canon and Creed

A theological interpretation of scripture, whatever its iteration, does not bring a particular modern "criticism" to the biblical text but rather a range of theological interests as ancient as the church. Its practitioners not only recognize the Bible's theological nature as a witness to God's saving work in history, similar to that of NT writers, but also expect that the interpretive ends of careful exegesis are also theological and ecclesial in nature. That is, if scripture is approached as a revelatory text, then its application by faithful readers should anticipate the retrieval of exegetical materials that will fund theological understanding whose effective yield is life with God. Among the most important ways to demonstrate this deeply spiritual sensibility is to regulate a reading of scripture by the church's apostolic rule of faith.[3] What follows attempts to briefly introduce this claim, which organizes this particular study of the NT theology of the church.

The practical problem of such a task is the surplus, not scarcity, of the theological resources at a reader's disposal. In fact, one could say that the NT from beginning to end is about the church—what it means to be God's people and do as they ought. In part, this is because the Bible is the church's book, shaped and sized from beginning to end to size and shape the church. Every scripture is divinely inspiring to form God's people into a covenant-keeping community, a light to the nations. There remains, then, a practical problem of how best to organize these diverse textual materials into a working resource for faithful readers to use with theological profit.

The decision to use the Niceno-Constantinopolitan (381 CE, hereafter "Nicene") creedal formulation of the church as "one, holy, catholic, and apostolic" as typological of a biblical conception of the church may strike some readers as odd, since to use a creed to order scriptural goods is to use something external to scripture itself.[4] But this criticism, if made, seems surprising since the tendency since the Reformation, especially among the "free" traditions of Protestantism, is to dismiss the creed as a mere summary of the real thing: why settle for the creed when you can read *sola scriptura* in full measure? But this move, which supposes that the creed is scripture written in shorthand, is reductionist, not only because it mistakes the proper function of creeds but also because it often overlooks that the creed is not a faithful summary of scripture's metanarrative since it nowhere mentions Israel. Not very legible shorthand!

Others may object to this typological move for theological reasons, arguing in forensic idiom that the four marks (one, holy, catholic, and apostolic) describe the church not as the world sees it but as God does because of Jesus. The confessing church, they claim, is not to mark out a social institution but a spiritual one known only to God; its purpose is doxological, not ecclesiological. Or similarly, the marks actually belong to God's kingdom. In this regard,

---

3. Robert W. Wall, "Reading the Bible from within Our Traditions: The 'Rule of Faith' in Theological Hermeneutics," in *Between Two Horizons: Spanning New Testament Studies and Systematic Theology*, ed. Joel B. Green and Max Turner (Grand Rapids: Eerdmans, 1999), 88–107. See also my commentary, Robert W. Wall, *1 & 2 Timothy and Titus*, Two Horizons New Testament Commentary (Grand Rapids: Eerdmans, 2012), in which I attempt to illustrate this interpretive practice with a biblical text.

4. In my reading of the evidence, the Nicene Creed works best as a creedal rubric for biblical theological interpretation not because it is the earliest but because it is based on a broad theological consensus that emerged from the first seven great ecumenical conferences of the ecumenical church (West and East) at Nicaea (1 and 2), Constantinople (1, 2, and 3), Ephesus, and Chalcedon. In this sense, then, it represents the church's most mature creedal analogy of apostolic faith at roughly the same time that the church recognized the final form of its biblical canon.

the church's confession of itself stipulates the four principal predicates of its peculiar vocation to represent God's reign in the world.

Both the Nicene Creed and NT canon were formed along parallel historical tracks as analogies of apostolic faith. Both are read and used together in Christian worship, the one targeting the other. The question concerns the nature of this interdependency. This book is organized by a particular answer to this question: the creed is *hermeneutical* of the canon. That is, the creed helps the interpreter locate and extract theological goods from the canon for use in a variety of Bible practices. In this sense, the Nicene Creed's four rubrics provide sufficient cover for a reading of the biblical text that elaborates what the community confesses to be true.

In this regard, surely the essential function of the creed's dense formulations is to delineate the church's theological consensus. Any truly ecumenical dialogue among different Christian communions begins there. Simply put, the creed supplies the church's theological agreements about what the church is: one, holy, catholic, and apostolic. Scripture is wrapped around these agreements to provide various witnesses to what each mark might mean. In this sense, any one of these biblical witnesses (e.g., Pauline or Petrine) articulates an indispensable yet insufficient definition of the church. The norm is a whole consisting of different yet integral parts (e.g., Pauline *and* Petrine).

At its core, the idea of the "church" translates the common Greek word *ekklēsia* and refers to a gathering place or voluntary assembly. The prefix *ek-* denotes a separation from something or someone in order to form a connection with something or someone else. The verbal noun to which *ek-* is attached, *klēsis*, imagines that this act of separation responds to a summons, call, or invitation. Especially, the Pauline use of "call" demonstrates the nature of the covenant relationship between God and God's people shaped by this divine summons.

At the same time, God "calls" people to obedience in the proclaimed gospel—an act of freedom made possible by grace but never coerced by it; this is a call of conversation to the risen Christ. In this sense, the act of freely trusting in God's decision to accept Christ's faithfulness even unto death as an acceptable sacrifice for humanity's sins is an act of separation from prior allegiance—a "repentance" or change of mind that chooses Christ in defiance against "pointless thinking" ignorant (and worse) of the gospel truth (Eph 4:17-19). Logically, this idea of "call" is routinely used in the NT as a metaphor of divine election: converts to Jesus gather together as an elect community with a special (or sacred) vocation to heed as agent and herald in the economy of God's salvation (see previously under "Does God Need the Church?" section). This act of separation, then, is more functional: the church separates itself from other works in order to engage in the covenant community's peculiar moral and religious practices.

Both the biblical canon and ecumenical creed provide normative witnesses of this called community to help forge its identity as a people belonging to God. The question remains: What is the relationship between them? In particular, why should the interpreter use the creed's confession of faith to order the canon's theological goods? While each performs different liturgical and curricular roles within the community, there are good historical and theological reasons for linking the two together, one glossing the other.

In the first place, they share a common referent: each is analogical of the apostolic rule of faith. In this sense, both articulate in different forms what the apostles witnessed of the historical Jesus concerning "the word of life" (1 John 1:1). The creed is a summary not of scripture but of an apostolic grammar that announces God's self-presentation incarnate in Jesus.

The Nicene Creed is selected for use because its ecumenical scope is coextensive with the canon of scripture. The creeds found in scripture (e.g., 1 Tim 2:4-7; 3:16) and then in various regions of the earliest church were localized to particular apostolic traditions or geographic regions. The gathering of bishops in Nicaea in 325 intended to bring unity to an increasingly diverse and expanding church threatened by intramural contests of one kind or another; in this sense, scripture and creed are similar innovations that serve similar ends: the formation of a common faith of the church, catholic and apostolic. For this reason, the formula "I believe," which characterized most earlier confessions linked as they were to the baptismal vows of individual converts, was replaced by "we believe" to fix and assert the core theological agreements of the entire community. In this sense, the authority of the community's creed and its scripture, both confirmed by the episcopacy, is based upon its epistemic role to unify a divided church and its spiritual role to form the identity of Christ's disciples.

Even the history of forming each follows roughly a similar chronology, stimulated by a range of similar crises, mostly intramural, and concluded roughly at the same time in the fourth century. The subsequent shift of language at Chalcedon (451 CE) from "we believe" to "we teach" probably reflects the fixing of the Nicene Creed's shape and dogmatic centers for reasons similar to scripture's canonization, which had already fixed its contents, if not quite yet its final form, a generation before Chalcedon. But the variety of contested issues, historical, literary, and theological, that swirl around the modern discussion of canonization or the Niceno-Constantinopolitan councilor procedure will not concern us. I would only allow that the legal address of both creed and canon is the church; the authority we grant both the confessed creed and the studied canon is rooted in the belief that the Spirit also dwells there with faithful congregants confirming the truth of each analogy of faith.

Even though canon and creed are of a piece, sharing both common referent (rule of faith) and purpose (faith formation), one observes that they are used differently by the church as Spirit-directed auxiliaries of Christ's continuing communication with his disciples. Even if Robert W. Jenson is right in arguing that one should not be read or confessed without grasping the other,[5] how so? Put simply, this book's heuristic use of the creed to order scripture's teaching about the church seems apropos of their working relationship, and so we will proceed accordingly.

According to the Nicene Creed, four material marks define the nature of the Spirit-directed church: one, holy, catholic, and apostolic. Many admit that they are ready markers of the church's failure to live up to God's calling, and so the creed rehearses each mark as a reminder of what the community isn't, making it ever more aware of its need for God's grace both to forgive and to transform a redeemed people with Christ into the people they have already become in Christ. In this sense, they present as a normative ecclesiology a vision of God's people put to rights. The measure of Christian hope this vision presents is nicely captured in the final chapters of Revelation where the eschatological community at last dwells in the New Jerusalem as one holy, catholic, and apostolic people. But there is no sharp dualism here; this future hope is the conclusion of a process of becoming that people, already realized in small steps as a faithful congregation becomes more united, more holy, more inclusive, and more obedient to apostolic teaching.

Note that I mention that this is so of a "faithful congregation." Creeds tend to write things large. But scripture mostly addresses local congregations of believers. The reader should keep in mind that, like politics, all hermeneutics is local hermeneutics! Individual congregations of a particular communion will recognize these marks differently and will doubtless find their own challenges in making good on what each represents. Yes, we can speak, but only with abstractions, of a global church. Believers belong to local congregations, and there is where the biblical rubber meets a road paved with all kinds of cultural pressures and theological traditions that require their own applications of NT instruction.

---

5. Robert W. Jenson, *Canon and Creed*, Interpretation: Resources for the Use of Scripture in the Church (Louisville: Westminster John Knox, 2010), 11–18.

So these marks are understood and practiced in various ways, whether as social benchmarks or moral practices. But they are, first and foremost, core beliefs of what God has in mind for God's people and thereby constitute a theological way of thinking about the church's creaturely existence as the body of Christ. Each marker also elaborates on the essential meaning of the "church" as a people who have responded in faith to God's summons to separate themselves from all of those prior allegiances that are contrary to the economy of God.

A final caveat about the creedal typology of the church that emerges from my discussion that follows: The reader will note a keen "Protestant" (or Pauline) emphasis on the missional church—an activist community called and sent out into the world as an agent and herald of God's victory over death. But these are also marks of the worshipping community that gathers as a people in the company of the triune God who is perfectly one, holy, catholic, and apostolic. Simply put, then, these are also the marks of worship that direct a people to God who alone is worthy to receive their praise, honor, glory, and blessing.

The Church Is One

Following the theological discourse regarding in what sense God may actually "need" the church (see previously under "Does God Need the Church?" section), the reader may rightly understand oneness in terms of the community's distinctive role as the chosen herald and agent of God's saving grace; there is no other community like it—in terms of its uniqueness rather than its unity (as most understand this mark). Its way of life and worship is viewed by outsiders as peculiar: the church as the one and only of its kind.

Yet, scripture teaches that God despises division within the covenant community. For this reason, Paul encourages his readers to "make an effort to preserve the unity of the Spirit with the peace that ties you together" (Eph 4:3). A divided body of Christ dulls the spiritual senses, making it difficult to discern the ways of God (Isa 29:9-24). In general terms, then, the church is a community called out of the world in such a way that the nonbelieving world recognizes that it does not belong to the world and, consequently, hates Jesus followers because of it (cf. John 17:14). Given the world's perception, it is difficult to imagine a conception of church unity that is a property of the "invisible" church. The church is indivisible but surely not invisible! Its public solidarity in faith and mission is a mark of the church's creaturely existence in the world. Jesus even goes on to allow that the community is sanctified by his revelatory word (John 17:17), which makes the separation between community and the world blatantly self-evident. So evident, in fact, that the world, even though hostile toward God and God's people, might eventually come to believe that God so loves the world so that none should perish but all should have eternal life by trusting in God (John 3:16; cf. 17:23).

The historic antipathy against the schisms and sects of a divided church is deeply rooted in a similar notion of separation such that no community can name itself truly "Christian" if it has separated itself from the manner of life and substance of faith defined by the church's biblical canon and ecumenical creed. Put differently, a reformation movement that ultimately separates itself from "the church" is led by the Spirit to do so, only because that church is demonstrably false as evinced by either confessing a creed of falsehoods (or no creed at all) or by refusing to accept the teaching of the biblical canon as God's word. God's call is to a singular hope, faith, and baptism and to one Lord and God (Eph 4:4-6); but it must be the mature understanding of this unity of faith precisely to resist a schismatic church (Eph 4:14-16).

In any case, the mark of Christian unity is not a uniformity of worship styles or even theological grammars. The pluriformity within the one church is mirrored by the pluriformity of witnesses found within scripture. Recognizing that its own diversity harbors within it the threat of division, believers assemble together in all their variety under a common confession of core theological agreements and related moral and spiritual practices stipulated by scripture, such that there is a striking family resemblance between the exuberant Pentecostalism of the developing world and the traditional Catholicism of the first world.

As we make our way through the NT, we will seek to gather all of those ideas and images of a community of believers who gather together with one heart and soul, whose peculiarity in the world is noted by whom it worships and also by its resurrection practices. At the same time, readers should take note of those warnings against a divided people whose disunity results from divisive practices or wrong beliefs. For this reason, the essential question invited by this mark is this: How does the church's solidarity distinguish its membership from other social groups?

The Church Is Holy

The church is holy because the Spirit of the risen One who calls it into existence is holy. The church's membership constitutes a "holy nation," because it is elected by and belongs to a holy God (1 Pet 2:9; cf. Exod 19:6; Isa 43:20-

21). This marker, then, is not self-evident because the church's ordinary life is rarely pure; the church is holy because God is eternally holy and so wills God's people to be and do "holy" in its worship, its internal practices, and its mission to the world. In Martin Luther's memorable (if not also theologically difficult) phrase, the church consists of saints who are also sinners at the same time: *simul justus et peccator* (Latin for: "at once justified and a sinner").

God's holiness is central to any definition of who God is and what God does. And while God's holiness sometimes refers to divine rectitude, more essentially, it provides sharp commentary on the public manners of a creator God who is wholly unlike any other creature. Walter Brueggemann aptly observes, "The God of the Bible is the strangest thing about the whole Bible."[6] Holiness is what God is; what God does, especially in partnership with the church, is also holy.

In this regard, it is a categorical mistake to suppose that God's holiness separates God's presence from everything else—since God is other than everything else. If we believe that the church is holy because a holy God is present in its midst, then the holiness of God is recognized not so much in the abstraction of God's distant otherness but rather in the experience of a holy God's abiding presence with the church. The Holy Spirit convicts the community of its sinfulness, not by appealing to a legal standard but by its internal testimony that they are a community of God's adopted children (Rom 8:14-17), who, as obedient children, must be holy in every aspect of life, because they are called to holiness by a Father who is holy (1 Pet 1:14-16).

The church can confess itself as a holy people because of its abiding relationship with a holy God, who is known and made effective only by their humble reception of God's Holy Spirit. Both of God's decisions to choose a people and then to abide actively with and for that people are self-willed and gifts of grace. Again, the church is holy only because the God who created and now covenants with it is holy. But it would be a mistake to understand the church's holiness in such passive terms. God has called the church to practice holiness precisely because this God is holy: holiness is an obedient response to be holy in the image of a holy God. To crib Brueggemann's phrase, "The strangest thing about the world is the sanctified church." In this sense, the idea that the church's calling (*klēsis*) includes the act of separation (*ek*) denotes its public presence as a nonconforming counterculture in the world (cf. Rom 12:1-2).

---

6. Walter Brueggemann, *The Bible Makes Sense*, 1st ed. (Louisville: Westminster John Knox, 1977), 61.

15

There is nothing here that supposes a passive (or magical!) view of holiness that insists that the profession of our faith keeps us holy no matter what we do. Scripture's prophetic role in "showing and correcting mistakes" (2 Tim 3:16 AT) illumines the role of those biblical instructions and protocols of discipline that attend to the community's practices of holiness. The real expectation that follows from the church's separation from its pagan past into a covenant relationship with a holy God also obligates covenant-keeping practices that include a holy life—what I have called elsewhere "participatory holiness." The confession of a holy church, then, not only admits to the sanctifying presence of the Holy Spirit in its company, but also embraces a new competency made possible by new birth to enjoin a life that purifies oneself (1 John 3:3) for a life that refuses to engage in any activity that offends the sensibilities of a holy God.

Those biblical ideas and images of the community's holiness, then, seek to elaborate those places rubbed raw by its persistent friction against those worldly systems and practices opposed to God's will. A NT ecclesiology should help define the church as countercultural, whose public witness and worship both instantiate the presence and power of a holy God and challenge all those idolatries and sins that undercut the creator's very good intentions for human life. In this sense, this mark raises another question: Do the practices of our congregation draw us into loving communion with a holy God?

The Church Is Catholic (i.e., Universal)

The geography of the church's mission is coextensive with the *missio Dei*: its reach is cosmic, even extending to the invisible "powers of evil in the heavens" (Eph 6:12) to which the church announces the victory of God (Eph 3:10; cf. 1 Pet 3:19). In this sense, the mark of oneness includes this same spatial sense: the church's unity extends to every nook and cranny of creation; it can't be restricted to a particular region or ethnic group: there is but one holy church throughout the cosmos. (For this reason, Israel's promise, which is the central trope of divine blessing in the OT, is spiritualized and universalized in the NT.)

One of the most evocative biblical images of the boundaries of the church's catholicity is the vision of the great crowd in Revelation 7. Here is gathered at history's conclusion a truly inclusive and diverse group, who together celebrate the victory of God. They all are gathered before the Lamb in common garb—white gowns washed clean by the Lamb's blood—and use the same liturgical gestures to worship and bless God. Their roots underscore their common history: they have all come from "great hardship" (7:14) and stand in the shelter of the throne to find unending food and drink and relief from the scorching sun (7:15-16). The Lamb who has purified them now stands in their midst to comfort and lead them. This lovely picture reminds us that the church's catholicity is grounded in this common hope of a people made whole by the mercies of God.

John Wesley's famous sermon on "the catholic spirit" defines catholicity by excluding certain kinds of groups from the church's global reach; the church's membership is not all-inclusive. According to Wesley, the limits of Christian unity are established by the "main branches" of the Nicene Creed; all those who own these essentials no matter their denomination or opinion regarding "nonessential" practices and beliefs are considered members of the Christian church. The global reach of the church's witness assumes that within its whole body one will find a rich diversity of believers to whom Christian fellowship should extend. Catholicity, then, would refer to the total diversity of what is found therein, held together by common creed and canon. The definitive meaning of "catholic" is whole; the church catholic is truly whole only when it includes all of these diverse communions of true believers in Christian fellowship.

Perhaps using Wesley to score this point suggests that we distinguish between ecclesiology and ecclesiastical, between matters of ecclesial identity and mission, on the one hand, and church order, clerical office, pastoral discipline, institutional organization, and the complicated apparatus by which the institution interacts with the state and with the society it inhabits, on the other hand. Naturally, this distinction is artificial and overly schematic, and there is a lot of overlap or two-way traffic between them. That is, a statement about who the church takes itself to be is going to shape how it organizes itself, how it chooses its leaders, and so forth. Affect but not completely regulate. Other factors such as the sociological, political, economic, cultural, and linguistic shape ecclesiastical organization as well, and in many cases prudent decisions about church order reflect the influence of these other, nontheological factors on how the church thinks about its identity and mission.

A NT theology of church may gather a range of biblical metaphors for the church catholic that creates a kind of polydimensional field, such that each metaphor shapes, corrects, and anneals the others in a particular social location. What happens, for example, if one thinks of the church primarily as a human body rather than as a familial household when applied to a particular congregation's real world questions about liturgical practices, mission, and fellowship? How does a particular social/religious location shape a congregation's celebration of the Eucharist *as* the body of Christ *or as* a household of faith?

17

If the mark of holiness is typically found when the church collides with the world, the mark of catholicity is often under pressure within the church when communions of competing forms of worship, moral practices, and theological grammars collide. In fact, to absolutize a particular communion's opinion or expression is idolatry. Rather, mutual understanding and Spirit-led ministry of reconciliation make the mark of catholicity a hard but real possibility.

The reservoir of NT ideas and images that elaborate the church's catholicity will typically be found attached to mission practices and in stories and instructions that delineate the community's identity by the dynamic of inclusion and exclusion, sometimes in a way that requires conflict resolution. The recovery of the old idea of "catholic" as a reference to the whole—to the whole world, every population group, the whole truth—provides a solution. The question provoked by this mark, then, may sound like this: How diverse is the reach of our congregation's membership?

The Church Is Apostolic

The church is the community of the apostles. Its identity is forged by their personal witness of the incarnate Word, who alone is the plumb line of Christian proclamation and the criterion of the community's *koinōnia* with God (see 1 John 1:1-4). As Brevard S. Childs puts it, "apostolicity became a dynamic term to encompass historical, substantive, functional, and personal qualities of the most basic core of the faith."[7] In this sense, the church's affirmation of its apostolic identity admits that by analogy of the rule of faith, canon and creed are both principal carriers of the apostolic witness to the incarnate One.[8]

There is also a sense that the apostles themselves serve the church as exemplary disciples. The word *apostle* means "one who is sent." That is, the apostolic church separates itself in obedience to God's call to go out with God's word in hand to do God's business in the world. Not only are the raw materials that form the church's core beliefs based upon the gospel handed down by the apostles, which we call "the rule of faith," but they also supply moral and missional examples—patterns of life and faithfulness—that continue to

---

7. Brevard S. Childs, *The Church's Guide for Reading Paul: The Canonical Shaping of the Pauline Corpus* (Grand Rapids: Eerdmans, 2008), 21.

8. I am aware of the debate between Protestants and the Roman and Eastern Church over how this apostolic witness is maintained and transmitted from one generation to the next. Protestants locate the notion of "apostolic succession" in scripture, so that each generation receives the gospel of the apostles in the teaching of scripture. Roman and Orthodox communions rather locate this witness in an ecclesial office, whether pope or patriarch. In either form, the apostolic witness to the incarnate One is safeguarded by the Holy Spirit.

define the church's public life in the world. It may even be true that, especially according to Acts, the apostles demonstrate how to receive, rely upon, and read the synagogue's scripture with a christological lens as an essential witness to the ways of God. In the NT, portraits and writings of their faith, then, meet the heart of the church's faith.

In this sense, the word *apostle* trades on the OT idea of a prophetic vocation: apostles were also carriers of the divine word, whose public proclamation raised difficult questions, identified idolatrous alliances, and called a people to make risky reversals in lifestyle for God's sake. Prophets cared less about looking good and more about Spirit-filled worship and the service of Israel's God. Of course, their endgame was Israel's repentance and renewal, rooted in the promise of covenant blessings from a faithful God. To confess the church as apostolic is to stand in this prophetic tradition of proclaiming and obeying God's gospel at considerable cost.

Reading the NT with this "apostolic" lens makes one especially alert to the canonical portraits of the apostles themselves, mostly from glimpses of them but then also from the fuller profiles of Peter and Paul in Acts and the Pauline autobiography in the letter corpus. Perhaps more implicit are those instructions and exhortations that view the congregation in prophetic terms: as a carrier of God's word or when acting out God's redemptive will to share possessions with the needy, embrace the marginal, or heal the sick. Simply put, then, this mark raises the question of the continuity between the beliefs and practices of our congregation and the risen Lord's apostles to whom he granted authority to lead the messianic community in his absence.

A final matter must be mentioned in this regard. Acts, which introduces the Spirit-led apostles to the reader, makes it clear that Paul's testimony of the risen Jesus differs from those apostles who knew the historical Jesus. That is, Paul did not accompany Jesus from the beginning with the Twelve (Acts 1:21-22); the apostolic tradition received from Paul is secured not by his memories of the historical Jesus and his messianic mission but by his vision of the risen Jesus (Acts 9:1-21) and memories of his mission to the nations (e.g., 2 Tim 3:10-14). The result is a more robust conception of an apostolic testimony based upon different experiences of knowing Jesus, which frames the church's reception of scripture as apostolic.

Why a *New Testament* Church?

Doesn't the scope of this study of God's people, reduced as it is to just NT books, collide with the scripture's nature, which consists of the OT and the

NT as integral parts of an interdependent whole? The reader may well question whether the NT idea of the church can be fully understood apart from the OT idea of Israel. Put more sharply as a question: Should a NT theology of a "one, holy, catholic, and apostolic" church draw upon an OT theology of a one, holy, catholic, and apostolic Israel?

In particular, one may first ask whether the juxtaposition of two testaments in a single biblical canon commends their theological unity (or continuity); this remains, of course, a hotly contested issue among biblical theologians.[9] Even when one's approach to biblical theology assumes the interpenetrating unity of the OT and the NT, the "center" of such a unity is debated, whether cast as a set of theological agreements internal to both testaments or external to a single rubric, such as the apostolic rule of faith. The question is especially nettlesome if the reader's intention to bring coherence to the Bible reduces the clear impress of its disparate witnesses, prophetic and apostolic. (Fortunately, this isn't the task of this book!)

Suffice to say, and only in passing, the predicate of scripture's theological coherence is its single referent: the one and only God of Israel who is incarnate in the historical Jesus. Moreover, since canonization produced a single book that holds within it an intractable diversity of theological traditions, the theological goods retrieved from any one collection must never be pressed into service in isolation from the rest of scripture. Or as Childs puts it, "The Old Testament bears its true witness as the Old which remains distinct from the New. It is promise, not fulfillment. Yet its voice continues to sound and it has not been stilled by the fulfillment of the promise."[10]

In this regard, the early church's preference for the chronological ordering of books in its Greek Septuagint (LXX) over the synagogue's tripartite Hebrew Bible is more than mere language games; the sequence of books in the LXX allowed the church to juxtapose the OT collection of prophets, which is placed last, and the fourfold Gospels of the apostles, placed first in the NT, to help secure the interdependency of both when read as the interplay of God's promises to a future Israel, which God now fulfills through messiah Jesus— or by whatever other diachronic scheme one might propose that relates the OT and the NT together as of a single piece and so secures the continuity between them.

---

9.   See, for example, James Barr, *The Concept of Biblical Theology: An Old Testament Perspective* (Minneapolis: Fortress, 1999), who defends the essential *discontinuity* between Old and New Testaments and so, then, the inherent difficulty of producing a fully *biblical* theology.

10.   Brevard S. Childs, *Biblical Theology of the Old and New Testaments: Theological Reflection on the Christian Bible* (Minneapolis: Fortress, 2011), 77.

But, second, the more substantive concern is provoked by the subject itself: the church. In this case, the division of the two testaments has sometimes had the effect of dividing off the NT idea of the church from the OT idea of Israel as though the church's beliefs and practices are substantively different from (or simply consistent with) Israel's. While this is clearly the case in part—since the church never presents itself as a nation-state or heir of a promised land and various moral and religious practices, stipulated by Torah, are discontinued or upgraded because of Jesus—the differences between the church and Israel mostly mount a false dichotomy. The principal ways by which the OT speaks of an electing, covenant-keeping God are retained by the NT: even if one claims (as I do) that God's incarnation in Jesus is a qualitatively superior self-presentation than God's sojourn in Israel, one should admit there is no substantive difference between them. What God did in Israel according to scripture is of a piece with what God continues to do more effectively in Christ.

One tragic result of this divided house is the church's historic promotion of supersession, a teaching that has hounded the church like a toothache from the moment the earliest church's mission to Jews failed and argued that God replaced Israel with the church to explain this failure. Supersessionism is the belief that the church has replaced Israel as God's covenant partner; that is, God's call of and promises to Israel according to the OT have been transferred to the church. We should admit that the NT itself is well aware of the community's struggle to find its identity as God's people apart from the synagogue, which had first mothered it but then turned against it. On the one hand, to be the church continues in Israel's airstream, but, on the other hand, to be the church also embraces a new Spirit-breathed reality inaugurated by the messiah and animated at Pentecost that distinguishes the church's future from the past of Israel. A separation of some kind between the church and the synagogue seems inevitable because of the conflict between them provoked by the risen Jesus and his apostolic witnesses.

Still, there is no more trenchant denial of supersessionism than that found in the NT book of Acts, which was written (and still is read) as a normative response to the church's own "Gentilizing" of its Jewish legacy. The thoroughly Jewish portrait of its central characters and even of the church's practices secures a robust sense of continuity with the church's Jewish legacy. What is remarkable about Acts, and especially its portrait of the apostles, is that the church's missions and the intellectual authority of its kerygmata never suggest a complement of apostolic writings. It is rather evinced by the church's Spirit-led, christological reading of Israel's scripture (e.g., Acts 17:1-4).

21

Although modern criticism sometimes presents as a problem of reliability that Acts neither portrays the apostles as letter writers nor quotes from their canonical letters, I would suggest that this is precisely the point! Acts does not plot a battle for the Bible but for a particular way of reading it. That is, we don't need to add a testament of apostolic witnesses to Israel's scripture as long as we read it rightly by the light of Christ and the power of the Spirit. So, even though typically asked with a NT slant, Acts invites a different slant: Does the OT theology of Israel require the NT theology of the church to complete it? The church ultimately decided that it does. But at the same time, the church's preservation of the Hebrew Bible as its OT assumes not only the integrity of its revelation of God but also that this revelation performs a canonical role for Christians.

Of course, the creed nowhere mentions Israel, which remains deeply troubling, even though perhaps a reflection of its different role within the church than the biblical canon. The effect of this omission, however, implicates the church's long-standing struggle with supersessionism. According to our juxtaposition of canon and creed, then, it is the OT's narrative of Israel that reminds the church of its importance in any normative account of its identity as God's people. We should allow that the Nicene Creed's marks of the church are also true of biblical Israel; that is, the OT testifies in different voices to one, holy, catholic, and apostolic Israel. Perhaps the marks of Israel, however, are best understood within the bounds of a single biblical canon as the *promised* marks (in every sense) that the community baptized into Christ brings to realization.

A Canonical Approach to the NT's Church

The path is now cleared to introduce the interpretive approach of this book. I have attempted, in several publications, to introduce readers to my so-called canonical approach to theological interpretation and will only sketch its relevant bits in this section.[11] By "theological interpretation" I mean to emphasize scripture's role in providing the community with a pluriformed and Spirit-sanctioned witness by which it learns all about God. Without discounting the usefulness of any other interpretive approach, mine follows from a particular conception of the Bible's nature: that is, the Bible is the

---

11.   For a recent description of the orienting concerns of a canonical approach to theological interpretation, see my discussion (and various responses to it), Robert W. Wall, "The Canonical View," in *Biblical Hermeneutics: Five Views*, ed. Stanley E. Porter and Beth M. Stovell (Downers Grove, IL: InterVarsity, 2012), 111–30. For a recent attempt to apply these concerns to biblical texts, see my theological commentary, Wall, *1 & 2 Timothy and Titus.*

church's canon, an authoritative analogue, with the creed, of the apostolic rule of faith. There would be no Bible without the church that formed it and is formed by using its sacred writings in worship and catechesis.

My principal interpretive prompts, then, are retrieved from a narrative of the canonical process (diachronic), when collections of biblical writings were edited into their final form and then fitted together in a way that is maximally effective in using the biblical canon to form a faith community's loving communion with God and its neighbor (synchronic). Actually, the term *canonical* is a theological trope for a range of theological issues and Bible practices that compel the interpretive approach used in this book. Most of these issues are indexed by the study of the reasons scripture was formed in antiquity and by attention to the theological aesthetics of its final literary form. In my estimation, the phenomena of the canonical process were hardly arbitrary, producing an ancient book by accident or without anticipated relevance for future readers—a kind of museum piece to come and visit when company is in town. Rather, the choices the ancient church made in forming the Christian Bible, whatever their motivation at garden level or ground level, may be understood as a Spirit-led process of theological discernment for the formation of the church in every age. Based upon these practices, those writings observed as best in doing this kind of heavy lifting were selected, collected, and arranged for use as, in Tertullian's (ca. 200) apt phrase, a *gubernaculum interpretationis* (governor for interpretation).

The most important moment of the Bible's earliest history, then, is not when it was composed and first read, but when the church recognized, upon repeated use and in a variety of settings, its persistent usefulness as an ecclesial canon. This shift of the historical project from the moment of composition to the postbiblical moment of canonization is both practical and theological in sensibility. In some cases, more is known about a book's canonization than the circumstances of its composition. Book titles or attributions of authorship and audience may have more relevance for its use as scripture than for the historian's reconstruction of its origins. More relevant for scripture's continued use than questions of authorship or date of composition, which are indeterminate in most cases, are answers to this question: What did the church recognize about a particular collection of writings that prompted its postbiblical reception as scripture? Often in answering this historical question, readers come to understand more clearly how to continue to use biblical writing for their theological formation.

The Bible's final form and the sequence of its canonical collections in particular, are themselves a visual aid to the most effective pattern of reading it as scripture. For this reason, I refer to this property of canonization that guided the production of a literary product with a particular literary shape as the "aesthetic principle." Nicholas Wolterstorff advances a philosophical conception of "aesthetic excellence" that posits ultimate importance on the salutary effects of the form of a work of art that enriches the public good. If the purpose of an art form is self-interested or trivial rather than inspiring its audiences to do good or to live more virtuously, then the aesthetic of its form is of lesser quality. How individual biblical bits work together to constitute a canonical whole is a decisive measurement of an object's performance as the trusted witness to God's word, whether it will be well-received and well-used by its future practitioners.[12]

This idea of aesthetic excellence provides a useful typology for explaining why the church came to valorize a particular shape and size of the biblical canon over other possible forms. Those inherent properties of shape and size, texture and color that naturally draw readers to an artistic work of higher quality also draw people to scripture. As a literary achievement, the biblical canon is a genre of collections made up of artfully told stories, memorable lyrics, vivid poetry, exacting law codes, practical letters, and even apocalypses, all of which aim readers at ultimate meaning. And these well-told parts are nicely fitted together into a complete and sufficient whole in order to perform its authorized roles effectively in the formation of Christian disciples.

Most modern constructions of the canonical process follow individual books through their earliest history, whether in the West or East, whether evinced in manuscripts, allusions and citations of the earliest Christian writings, or various "canon lists" that the early church produced to keep track of decisions made. While providing an important sociological layer to the context within which the canonical process is studied within antiquity, this kind of work largely ignores the phenomenology of the canonical process itself: almost every individual book entered the biblical canon as an integral member of a whole collection (e.g., Torah, Psalter, Book of the Twelve, Fourfold Gospel, Pauline collection, Catholic Epistle collection, and so on). The final redaction of a collection, therefore, evinces an aesthetic that is maximally effective for performing the authorized roles of a biblical canon.

The approach of this book follows the internal "canon-logic" envisaged by the working relationships between canonical collections. Obviously, this

---

12. See Nicholas Wolterstorff, *Art in Action: Toward a Christian Aesthetic* (Grand Rapids: Eerdmans, 1980), esp. in his proposal of a distinctively "Christian aesthetic," pp. 65–174. Wolterstorff is therefore not primarily interested in whether art can be used as a source of Christian theology or an auxiliary of divine revelation, although I take it he would allow that great art which deals with themes central to the Christian faith might better function in drawing people to God.

approach differs from the "chrono-logic" of critical orthodoxy, which orders individual biblical writings (often within a collection) according to the date of their composition. Most attempts at constructing a NT ecclesiology treat the diverse ideas and images of the church as an evolving conception, beginning with the first written (typically Pauline) and concluding with the last composed (typically 2 Pet). Reading the final form of the NT sequentially, however, implies a different kind of internal logic, which underwrites the importance of juxtaposed collections in a way that privileges prior collections when reading the next one. Most essentially, then, the fourfold Gospel is considered first and necessary reading for Acts, Acts is read as the Bible's introduction to the two letter collections that follow, and Revelation is read last to sound scripture's concluding note.

The elevated importance we grant to the sequence of writings within a canonical collection does not envisage a linear progression of thought that only looks forward. Rather, scripture's pluriformed witness to God's word unfolds in a more dynamic way, by a reading whose sequence is both forward and backward. Not only do successive collections (and sometimes writings within collections) elaborate prior points (reading forward), but the reader will also be prompted by the repetition of these scored points to recall their antecedent iterations in ways that expand their meaning in earlier settings (reading backward).

Finally, similar to the artist who changes the wording of a poem or a line of a painting because it improves the poem or makes the painting's image more arresting, we might allow that the indwelling Spirit forms a community's capacity to recognize which particular bits in what forms are necessary in constructing a single biblical canon that is most effective in accomplishing its holy purposes. The church's decisions in forming the collections of the biblical canon, if they are directed by the Holy Spirit, will effectively help to accomplish God's redemptive desires for the world. In other words, if a loving God has created us for loving communion with God and each other, then the church's production of scripture in its present canonical form and so the church's practices of scripture—its careful exegesis, its theological interpretation, and its vibrant proclamation—must target this same holy end.

Toward a NT Theology of Church

The practices and orienting concerns of theological interpretation cohere to a theology of the Bible as the church's scripture. The reception and uses of scripture at its ecclesial address, indexed by the hermeneutics of the canonical process and the final literary form of its canonical product, are of a piece with what the one, holy, catholic, and apostolic church confesses about itself. There is no Christian scripture apart from the church, and so no theological reading of scripture is disinterested in the holy effects an interpretation has upon its faithful readers, in the catholic reach of its application to different Christian communities in different time zones and in its coherence to what the apostles witnessed and proclaimed of the incarnate One. Quite apart from, and in no way in competition with, an interpreter's linguistic acuity or historical critical fluency, theological interpretation emphasizes how Christians practice and perform their scripture to form their spiritual wisdom and to guide their lives with God and one another.

It should come as no surprise, based upon these other concerns, that the canonical approach recognizes the importance of congregational worship in forming the believer's capacity for faithful interpretation. Not only do various Bible practices find their home in a congregational setting (e.g., Bible readings, liturgical use of scripture, sacrament of the word, and singing of the Psalter) and purpose to aim believers at God, but it is also in the company of the saints that the spiritual authority of the biblical interpreter is honed and confirmed. Along with the intellectual equipment required to work with biblical texts skillfully, the virtues necessary to read sacred texts after the mind of Christ are formed within the body of Christ. The congregation recognizes a capacity for self-criticism and the maturity of one who can avoid sinful tendencies in interpreting biblical texts. This concern for the formation of the faithful interpreter, although ancillary to a primary concern in the formation of the biblical canon, is an important feature of the canonical approach as a species of theological interpretation.

If scripture's principal address is the church, the interpreter's principal concern should be to facilitate Bible practices within a congregation of believers. The terms of scripture's authority (e.g., divine inspiration, special revelation, and sacrament of the word) are defined in functional rather than in dogmatic terms, and believers will come to question the scripture principle if they perceive that its teaching either lacks relevance for their contemporary situation or is simply incomprehensible to them. When such a situation persists, believers will set aside scripture for other resources, sometimes found outside of the canonical heritage and even secular in cast, which can lead to serious distortions of the apostolic faith.

The act of sound interpretation, when provoked by this theological crisis, intends to demonstrate the Bible's authority for a particular congregation of readers by first clarifying what the text actually says (text-centered exegesis) and then by recovering from the text that particular meaning which addresses their current theological confusion or moral dilemma in productive ways—that is, in ways that end theological confusion and resolve moral dilemma in a truly Christian manner. Of course, the legitimacy of any biblical interpretation as truly Christian is not determined by its practical importance for a single readership but by general agreement with the incarnate Word of God, Jesus Christ, witnessed to by his apostles, and preserved by the Holy Spirit in the biblical canon and ecumenical creeds of the one, holy, catholic, and apostolic church. The substance of a NT theology of the church, by any name, should agree with this normative definition.

Chapter Two

The Fourfold Gospel

he story of Jesus is the primary subject matter of the Gospels, and the story of Jesus is also the story of his disciples who are called to follow him. If the interpreter supposes that the task is to reconstruct the life of the historian's Jesus, then the interpreter could legitimately question the relevance of the Gospels for any study of today's church. After all, the church did not originate with Jesus; he founded a messianic movement rather than an organized religion.[1]

The apostolic testimony of this movement is hardly monolithic, nor is the post-Easter community's experience of its risen Lord homogenous. The Evangelists and their respective communities shaped portraits of Jesus according to different theological interpretations of his life and in response to different encounters of his abiding presence in each community's worship and witness.[2] This pluriformed witness of Jesus, fixed by its canonization as a fourfold Gospel, not only informs the range of Christologies found within the NT but has produced an implicit ecclesiology based upon its portraits of Jesus and his relations with the disciples. This ecclesiology frames our reading about the earliest church in Acts and the instructions that target the congregations addressed by both the Letters and the Apocalypse. A study of the

---

1. For this history, see Craig A. Evans, *From Jesus to the Church: The First Christian Generation* (Louisville: Westminster John Knox, 2014).

2. See, in particular, Francis Watson, "*Veritas Christi*: How to Get from the Jesus of History to the Christ of Faith without Losing One's Way" in *Seeking the Identity of Jesus: A Pilgrimage*, ed. Beverly Roberts Gaventa and Richard B. Hays (Grand Rapids: Eerdmans, 2008), 96–115.

fourfold Gospel, then, is hardly incidental to our study but is rather foundational for answering the question, "Why the church?"

In fact, a canonical approach to the four Gospels is cued by the collection's singular title, *Gospel*: indeed, the church receives multiple biographies of Jesus as witness to one Gospel. As Brevard S. Childs puts it, "the major formal sign of canonical shaping of the collection is the juxtaposition of the four books with titles which introduce the books as witnesses to the one gospel."[3] Although the sources and nature of the Gospels as narrative literature, and especially the evident differences between them, have occupied modern Gospel criticism, scripture's title of this fourfold collection points readers to their unifying story of Jesus and its implications for Christian faith and witness. In fact, nowhere in scripture is Christology and ecclesiology so intimately paired as here.

Even though the church had recognized a plurality of stories about Jesus by the middle of the second century, when using these stories in worship, catechesis, and mission, the church also recognized that no one of the four authorized Gospels adequately narrates the whole story (cf. Luke 1:1-4). Four *different* stories of Jesus's life, arranged and received in precise order, best approximate the full presentation of Jesus's life as the apocalypse of God's salvation.[4]

The rearrangement of the four Gospels according to their supposed date of composition is an invention of modern critical orthodoxy. Accordingly, Mark is generally granted priority and studied first because most historians judge it to be the first Gospel written. Most scholars contend (on little actual evidence) that the second Gospel is the principal source behind the first and third Gospels, together forming a subcollection of three look-alike (or "synoptic") Gospels. Virtually every modern introduction tells us so, and so every one of them begins its treatment of the Gospels, and the contribution to NT theology of each, with Mark's story of Jesus's life. The effect of Mark's chronological priority is to elevate its theological priority, thereby narrowing a critical reading of Matthew or Luke's redactional layers as theological add-ons to Mark's normative Gospel. Of course, the contribution of John's non-Synoptic Gospel, especially evident in the modern quest of the historian's Jesus, is marginalized altogether because John's Jesus is so dissimilar by comparison with the other three Jesuses, especially when cued by Mark's narrative of Jesus.

---

3.   Brevard S. Childs, *The New Testament as Canon: An Introduction* (Philadelphia: Fortress, 1984), 155.

4.   See now, Francis Watson, *Gospel Writing: A Canonical Perspective* (Grand Rapids: Eerdmans, 2013), whose important study of the formation of the Gospel canon recognizes the importance of its internal diversity even though he fails to find that the canonization of a fourfold Gospel (probably already in the second century *contra* Watson) was a deliberate and theologically intentional decision of the church.

Contrary, then, to modern criticism's Gospel canon, the church's final redaction of its biblical Gospel was already recognized by Irenaeus in *Against Heresies* (180 CE). Even earlier manuscripts and subsequent canon lists suggest that Irenaeus's fourfold Gospel was copied on single codices for wide use, the written result of an extended organic process based upon its variegated uses in worship, catechesis, and mission.[5] Irenaeus did not understand the Gospel's unity as a linguistic matter—the church's earliest interpreters all recognized the disruptions and diversity between the four—but rather that each Gospel's portrait of Jesus is analogous to the christological agreements of the apostolic rule of faith.[6] What results, then, is a mutually glossing intertextuality, producing applications and implications of the single Gospel that are greater than the mere sum of its four discrete parts—perhaps producing commentary that looks something more like the longer ending of Mark!

Much has been made in recent years of scripture's intertextuality, which clearly means different things to different scholars. Literary studies of intertextuality argue that the very polyvalence of texts opens their interpretation up to an ever-unfolding meaning. In the present case, one Gospel's narrative is not fixed by its individual literary or theological shape, its Evangelist's intentions, or the cultural context of its first auditors-readers; rather, the inclusion of any one Gospel within a fourfold canonized whole and its subsequent placement at the head of the church's emerging second biblical testament, occasions a new (textual) context for reading and appropriating Jesus's story in worship and catechesis. No single redaction of a particular pericope from that story can be isolated from its other recensions found anywhere else in scripture. A shift from a biblical book's compositional occasion in the distant past to its current canonical setting as the real point of that book's origins as scripture alters how we think of its intended readers. Readers should assume that the production of a single biblical canon under the Spirit's direction brings together different texts in fresh ways that both relativize and thicken the meaning of any one passage. This thickened meaning, when aimed at new questions and concerns raised by a faithful

5. For this history, see Graham N. Stanton, "The Early Reception of Matthew's Gospel: New Evidence from Papyri?" in *The Gospel of Matthew in Current Study: Studies in Memory of William G. Thompson, S. J.*, ed. David E. Aune (Grand Rapids: Eerdmans, 2001), 42–61.

6. "Christ Jesus, the Son of God; who, because of His surpassing love towards His creation, condescended to be born of the virgin, He Himself uniting man through Himself to God, and having suffered under Pontius Pilate, and rising again, and having been received up in splendor, shall come in glory, the Savior of those who are saved, and the Judge of those who are judged, and sending into eternal fire those who transform the truth, and despise His Father and His advent" (Irenaeus, *Against Heresies* 3.4.2, in *The Apostolic Fathers, Justin Martyr, and Irenaeus*, vol. 1 of *The Ante-Nicene Fathers*, ed. Alexander Roberts and James Donaldson [Buffalo, NY: Christian Literature Publishing, 1885]).

reader, will more adequately disclose God's word for a new day "according to the scripture."

Irenaeus further understood that the Gospel's final form is itself canonical. Not only did he grant hermeneutical priority to the Gospel's fourfold form, but also he defined the source of heresy as a breach of this form. While his exposition of this point may strike us as fantastical today, the point itself should not. What Irenaeus observes is that when only one or a twofold Gospel is used to tell the story of Jesus (this might include today's privileging of the threefold Synoptic Gospel over the fourth), the theological form of the community's discipleship also becomes distorted.

A canonical approach to the fourfold Gospel differs sharply from biblical criticism's proposed (and various) solutions to the so-called synoptic problem or its division between the Synoptic and fourth Gospels.[7] The hermeneutics of the canonical process, cued by the church's Bible practices in worship and catechesis, prioritized Matthew, not Mark (even if written before Matthew) and so placed Matthew at the head of the Gospel canon.[8] At the very moment the apostolic traditions about Jesus were being shaped into a fourfold Gospel canon, then, Matthew had theological and ecclesial priority and its placement reflects this. (Augustine even referred to Mark as Matthew's "epitomizer"—a kind of "reader's digest" version of Matthew's normative rendering of Jesus!)

If our intuitive reading of the canonical Gospel to mine its theological goods is cued by the sequence of its four narratives, the potential is awakened for additional impressions of the distinctive contribution that each narrative makes to the whole witness. The placement of Matthew, named after an eyewitness, to head the Gospel, for example, may be viewed as strategic in two different ways. In the first place, Matthew's particular literary structure and theological perspective, especially its portrait of the relationship between the synagogue and the church, introduces a range of important theological questions, including, "Why the church?" to which Mark, Luke, and John continue to respond. Matthew is the only Gospel that actually speaks of the *ekklēsia* (16:18; 18:17); it does so in a way that both suggests what an

---

7.   Robert W. Wall, "A Canonical Approach to the Unity of Acts and Luke's Gospel," in *Rethinking the Unity and Reception of Luke and Acts*, ed. Andrew F. Gregory and C. Kavin Rowe (Columbia: University of South Carolina Press, 2010), 172–91. The fourth Gospel is often detached from the fourfold whole and placed in a "Johannine corpus" that includes the three Johannine Epistles and sometimes John's Revelation because they, like the Synoptic Gospels, share a common symbolic universe.

8.   Manuscript and citational evidence supports the conclusion that it was the most widely used Gospel in the early church's worship and catechesis; see Édouard Massaux, *The Influence of the Gospel of Saint Matthew on Christian Literature before Saint Irenaeus*, trans. Norman J. Belval and Suzanne Hecht, ed. Arthur J. Bellinzoni, 3 vols., New Gospel Studies 5 (Macon, GA: Mercer University Press, 1990–93).

apostle-led church will become after Jesus's departure and cues the images of this future community in the other Gospels. In the second place, Matthew's placement within the biblical canon occupies its most crucial seam between the OT and the NT. Its role as the narrative hinge on which the canon's two Testaments swing is illustrated by its deliberate use of the OT, which links the stories of Israel and Israel's messiah in a way that secures the theological continuity between the promises God makes to Israel according to scripture and their realization because of the faithfulness of the risen Jesus according to scripture. Indeed, it is a crucial portal into NT ecclesiology to understand Jesus's mission in the terms of the Bible's introduction of it in Matthew 1:21: "You will call him Jesus, because he will save *his* people from their sins" (emphasis added).

Although Augustine's reading of Mark as Matthew's epitomizer is no longer defensible, reading Mark after Matthew (even though probably written before Matthew) has the effect of making the theological contribution of each more emphatic. Although Mark's essential story line does not depart from Matthew's, nor does his portrait of Jesus disagree with Matthew's, its distinctive literary shape, framed by its "sudden beginning" and "open ending,"[9] captures the irony of this Gospel's portrait of the community's obedience of the hard command to follow Jesus. In particular, the beginning of Mark indicates that its telling is but the "beginning of the good news about Jesus Christ, God's Son" (1:1), while its ending suggests that the church's continuation of this same gospel, even though confirmed by both proclamation and stunning signs (16:15-20), is also accompanied (perhaps even threatened) by bouts of unbelief and stubbornness (16:8-14). The effect of reading Mark within this narrative frame after Matthew is to secure a more realistic appraisal of the church's grace-fueled capacity to follow after the risen Jesus in teaching the nations (Matt 28:19-20) what he has revealed in the Spirit to his disciples (Matt 11:25-30; 13:10-16; 16:17; 18:18-20).

Even though the distinctive theological contributions of Luke's Gospel are clear enough, the effect of reading the third Gospel after reading the first two seems less so to me. Following my contention of Matthew's theological priority and that the effect of reading Mark after Matthew checks-and-balances its implicit optimism of grace, perhaps Luke has a somewhat similar effect on its reader. For example, even if Matthew prophesies the existence of a post-Easter "church," surely the conception of discipleship in the third Gospel, if composed (but not canonized) with Acts's narrative of the church's

---

9. Luke Timothy Johnson, *The Writings of the New Testament: An Interpretation*, 3rd ed. (Minneapolis: Fortress, 2010), 149–50.

Pentecostal origins and subsequent mission in view, has the effect of filling out the sparse profile of Matthew's "church."

Not only does Luke's implicit ecclesiology have the effect of preparing the fourfold Gospel's readers for Acts (= the "scroll" of Acts 1:1), but it does so in a way that retains Matthew's insistence that such a Gospel is rooted in Israel's biblical story. In fact, Luke's more allusive but extensive use of Israel's scripture solidifies the continuity between the historical Jesus and Israel's messianic hope, especially as it fulfills the expectation of the victory of God's reign. Related to this is the third Gospel's more sociological understanding of God's kingdom indicated by a narrative interest in geography (especially Jerusalem as the city of divine destiny) and in the community's use of money. If inward righteousness marks out Matthew's discipleship, Luke's advocacy of the community's public acts of mercy has the effect of expanding the portfolio of church practice to include acts of social justice and egalitarian economics.

As with Matthew's priority, John's placement as the concluding narrative of the canonical Gospel may also be viewed as strategic, because it completes the story of the historical Jesus and the portrait of the community of his disciples. Putting the interpretive issue in terms of the fourth Gospel's relationship with the synoptic three shifts the reader's interest from the standard concerns of modern criticism, which seek to reconstruct the Gospel's compositional origins—its author and first audience, its sources, its occasion, and the like. A further matter, of course, is the well-known distinction, already in play during the patristic period, between the more human or "historical" Jesus of the Synoptic Gospels and the more spiritual "Christ of faith" portrayed in John's Gospel. During the modern period, this distinction is evident in the historian's quest of Jesus, which rarely considers John's Jesus as a viable source for this project.

A canonical approach recognizes that scripture's *Gospel*, including its fourth (or John's) telling, bears witness as a fourfold whole to the historical Jesus. This Jesus is at the same time the exalted Son-of-God messiah who is trusted and worshipped by his followers. In fact, the fourth Gospel makes this point more clearly than the other three, but the same is so of these three. Each witness tells the story of the incarnate One from a certain theological angle, but each witness is grounded in Jesus's earthly life—what was observed, heard, and touched by the Word of life (1 John 1:1). Any theological reflection upon the Gospel, then, begins from this premise: the Jewish Jesus of first-century Roman Palestine is the Son of God, the Christ of Christian faith.[10] The community of his disciples is of a piece with this biblical witness.

---

10. See the essays by Francis Watson, Dale C. Allison Jr., and Marianne Meye Thompson in Gaventa and Hays, *Seeking the Identity of Jesus.*

The most evident feature of John's community of disciples, besides its close connection with God's Son, is its more sectarian character and conduct. The advocacy of neighborly love in the first three Gospels, which includes the stranger and even the community's enemies, is withdrawn and replaced by a commitment to care for "one another" (i.e., other believers). The effect of doing so, especially following the inclusive ethos of the synoptic tradition, is to balance the church's mission to the nations with one occupied with the needs of one's own congregation. The juxtaposition of Synoptic and fourth Gospels, then, insures the fragile dynamic between the inclusive and exclusive dimensions of the community's missionary practice.

Finally, the fourth Gospel occupies another important canonical seam, this one between the Gospel and Acts. The Gospel's concluding episodes re-introduce the risen Lord and his remaining apostles to God's Spirit (John 20) and to a rehabilitated Peter (John 21), who will come to lead the messianic community in Christ's absence. John's ending adds a layer to Luke's images of the future church in a way that secures the link between the fourfold Gospel and Acts that clarifies what Jesus "did and taught," which is continued by his Spirit-led apostolic successors (Acts 1:1-2) and by their successors, including today's church catholic and apostolic.

The Church's Oneness according to the Fourfold Gospel

The Gospel of Matthew

Luke Timothy Johnson calls Matthew "the Gospel of the church," not only because it is the only Gospel to use the word *church* (*ekklēsia*; cf. Matt 16:18; 18:17 [twice]), but also because both its literary structure and portrait of Jesus intend to form a community of his followers.[11] The Gospel does not, however, envision a carefully organized or "institutional" church but rather uses the primary sense of the LXX word *ekklēsia*, which generally refers to intentional gatherings of God's people for different reasons. This rather modest clue that the presence of a future church is already latent whenever two or three disciples gather (cf. Matt 18:20) is made more important by images of the close connection between Jesus and the community of his disciples, characteristic of the first Gospel. The sense of the community's unique importance

---

11. Luke Timothy Johnson, *The Writings of the New Testament*, 165.

is not linked to any normative church practices or formal offices, nor to any titles of self-importance; nonetheless, these two mentions of "church" signal the importance of the stories in which they occur in defining Matthew's conception of the church's oneness.

The community's unique importance may already be assumed by the special relationship with Jesus and access to himself that Jesus grants only to his disciples. Ulrich Luz points out that the disciples receive "far more frequent special instructions in Matthew than in any other Gospel";[12] they are unique simply because they know more than other groups about God because of their proximity to Jesus who has brought God's heavenly kingdom near to them (4:17).

An easy entry into this conception of the church's distinctive importance is the Gospel's initial use of "church" in Matthew 16:18, which is introduced as an invincible community that even death, the creator's fiercest enemy, will not be able to overcome. The question remains: What accounts for this astonishing claim?

The story that encloses *ekklēsia* is full of not only theological promise but also exegetical problems. Generally observed, it narrates the circumstances of the first public confession of Jesus as messiah. Peter's identification of Jesus is decisive and definitive: he is "the Christ, the Son of the living God" (16:16). Matthew's redaction is more expansive than the other two Synoptic Gospels (Mark 8:29; Luke 9:20), which even more sharply distinguishes Peter's apprehension of Jesus's identity from the general public's (cf. 16:13-15) but which also aligns his confession with Israel's expectation of a kingly messiah.[13] Most scholars think Peter's confession climaxes the Gospel's first movement, which tells the story of Jesus's public ministry in Galilee that is plotted by the conflict that his actions and proclamation generate when an obdurate Israel fails at every turn to recognize Jesus as messiah, Son of the living God.

The question may reasonably be asked: How is Peter uniquely able to recognize what the elites of Israel do not? My question does not ask after Peter's personal authority, which is surely portrayed in this Gospel, but rather of the whole community of disciples he represents. Already in Matthew 14:28-31, Peter's bold but brief sojourn on the water and his subsequent failure of "weak faith" characterize the potential of *every* disciple to actively participate in the authority granted to Israel's messiah.[14] This includes the authority, granted

---

12. Ulrich Luz, *Studies in Matthew* (Grand Rapids: Eerdmans, 2005), 122.

13. According to John's Gospel, however, Martha, not Peter, offers the climactic confession of who Jesus is (11:27; cf. 20:31).

14. See Jack Dean Kingsbury, who regards Matthew's Peter as performing a distinctive but typical role as leader of the community of disciples: "The Figure of Peter in Matthew's Gospel as a Theological Problem," *Journal of Biblical Literature* 98, no. 1 (1979): 67–83.

first to Peter, to "fasten" or "loosen" on earth what God then confirms in heaven (16:19). Jesus subsequently extends Peter's authority to the entire community (18:18-20). In any case, the source of Peter's capacity to know Jesus's identity is divine revelation (16:17)—a line of evidence available only to those few Jesus selects.

In fact, twice before in the Gospel, Jesus indicates—apropos of his office as a teaching messiah (cf. Matt 28:19-20)—that he gives those who follow him insider information that distinguishes them from the rest of Israel. They alone have the eyes to see and the ears to hear the "secrets of the kingdom of heaven" (13:11), because he has explained it to them rather than deaf and blind outsiders for whom these mysteries are received as indecipherable parables (13:13). Even more dramatically, in a doxological refrain, Jesus says that while God hides "these things" from the power elites, the Son reveals them to those who come to him to find rest (11:25-30). That is, what accounts for the church's optimism in the face of death, where others fear to tread, is that Jesus's disciples know what the rest of Israel does not: Mary's son is God's Son, the messiah, who brings God's heavenly reign nearby (cf. 4:17) and in whom the prophet's promise of shalom is realized.

In this sense, then, what marks out the church from all other groups is what distinguishes Peter from public opinion: he confesses that Jesus is the Son of God, the messiah. Jesus tells Peter, after all, that he, not Peter, is the one who "builds" the church and it is "my church" that he builds (16:18). Paul would not disagree with Matthew on this point, since the public profession of Jesus as the risen Lord is the single membership requirement of belonging to God's people (Rom 10:9-13).

With this special knowledge of Jesus's true identity, however, comes a distinct authority, which Matthew describes by the cryptic phrase, "keys of the kingdom of heaven" that fasten and loosen on earth what is already so in the heavenly kingdom (16:19). And why shouldn't the disciples, in light of the instructions for their mission to Israel already given them in Matthew 10, tell others that Jesus is the messiah, especially since God has revealed his true identity to Peter who is blessed because of it? Why are they then told not to tell anyone else (16:20)? Answers to these questions concentrate on the larger theme of the nature or practices of the church's unique authority on earth and help define Matthew's contribution to scripture's understanding of "one" church.

Although the interpretation of this phrase remains contested, I prefer the more modest rendering, which follows the rabbinical use of applying an interpretation of Torah to particular situations (*halakhah*) in a way that "binds" faithful Jews to its performance as God's word. By analogy, the apostle's authority is *halakhic* in nature: Peter has the authority to render scripture in a way that clarifies God's word, which "binds" disciples to its covenant-keeping performance (see also 2 Tim 3:16-17). Since Jesus's comments to Peter are mostly self-referential, one assumes that Peter's apostolic *halakhah* is christological, confirmed in Acts, which gives it enduring authority for the messianic community. Subsequently, Matthew uses this same phrase of the entire congregation (note 18:18 where the plural number is used) when evidence of a believer's sin requires discipline that seeks his or her spiritual restoration (18:15-22; cf. 1 Tim 5:19-21).

The community's unity is thematic of Jesus's sermon on greatness (Matt 18), in which "church" is used a second time (18:17). The Gospel tells of other sources that form a unified community, especially the Lord's instructions to his disciples that are gathered up into five discourses all of which target the disciples (see Matt 5:1-2; 10:1; 13:10; 18:1; 24:1). It is this fourth discourse that concentrates disciples on the community's internal relationships and on two practices that build solidarity among a household of believers. (1) In response to the disciples' question, "Who is greatest in the kingdom of heaven?" (18:1), Jesus's initial use of the child as metaphorical of low social standing suggests that a lack of status-consciousness among individual members is necessary to mutual accountability and requisite for building church unity (18:1-9). (2) An essential commitment to the restoration of the lost as well as to the least is another critical practice, especially when the church is divided. Matthew's redaction of the Lord's parable of the lost sheep emphasizes the restoration of the believer (18:10-14), whereas Luke focuses on the repentance of the nonbeliever (cf. Luke 15:1-7), as a prologue to his instruction on church discipline (Matt 18:15-17). That is, the community in which Jesus is found (18:20) must be characterized by the application of *halakhah* (18:18-19; see the previous paragraph) that seeks to correct the wayward believer and then readily extends forgiveness (18:21-35).

Although Matthew's profile of disciples puts into play a positive conception of a community awakened by divine revelation, they (cued by Peter) are susceptible to a failure of incomprehension (cf. 16:21-23; 26:6-13, 40-46). Nonetheless, they understand the teaching and messianic identity of Jesus and accept it, even if on occasion with "weak faith" (8:26; 14:31; 16:8; 17:20). Clearly, the community's unity is predicated on their embrace of what they learn from Jesus and know/confess about him (cf. 10:37-42; 11:25-30; 16:16-20; 18:18-20; 19:28; 21:6; 28:18-20). Given Matthew's priority, the centrality of Jesus, especially as the definitive teacher of God's way of salvation (Matt

23:8-12), remains the baseline definition of the church's oneness within the fourfold Gospel. The community is formed around him and its unity/uniqueness is based upon its coherence to him—to who he is and what he does.

The Gospel of Mark

The literary shape of Mark's "sudden beginning" sharpens the reader's awareness of the distinctive marks of belonging to the community: a radical change of mind occasioned by faith that the apocalypse of God's promised kingdom is now near (1:15) and by obedience to the call to leave everything else immediately to follow after Jesus (1:17-18). Some did; most did not.

What is clear from Mark's telling of the story, however, is that, unlike the optimism of Matthew's community, the disciples of Jesus who populate this Gospel are as obdurate as everyone else in Israel about who Jesus truly is. Unlike Matthew's Jesus who expects his disciples to understand his parables (Matt 13:18), Mark's Jesus does not (Mark 4:13); their "hearts," Jesus says, are hardened (Mark 6:52; 8:17), which Matthew's Jesus omits (cf. Matt 14:32; 16:9), even if allowing on occasion that his disciples fail to understand him (Matt 15:16-17; 16:8-9). Were it not for the addition of the longer ending to the second Gospel, the community would seemingly have no future, especially when compared to Matthew (see Matt 17:9; 18:19-20; 19:28; 24:14; 27:64; cf. 28:18-20—all passages not found in Mark).

Although the Gospel's early portrait of the disciples is quite positive, the striking way in which Mark scores the relationship between Jesus and his disciples following Peter's confession of him as the messiah (Mark 8:29) on their way to Jerusalem underscores the community's growing ignorance of who Jesus really is. In a triad of purposeful exchanges unique to this Gospel, Jesus first predicts his execution but then his resurrection (8:31; 9:31; 10:33-34), which provokes responses among the disciples of evident misunderstanding (8:32; 9:31; 10:35) that only the resurrection will eventually begin to correct (cf. 16:9-20). As Jesus gets closer and closer to his city of messianic destiny, his disciples' understanding of who Jesus is seems to diminish by degrees until no one is left standing with the suffering, crucified one (cf. 14:50-52, 66-72).[15]

The disciples' diminished understanding of and distancing from Jesus not only corrodes their capacity to participate in his messianic mission but is

---

15. For a comparison between Mark and Matthew on this point, see C. Clifton Black, *The Disciples according to Mark: Markan Redaction in Current Debate.* Journal for the Study of the New Testament: Supplement Series 27 (Sheffield, England: JSOT Press, 1989), 43–46.

also reflected in increased bickering among them (8:32-33; 9:33-34; 10:35-41). The distinctiveness shaped by their association with Jesus becomes less and less so, a regression most clearly instantiated in a growing misapprehension of Jesus as the suffering son of man, who ultimately becomes more like his Jewish opponents who have already rejected Jesus's messiahship and instruction on this basis.

After Mark's more negative portrayal of the disciples, whose growing alienation from Jesus and each other is made complete at the crucifixion (even if then restored in sputters and spurts following Easter; see 16:9-20), Luke's more balanced conception of the community's life returns readers to where they began: in Matthew. Most scholars would argue this is because the Evangelist's conception of the community of disciples corresponds with the church of Acts (rather than within the "church" traditions found in Matthew) in order to maintain the narrative unity of a "Luke-Acts."[16] Even so, the canonical process recognizes the integrity of Luke within a fourfold Gospel, although not from its codependence on Acts (see earlier, pp. 25, 33–34).

The Gospel of Luke

In any case, if both the unity and unique characteristic of the community's oneness is due to its close connection with him, no passage is more crucial for Luke's contribution to this discussion than its expanded narrative of Jesus's programmatic ministry in Nazareth (Luke 4:14-30; cf. Matt 13:53-56; Mark 6:1-6). In particular, two core themes are entwined in this story: Spirit-filling and God's word, the two essential properties of prophetic ministry. Luke's Jesus is baptized with the Spirit (rather than by John; Luke 3:21-22) who accompanies Jesus into the wilderness for a season of spiritual testing (4:1) and then back to Galilee (4:14) and the synagogue in Nazareth where he pronounces this same Spirit of prophecy, glossed by Isaiah 61, which now infuses his public ministry in preaching good news to the poor and powerless (Luke 4:16-21).

The effect of his commentary on Isaiah's prophecy is to divide his audience of Jews, some of whom receive his words gladly while others question his teaching authority. Jesus goes on to link his message with the prophetic missions of Elijah and Elisha to non-Jews (see under the later section "The Church's Catholicity according to the Fourfold Gospel"), which incites the crowd to reject Jesus; in doing so, it more clearly delineates the division within Israel between God's messiah and Israel's rich and famous.

---

16. For instance, Charles H. Talbert, *Literary Patterns, Theological Themes, and the Genre of Luke-Acts* (Missoula, MT: Scholars Press, 1974), esp. 125–40.

The community's solidarity with Jesus's controversial mission to the poor and powerless, on the other hand, is predicated on actively sharing in his mission (cf. Luke 9:1-6, 10-17). Although not yet actively engaged in his mission, Jesus makes his intentions clear in the instructions he gives the Twelve immediately following their selection and naming (6:12-16, 17-36), a story shaped by Luke's christological interests. If Jesus brings good news to the poor and powerless, then the community of his followers will likely realize what he heralds: it will be to the poor, hungry, and persecuted, rather than the rich, well-fed, and influential (see 6:20-26)—a reversal of social convention (cf. 1:46-55). The mechanism that forms such a corporate life is a revolutionary love that includes enemies and that gives without karmic expectation of payback (6:27-36).

In fact, wealth/poverty is thematic of the messiah's instructions to his disciples in the third Gospel, to illustrate not so much the cost of discipleship but rather the solidarity with the Lord whose gospel targets the least, last, lost, and lame. Likewise, any division among the people provoked by his preaching of God's word does not serve his social criticism, but reveals a people's separation from God's favor.

The Spirit who anoints Jesus for this prophetic ministry is the same Spirit whom the Father will give to those who ask (Luke 11:13). In context of Luke's redaction of the Lord's Prayer (11:1-4), the community's petition is not for the Spirit but for its daily provision and its debt reduction (both spiritual and financial). The community's reception of the Spirit enables it to engage in that mechanism of life that forms a united community, which shares its goods as well as its confession of faith. In both ways, its witness is distinct and provocative.

The Gospel of John

John's notion of the community's oneness lies at the heart of Jesus's conception of discipleship according to John 13–17 and especially his pastoral prayer (John 17) for those who confess that he came from God (16:30; cf. 17:6-8). Already, the corporate character of discipleship and its solidarity with Jesus is clearly reflected in Jesus's use of the image of a "good shepherd" (10:1-18, 22-30), who is entrusted to lead and protect a flock of sheep self-sacrificially so that "there will be one flock, with one shepherd" (10:11-16). The definition of a "good" shepherd as one who gathers and protects his sheep from danger is glossed by Jesus's prediction that his execution would cue the gathering together of God's people who are presently scattered (11:52; cf.16:32; Mark 14:27-8).

More important, the oneness of the flock is based upon its recognition of and following the lead of its one shepherd. That is, it is the community's confession of a particular Christ, "the one who enters through the gate" (John 10:2), which shapes its oneness. This includes those nameless "other sheep," who are eventually brought into this same fold upon listening to the shepherd's voice and then following him. Finally, the unity of the community and Jesus is predicated upon his preexistent relationship with God: even as they are eternally one (10:30), so, also, is the community's relationship with the one it follows (10:15, 27-29).

These same notes are sounded more clearly in the two sets of prayerful petitions the Lord offers his Father for his disciples (John 17:9-19, 20-23), which conclude his Last Supper with them when Jesus prepares them for their mission following his departure when they no longer can follow him (John 13–17). Jesus's abrupt announcement of the cessation of discipleship (13:33) has already provoked considerable unrest among his followers and occasions his final instructions. A realistic implication of Jesus's departure is that his sheep will soon be scattered (16:32), and it is against the horizon of this possible outcome that John's conception of the church's oneness is drawn.

God's safekeeping of the community's unity against any threat of "scattering" it (and so subverting its mission in the world) is based upon God's unity with the Son (John 17:11b). The community's future is in lockstep with the future of Jesus. And because God is committed to Jesus, and Jesus to his disciples, any influence from the evil one (who is a nonplayer in John's narrative world) or from the world system (17:14-16) is vacated. The mutuality that characterizes the Son's relationship with his Father (17:10-11) by extension characterizes the Son's relationship with his disciples (17:12). And so even as Jesus's departure signals his glorification by the Father and the Father's by him (13:31-32), so also, rather than posing a threat to the community's unity, his departure signals the glorification of those who follow him. Jesus's eternal oneness with God and his enduring oneness with his disciples shape what happens next.

Jesus's rehearsal of his mission, according to John (17:12-16),[17] frames his petition to consecrate the community for its practice of truth telling (cf. 8:32), for which it will be sent out into the world (17:17-19). This is the essential mark of the church's uniqueness. This petition is anticipated by Jesus's

---

17. In particular, the petition for protection from the "evil one" reflects a stark difference between John and the synoptic traditions: Jesus does not confront the evil one directly in John's narrative world, in which there is no temptation or exorcism story (cf.13:27). Jesus is relatively safe in asking God for this protection since from his experience he knows that God has kept him safe from the evil one, and what has been so for him will continue to be so for those who continue to follow him after his departure.

address of God as "the one and only true God" (17:3, paraphrase) and by Jesus's declaration of himself as "the truth" that leads to God (14:6; cf. 14:17). What is shared between Father and Son is also shared with his disciples. Significantly, the connection of truth telling with the act of consecration (*hagiasō*, 17:17, 19), stated in the past (active aorist) tense, secures this sense that Jesus has already sanctified and set the community apart for a distinctive work in the world—a work that continues what the messiah has been set apart by God to do for them (cf. 10:18).

The second set of petitions (John 17:20-23) broadens the scope of the community to include those members added after Jesus's departure because of the witness of his apostles. Remarkably, their witness is not kerygmatic— Jesus does not say the world will come to know him in response to the community's proclamation of him (as in Acts or Pauline missionary traditions); rather, the world's attraction to and knowledge of Jesus are prompted by the testimony of the community's solidarity with each other! The nature of this distinctive unity is not included in Jesus's petition, but the Gospel's wider context suggests that it is the demonstration of love for one another, since earlier in this discourse Jesus tells his disciples that the unity of God's love for him characterizes his love for them (15:9), and that unity with him features love for one another (15:10-17).

Perhaps this idea of the church's oneness and its attractiveness to the world, such that it defeats the advances of the evil one, provides an illustration in response to Lohfink's question about whether "God needs the church." John asserts that "God so loved the world" (3:16)—even if not with the intimacy that God loves Jesus or Jesus his disciples—but the world comes to know this as true by observing a congregation whose members are fiercely united in their love for each other. Without wishing to overdetermine this point, Jesus seems to indicate two concurrent directions of oneness that bring this testimony of love to perfection (or maximal effectiveness; 17:23; *teteleiōmenoi eis hen*): God is at work in Jesus who is at work "in" the disciples (17:23), while at the same time the disciples are at work in Jesus who is in God (17:21; cf. 14:20). This robust mutuality of love lies at the heart of this Gospel's sense of the church's oneness without which the world will not "know" Jesus.

To sum up, what is clear from the fourfold Gospel is that the uniqueness of the community's identity and mission in the world is predicated on its distinctive, personal relationship with Jesus, the one and only messiah. Furthermore, the community's unity is shaped by its common response to obey Jesus's calling and command to follow his lead as practitioners of God's word.

The Church's Holiness
according to the Fourfold Gospel

The definition and practice of holiness had elevated religious and political importance to the Judaism that helped shape the mission of Jesus and his disciples. The contest between the various Judaisms of his day was largely over delineating the boundaries of a decisively Jewish identity within a social world shaped (or misshaped) by the Roman occupation of Palestine. No religious Jew disputed that Israel's God is holy or that a holy God dwells comfortably only with a people intent on meeting the prescribed standards of purity, both corporate and personal. The battle zone was over definition, and the holiness of God's people is a pivotal topic in the Gospel's narrative. Its plotline is often drawn by Jesus's provocations with Judaism's religious elites over what rituals and routines maintained the identity and vital practices of a holy people, clearly separate from Palestine's pagan occupiers. Sometimes the conflict was over biblical interpretation or social practice, but always at the epicenter of the conflict was Jesus the messiah, whose teaching and life defined a holy God's will for God's holy people.

Indeed, the community's life together and in the world is patterned after the one who calls it into existence. We can speak of the holiness of this community because the Jesus of the fourfold Gospel is "God's holy one" (John 6:69; cf. Mark 1:24/Luke 4:34; Luke 1:35). Jesus's holiness is central to who he is, and the community is holy because Jesus is present where two or three are gathered in his name (cf. Matt 18:20). Yet the Gospel also makes it plain that this community, which is called out of the world in repentance and then led by the Spirit back into it for mission, practices holiness in the manner of Jesus. He both defines and embodies the holy life, and to follow him is to follow in the way of holiness (cf. Matt 21:32).

The Gospel of Matthew

The literary structure of Matthew introduces and frames the fourfold Gospel's discussion of this point. Jesus is first introduced as "God with us" (Matt 1:23) and then concludes the Gospel by telling his disciples that he chooses to remain "with you every day" to the very end of this age (28:20). The telling of the entire Gospel, then, is enclosed by this core belief that God's people are earth's dwelling place for God's Son. Moreover, God's kingdom, which demands that its citizens live by "God's righteousness" (6:33; cf. 21:31-32), is given to the "people " (i.e., the church; 21:43a) whose sins are forgiven (1:21) and whose repentance (4:17) now "produce[s] its fruit" (21:43b).[18]

Matthew expands the idea of the church's holiness by linking it with "righteousness."[19] In doing so, the Gospel rests a people's holy life upon God's righteousness. That is, the central demand of the repentant community to live into a greater righteousness (Matt 5:20) is not detached from its central belief in the righteousness of God's kingdom but integral to it. God's people are called to a manner of holy life and worship befitting the righteous place that awaits their future life with God.

As we would expect, the Gospel's use of "righteousness" sometimes implicates God (cf. Matt 6:33; 21:32): when believers gather in the presence of God, whose kingdom (6:33) and ways (21:32) are righteous, they are righteous by association, because God is righteous. Nonetheless, the principal meaning of righteousness in Matthew defines the character of God's people: a righteous people does God's will as exemplified and taught by Jesus, whose messianic mission "fulfills" (3:15) or satisfies scripture's moral requirement for life with a holy God (cf. 6:33). In this sense, righteousness regards the faithful practice of a covenant-keeping community (cf. 6:1); it is living right in the manner of the messiah who not only provides evidence of genuine repentance but also testifies to the apocalypse of God's salvation promised by "the Law and the Prophets" (cf. 5:17-20).[20] For Matthew, then, righteousness is the essential mark of Christian community (cf. 7:21-24; 12:46-50).

The working relationship between Matthew's Jesus and his disciples is mostly a didactic one; hence, the Great Commission of a church that passes on "everything that I've commanded you" (28:20) continues Matthew's sense

---

18. Jack Dean Kingsbury argues that Matthew's narration of Jesus's presence "with" people is carefully limited to the circle of disciples to make the theological point that the church's worship and witness is conducted on the continuing authority of the exalted Jesus by whom God's righteous rule is empowered; see Kingsbury, *Matthew*, Proclamation Commentaries (Philadelphia: Fortress, 1977), 78–81.

19. See Donald A. Hagner, "Holiness and Ecclesiology: The Church in Matthew," in *Holiness and Ecclesiology in the New Testament*, ed. Kent E. Brower and Andy Johnson (Grand Rapids: Eerdmans, 2007), 40–56. Matthew's use of righteousness follows its Jewish conception as an ethical way of living that agrees with God's will disclosed in Torah. This is different from Paul's use of "righteousness," which concerns the community's right standing with God as one effect of Jesus's death. See Benno Przybylski, *Righteousness in Matthew and His World of Thought*, Society for New Testament Studies Monograph Series 41 (New York: Cambridge University Press, 1980), who regards Matthew's use of "righteousness" as continuing the synagogue's traditions of covenant keeping but detaches it from Matthew's understanding of God's way of salvation. The polemic against a nomism that substitutes prescriptions of covenant keeping for a vital relationship with God (Matt 6:1; cf. 5:20) in no way obviates the centrality of a holy life for Matthew as the evidence of a disciple's genuine repentance.

20. The plural number used in Luke 3:15 has also in mind the Baptizer's mission as the messiah's precursor. This is an important note since it is John, Jesus later says, who came "in the way of righteousness" (21:32 NRSV), the prophetic one preparing the way of righteousness of the holy other.

of Jesus's mission. Basically, the profile of a disciple in Matthew is one who *learns* all about Jesus. For this reason, the structure of Matthew's narrative intrudes upon itself before returning to its plotline to insert five expansive sermons (Matt 5–7; 10; 13; 18; 24–25) that gather Jesus's instruction around core topics of discipleship. Mostly, this instruction helps disciples discern those practices that produce good fruit (cf. 7:15-20; 12:33; 13:23; 21:43). Not only is the production of good fruit the test of true repentance, but it is also the hard evidence that distinguishes the church from unrepentant Israel (so 21:42-46) and, within the professing church (see 7:21; cf. 16:16), between its true and false members (7:21-27).

Although this conception is worked out in all five discourses, the first one, the Sermon on the Mount, is most instructive for our purpose, since it supplies road markers that guide the community "in the way of righteousness" or holiness (Matt 21:32 NRSV).[21] It is primarily here that the first words spoken by Matthew's Jesus, which claim that "righteousness" is "fulfill[ed]" by his messianic mission (3:15), are picked up again (5:17, 20) to define more concretely the practices of the narrow way—the way of righteousness—that leads God's people into the apocalypse of God's salvation (cf. 7:13-14, 21-28). In fact, within a narrative context in which sermons provide commentary on preceding narratives, this sermon provides the criterion of genuine repentance—that is, the "fruit" that the Baptizer earlier insists demonstrates repentance (3:8). In this sense, a "greater righteousness" (5:20) is also "greater" in a practical sense, because it obeys Jesus's call to repent (4:17) by following his instruction and example (4:19).

The Sermon defines this "greater righteousness" by combining three integral elements of holy living that are of a piece with the life of Jesus who fulfills "the Law and the Prophets": character (Matt 5:3-12), conduct (5:21–6:18), and criterion (6:19–7:28). The *character* of the kind of community that can actually live in the manner demanded by Jesus is set out. In this regard, right living is a matter not of ritual purity but of the cultivation of those inward pursuits that align with the purposes of God's reign. The differences between Matthew's and Luke's versions of the "beatitudes" (Matt 5:3-12; Luke 6:20-26) are well known and their sources and redactions are understood in different ways. What seems clear from their comparison is Matthew's interest in the inward life of the repentant disciple (5:6)—a righteousness of "being" as the

---

21. The literature on the Sermon on the Mount is vast and deep, and I would encourage you to dip into it. The church's moral formation begins there. Perhaps the most fluent interpretation of the Sermon for our purposes is by a contemporary pastoral theologian, Ellen T. Charry, in her superb book, *By the Renewing of Your Minds: The Pastoral Function of Christian Doctrine* (New York: Oxford University Press, 1997), 61–83.

precondition of performing God's will (cf. Matt 12:46-50). The placement of the beatitudes at the head of the Sermon implies the appellative, "blessed," which designates the spiritual qualities necessary to perform God's will.

The *conduct* of this "greater righteousness" is first illustrated by a series of six so-called antitheses (Matt 5:21-26, 27-30, 31-32, 33-37, 38-42, 43-48), which adapt Israel's "Law and Prophets" (i.e., Jesus's Bible; 5:17-18) in fresh ways for the messianic age Jesus has inaugurated. While not abolishing scripture's teaching, he does suggest that his interpretations "fulfill" or rightly understand God's will revealed in Israel's scripture (5:17-19). The messianic definition of holiness for God's people, then, is not brand-new instruction, since it concerns the very same patterns of corporate life that concern God on Mount Sinai. But the patterns of righteousness that he now stipulates are "greater" in the sense that traditional practices or biblical interpretations are set aside in favor of more radical applications of scripture's two love commandments: to love God means that the community does so bodily and publicly and also with the thoughts and inward intentions of the "heart" (5:28; cf. 6:15); to love one's neighbor means that the community embraces its enemies (5:44) in like manner as God, who sends needed provisions to "the righteous and the unrighteous" (5:45).

To these more expansive (or "greater") patterns of moral conduct are added three traditional piety practices that also display righteousness but in a manner that cultivates the disciple's personal relationship with God (Matt 6:1): almsgiving (6:2-4), prayer (6:5-15), and fasting (6:16-18). How the disciple handles personal possessions (6:19-34) is also crucial in the pursuit of God whose kingdom is righteous (6:33).

Finally, a *criterion* is stipulated, which measures by a stark standard, that offers a choice between two competing ways, one that leads to destruction and another, more difficult way that leads to life (Matt 7:13-14). While we are always motivated by inward affections, one recognizes good choices by the fruit they produce (7:15-20). Thus, even though one professes faith in Jesus as Lord (7:21a) and produces good works in his name (7:22), only those who bear the fruit produced by doing God's will (7:21b) according to Jesus's instruction (7:24a) will enter God's kingdom "on the Judgment Day" (7:21-22b, 24b-27). Nowhere is the contrast between Pauline and Matthew's definitions of righteousness clearer. While the criterion for Paul is whether or not faith is placed in the faithfulness of the crucified Jesus, lest one boasts in someone or something other than God's grace, the "greater righteousness" taught by Matthew's Jesus stipulates a different choice: whether it produces good fruit in a manner commensurate with the righteousness of God's kingdom.

Moreover, the interpenetrating relationship between the community's character ("being") and conduct ("doing") extends to personal and public locations and to religious and ethical practices in a way that the community's present choices have implications for its future with God. In this sense, then, the community's holiness factors into the Gospel's eschatology in a way that is not detached from soteriology. Only the community that chooses to live the robust righteousness stipulated by Jesus will enter into God's kingdom "on the Judgment Day" (cf. 7:21-28).

The Gospel of Mark

The use of irony in Mark's telling of Jesus's story is nowhere more evident than in the demoniac's recognition of Jesus as "the holy one from God" (1:24). Clearly, the "sudden beginning" of this Gospel shapes the reader's impression of Jesus's centrality to the gospel of God: it is he, as God's Son, who provides its genesis (1:1) and it is he who first announces its glad tidings that he has brought near the kingdom that God promises Israel according to scripture (1:15). The failure of Jesus's followers to recognize the purpose of his messianic mission reinforces the Gospel's portrait of Jesus as of singular importance. The reader understands why a misunderstood Jesus is finally executed by Rome but also why the execution of God's Son supports God's initial audition that he is the Son who is "dearly love[d] [or faithful]" (1:10-11) and that his death is messianic on this basis.

The irony is not only that Jesus's demonic opponents get his identity right from the very beginning of his messianic mission when those closest to him do not; the compressed manner of Mark's storytelling juxtaposes who Jesus is—the "holy one from God"—with his announcement that he has brought God's promised kingdom "here"—that is, in the presence of him, "the holy one from God" (Mark 1:15, 24). Set within a narrative that gathers various individuals—Simon, Andrew, James, John, Levi—to follow him, Jesus constitutes a community of disciples who draw near to him, who become holy because they keep company with "the holy one from God" (cf. 3:31-35). Of course, the irony of this relationship is that Mark's profile of this holy band of disciples is especially unholy in practice and obdurate in understanding, which underwrites the Gospel's theology of grace: the community is holy because the one who calls and convenes them is holy.

The story setting in which the episode of Jesus's calling of Levi is placed (Mark 2:1–3:6), concluding with the repetition of the opening scene when only a demoniac knew Jesus's real identity, suggests other details of the community made holy because of their nearness to the holy one sent by God. In the first place, it is clear from Jesus's example that the predicate of a holy people is not conformity to the practices of institutionalized purity. Jesus forgives and heals without priestly sanction and outside temple protocol (2:1-12). He eats with Levi, a tax collector, in his home with "many tax collectors and sinners" (2:15), which resets the social boundaries to include the very ones excluded by institutional practices that define and make people holy— Sabbath keeping (3:1-6), Torah keeping (2:23-28), and exorcism (3:7-12).

Here again, however, Mark concentrates the reader on Jesus. In breaking down the leading symbols of his Jewish world and its institutionalization of purity, we should expect Mark's Jesus to follow Matthew's Jesus in making right living a matter of the heart (5:8, 28; 6:21) in addition to those public practices based upon his messianic reading of Torah (see the section on the Gospel of Matthew under "The Church's Holiness according to the Fourfold Gospel"). Once again Mark's Jesus rather calls attention to the "hardened hearts" of his disciples (6:52; 8:17 AT).

Significantly, whereas Matthew's Jesus calls his disciples to the moral and religious rigors of a "greater righteousness," with a healthy supply of wisdom and mercy to perform it (Matt 11:25-30), Mark's Jesus claims that he does not call "righteous people, but sinners" (Mark 2:17). It is this motley gathering of sinners and tax collectors, the diseased and working-class poor that Jesus forgives, heals, and calls out of Israel to be near him, the holy one/Son of God, that transforms how we think of a holy people. Precisely because Mark assigns a people's holiness to their proximity to the holy one of God— whether they keep his company and believe the gospel he proclaims (1:15; cf. 1:1)—the rules of engagement also change. To separate from impurity and draw close to the holy one is a real possibility for anyone who chooses to leave immediately what they are doing to follow Jesus.

Mark seems to invite us to take a step back from Matthew's Gospel, especially from its grand presumption that to follow Jesus onto the "way of righteousness" includes living like him, to concentrate on the ultimate importance of "Jesus Christ, God's Son," whose messianic mission marks the "beginning of the good news." But perhaps this Jesus-only beginning is glossed by the Gospel's so-called longer ending that tells the story of the disciples' genuine repentance (at long last!). The reader is left to suppose that only after the departure of the risen One are the repentant disciples willing and able to confirm their proclamation of Jesus's gospel "by the signs associated with them" (Mark 16:20). They are then a holy people not because the departed Jesus is with them but because they are now enabled to engage in holy practices.

48

The Gospel of Luke

Luke's distinctive portrait of Jesus as God's prophetic messiah, which he announces in Nazareth at the beginning of his mission (Luke 4:16-21), is introduced by a series of programmatic Christmas carols (1:47-55; 1:67-79; 2:14; 2:29-32) that point out Jesus's importance in the history of God's salvation and that point readers forward into his story as Savior, Christ, and Lord (2:11). In particular, two typologies of holiness are introduced by the lyrics of these carols that are especially important in understanding Luke's contribution to our confession of a holy church.

First, Mary's doxology (Luke 1:47-55) predicts the "great reversal" of various social forces at work that undermine God's intentions for Israel (personified as "arrogant," "powerful," and "rich") by "the mighty one" whose name is "holy" (1:49). In context, Mary is herself the beneficiary of this reversal since she is poor and powerless, but God has noticed and appointed her (1:48) to do something great: to give birth to God's holy Son (1:49; cf. 1:35). Subsequently, Jesus tells the Pharisees, who are gatekeepers of God's holiness, that God's kingdom is "among you" (17:20-21). Most understand Jesus's provocative one-liner as self-referential: God's reign is embodied in his persona and the practices of his ministry.[22]

Critical, yet often overlooked by commentators of Mary's *Magnificat*, is the apposition of God's "might," sufficient to overturn the forces of evil to put the world to rights, and naming this God as "holy." That is, it is her recognition of God's holiness, not only God's power, which prompts Mary's praise. John Webster rightly contends that "holiness is a mode of God's activity; talk of God's holiness identifies the manner of his relation to us."[23] Those who define holiness here in terms of God's transcendence or sovereignty—a God who stands *apart from Mary* (and us)—misread its meaning. While a holy God must reverse everything that is unholy, Mary names God "holy" because God freely bends down to her in mercy in order to purify and bind her to God's own redemptive purposes.[24] For this reason, Mary is right to respond to God and to God's appointment that she bear the messiah by purifying herself according to the Law of Moses (Luke 2:22-23).

The verbal aspect of the aorist that Mary uses when describing the pattern of God's mercy (Luke 1:51-55) may suggest that the practices of Jesus's messianic mission have already realized God's final victory over evil. The angel's

---

22. See Darrell L. Bock, *Luke 9:51-24:53* (Grand Rapids: Baker, 1996), 1414–19.

23. John Webster, *Holiness* (Grand Rapids: Eerdmans, 2003), 41.

24. Ibid., 45–52.

earlier declaration that the child promised to Mary will be "holy" (1:35) implies that holiness is the mode of his messianic activity. That is, the repetition of *hagios* to name both God (1:49) and God's Son (1:35) underscores their partnership in reversing evil for good. Hence, Jesus's announcement in Nazareth at the beginning of his mission that he is Isaiah's Spirit-filled prophet who comes to proclaim good news to the poor should not take the reader by surprise. To release captives, give sight to the blind, liberate the oppressed, and announce the year of Jubilee (4:18-19) show what the victory of a holy God looks like at garden level.

Consider the familiar stories of mealtime in this Gospel. What, how, and with whom people ate (or did not) in a Jewish world "encoded messages about hierarchy, inclusion and exclusion, boundaries and crossing [the] boundaries" of a holy God.[25] In particular, the levitical "holiness code" (Lev 17–26), expanded by rabbinical casuistry during Judaism's Second Temple period, provided Jesus's world with expansive instructions delineating the clean from the unclean in the conduct of meals. Because sharing meals are times spent with friends and family, finding Jesus at mealtime with a varied set of people embodies a prophetic sensibility that sets new boundary markers for a community that now includes the "unholy." His calling of Levi, for example, is framed by a meal when Jesus eats with Levi and other tax collectors and sinners (Luke 5:29-32; cf. 19:1-10). At another meal hosted by Pharisees, Jesus seats a range of rejects at his table: the sinful woman who bathes his feet whom he then forgives (7:36-50) and "the poor, crippled, and blind" outcasts (14:1-24; cf. 4:18). Moreover, when not properly cleansing himself for a meal, he chastises Pharisees for their elevated concern for practices of a public purity rather than for a purity of the heart (11:37-52).

These prophetic acts prepare the reader for Jesus's last meals with the community of disciples. Luke's telling of the Last Supper tradition (22:14-20) provides the context for settling rivalries over greatness (22:24). If Peter represents the others, the reader already knows that the disciples are not great because of their spiritual prowess (cf. 24:31-34) or because of their socioeconomic status (cf. 24:35-38).[26] Rather, a seat at the messiah's eschatological

---

25. Joel B. Green, *The Theology of the Gospel of Luke* (New York: Cambridge University Press, 1995), 87.

26. The Gospel of Luke's Jesus announces good news to the poor, since the benefits of God's kingdom also belong to the poor and powerless (6:20; 7:22; 14:12-14; 16:19-31). The community's possessions are not privatized but shared. This point, thematic of both Luke and Acts, challenges any connection between holiness and wealth, as though the believer's material possessions are divine compensation for holy living. This assumption is especially critiqued in Jesus's responses to the wealthy ruler (18:18-30) and probably also in his parable of Lazarus and the rich man (16:19-31).

banquet is based upon faithful service to God's reign (22:25-27). Likewise, the holiness of the community that keeps company with Jesus is not a matter of its social or religious purity but a matter of its steady loyalty to Jesus (22:28-30).

Similarly, when the risen Jesus is invited to share a meal by incredulous disciples who initially fail to recognize him (Luke 24:13-29), their "aha experience" happens "as he broke the bread" with them (24:30-35). In this case, however, their hospitality toward a stranger, a holy practice, prepares them for an awakening and spiritual reversal.

A second typology of holiness is introduced by Zechariah in his *Benedictus* (Luke 1:67-79): repentance for forgiveness *of sins* (1:77; cf. 3:3; 4:18; 5:20-24; 7:47-49; 11:4; 15:11-24; 24:47). What this typology emphasizes is not particular programs of holiness but the reorientation of sinful affections and attitudes that prompt the repentant community to separate itself from unholy things in order to walk in the peacemaking ways of a merciful God (cf. 1:78-79; cf. 6:36).

The shift of Zechariah's address to his son, the Baptizer, has the effect of relocating God's fulfillment of the biblical promise of a restored Israel to Jesus's messianic mission. John's preparatory mission supplies God's people with the "knowledge of salvation" through the forgiveness of their sins (Luke 1:77 AT; cf. 1:15-17) so as to "guide us on the path of peace" (1:79). In this case, the two catchphrases, "knowledge of salvation," found only here in the fourfold Gospel, and "forgiveness of sins," are linked together to indicate that the people's spiritual experience of forgiveness not only forms its knowledge of God's salvation—that is, the knowledge that God's promise of salvation is fulfilled comes from the experience of forgiveness or inward cleansing from sins—but also is the precondition of covenanting with a holy God in the way of peace, the mark of repentant/restored Israel (1:79).

Luke's Jesus picks up this typology of forgiveness to mark both the beginning (4:18) and ending (24:47) of his mission. God's people are characterized by their inward purification: their sins are mercifully forgiven and their covenant relationship with God righted because they have repented to follow God's Christ onto the way of shalom. But this prophetic calculus is not exclusively spiritual and inward; God's forgiveness of a repentant people's sins clears the way for the Spirit's formation of a prophetic community that loves even the enemy without expectation of return (6:27-36; 11:4).[27] Moreover, if the Evangelist composes the distinctive "central section" of his Gospel

---

27.   For the idea of a "prophetic community," see Luke Timothy Johnson, *Prophetic Jesus, Prophetic Church* (Grand Rapids: Eerdmans, 2011).

(9:51–19:44) by following the same sequence of topics found in Deuteronomy, as C. F. Evans has argued, then Jesus's instructions to his community of disciples follows the example of Moses who grounds a repentant people's confession of God in their covenant-keeping practices.[28]

The Gospel of John

Thomas L. Brodie argues that John's Gospel is plotted by the parallel story of the ravages of sin and division and a "greater" story, rooted in divine love, which focuses on holiness and unity.[29] Peter's confession of Jesus as "God's holy one" (6:69), even if without the Spirit's clarifying revelation, anticipates the messianic triumph over sin and disunity. In this sense, the fourth Gospel depicts Jesus's mission as a sanctifying act, culminating in his death as God's Lamb that purifies the world of its sin (1:29).

The movement from sin to holiness that Brodie speaks of is nowhere clearer than in his Passover commentary on the Paschal Lamb in John 13–17. Beginning with Jesus's foot washing of disciples, Jesus concludes his teaching by petitioning God as God's Son to sanctify the community of disciples he selects and sends into the world with God's word (17:17-19). Jesus's definitive claim that God's "word is truth" (17:17) is an admission that the world, contaminated by evil, holds no power over the community that possesses God's word. Holiness belongs to those who possess God's truth. The Gospel's narrative, then, plots the dynamic of a community that Jesus, the holy Son of God, calls into existence and then sends into the world as a sanctified people. The world's rejection of Jesus is a rejection of God's truth instantiated by Jesus, which sanctifies those who abide in him.

Unlike the synoptic narratives that delay and typically frustrate the disciples' awareness and confession of Jesus's messianic identity, Jesus's initial call to discipleship comes with a catalogue of christological titles that set out what believers already know about him before his journey to the cross begins: they follow him as the messiah, God's Lamb, rabbi, the prophet like Moses, and God's Son sent from heaven (John 1:32-51). In fact, the Baptizer, who bears witness to Jesus as God's Lamb, sends Jesus two disciples. In any case, these titles express the core beliefs about Jesus that would sharply distinguish his

---

28. C. F. Evans, *Saint Luke*, TPI New Testament Commentaries (London: SCM Press, 1990), 30–44. Cf. Robert W. Wall, "Martha and Mary (Luke 10.38-42) in the Context of a Christian Deuteronomy," *Journal for the Study of the New Testament* 35 (1989): 19–35.

29. Thomas L. Brodie, *The Gospel according to John: A Literary and Theological Commentary* (New York: Oxford University Press, 1993), 505.

disciples, who believe in him, from the rest of the world, which has rejected him (3:1-21; 17:14). Thus, the sense of Peter's initial confession of Jesus, expressed with indicative perfect active verbs, is that he fully "believe[s] and know[s] that [Jesus is] God's holy one" (6:69). Of course, Peter's boldness is glossed by the Evangelist's purpose statement that the Gospel story and especially its resurrection narrative are written to fund and confirm this knowing faith (20:30-31). The irony of John's story of Jesus is that this knowing faith, so clearly and confidently expressed from the beginning, is only possible *after* the resurrection upon reception of the revealing Spirit (7:39).[30]

Nonetheless, the *faith* community abides in Jesus as the holy one from God and is thereby sanctified and sent out (via the Spirit; cf. John 20:19-23) into the unholy, hostile world (17:20-26) by him to serve God just as he had (17:16-19). No Gospel so keenly makes this existential connection between the holy one and the community he makes holy by his abiding presence: the church is holy *because* it abides in the risen Jesus who is holy.

This interpenetrating union, promised during the Lord's "Farewell Discourse," comes with the promise of the Holy Spirit (John 14:15-17, 25-26; 15:25-26; 16:7-11, 12-15) for good reason: the truth about Jesus, who is then believed on to acquire life (20:31; cf. 3:6-8), is revealed/reminded by the Spirit (14:26; 16:12-17; cf. 7:39) who abides with Jesus in those whom Jesus chooses (14:16-17). This Holy Spirit is not only unavailable to the unholy world, but its availability to a particular community effectively separates it from the world even as holy remains holy by its *necessary* separation from profane things (i.e., "the world"; cf. 15:18-26; 16:7-11).

Although the fourth Gospel understands the community's holiness in terms of its Spirit-abiding relationship with "God's holy one" (John 6:69), this more existential conception of holiness is witnessed by public acts of self-sacrificial love for one another. In particular, since Jesus's holy character is disclosed for all to see by his act of self-sacrificial love on the cross (cf. 12:23-32)—an act that takes away sin/death that separates the profane world from its holy, saving God (11:4, 40)—the Spirit's animating presence in the community is conditioned upon its obedience to Christ's commandment to love one another (14:15-21). In this same way, the community's sanctifying presence in the world can be discerned in the world by its own acts of self-sacrificial love (17:18-23). The circularity of this idea that the obedient love that conditions the reception of the Spirit, whose presence conveys the truth about Jesus that cues the faith necessary for holiness, secures the

---

30. See Gary M. Burge, *The Anointed Community: The Holy Spirit in the Johannine Tradition* (Grand Rapids: Eerdmans, 1987), for the community's relationship with the Spirit according to John's Gospel.

inseparability between faith and loving one another. In fact, if Jesus is holy and if his holiness is exemplified by self-sacrificial love, then a community sanctified by his presence should be holy just as he is holy and so love one another self-sacrificially. Jesus's prediction is that the profane world will take note of such a holy people (17:23).[31]

Finally, there may be a connection, however muted, between this conception of holiness and the Gospel's well-known interests in Jewish feasts and Christian sacraments (cf. John 3:5; 6:35-58; 7:35-37; 13:1-14; 19:34). Both themes are vested with christological importance precisely because they both help identify the ultimate importance of Jesus. Both elements seek to narrow the distance between Jesus and the Israel that birthed him (feasts) and the church given birth by him (sacraments). The priestly insistence that a holy people and its holy places are holy because of the faithful presence of a holy God who made them so is carried over to John. Jesus self-identifies with the Jewish festivals that proclaim the holiness of land and of God's people as possessions of a holy God; he, too, is "God's holy one" whose presence sanctifies the community with whom he abides.

Likewise, the extraordinary allusion to the Eucharist in John 6:41-58, which stipulates that the one who eats Jesus's flesh and drinks his blood "remains in me and I in them" (6:56) and "will live forever" (6:58), completely overcomes the temporal and spatial distance between him and his disciples. Of course, the reaction to Jesus's "harsh" teaching is unbelief and dismissal (6:59-65). This intimate union between the Lamb, whose flesh and blood takes away sin, and those whose sins are forgiven is carefully limited to those who believe (6:64) and do not quit following him (6:66). Rather, they recognize him for who he is: "God's holy one" (6:69).

The question may be asked, what does the prior controversy over consuming Jesus have to do with this confession of his holiness as the messiah-Son sent from God? The implication is that a people's holiness is in some sense linked to the Eucharistic practice in which the mystery of consuming the body and blood of the living Jesus makes them one with God's holy one. This "harsh" practice publicly separates those who do not quit following Jesus from those who have. Many scholars also argue that John's Peter is merely confessing Jesus in different words than found on his lips in the Synoptic Gospels in a way that recognizes that his primary messianic task is priestly: Jesus is God's holy Son sent into the unholy world to purify it of sin (John 3:17; 10:36; 17:17-19). In this sense, those who do not quit on Jesus share in the results of his messianic

---

31. There may also be a connection between this conception of holiness and the Gospel's interest in Jewish feasts and Christian sacraments.

work and are cleansed of sin; unbelievers and those who quit Jesus belong to the world, unclean and unsaved (3:17-21; and so on).

The Church's Catholicity according to the Fourfold Gospel

The Gospel of Matthew

The beliefs that implicate the church's catholicity especially shape the fourfold Gospel's presentation of Jesus's mission sayings and final instructions to his disciples. Matthew's priority within the canonical collection is once again important for establishing the inclusive nature of the messiah's community and its mission to the last and least. This claim is surprising since Jesus's initial instruction to the Twelve, which picks up his earlier promise to "show you how to fish for people" (Matt 4:19), tells them to avoid particular people—those living in the Gentile and Samaritan regions of Roman Palestine (10:5)—and to "go instead to the lost sheep, the people of Israel" (10:6). On this basis, the antecedent of the angel's announcement that Jesus will save "his people" from their sins may be drawn narrowly to circumscribe only Jews (cf. 15:21-28; also, 8:1-13).

The Gentile magi's adoration of the infant Jesus in Matthew's story of his birth (2:1-12; cf. 8:11-12), however, already hints at the more universal scope of the messiah's mission. Moreover, the gospel Jesus instructs his disciples to proclaim to Israel, "The kingdom of heaven has come near" (10:7; cf. 4:23; 9:35), carries with it Israel's belief that God's rule encompasses the entire creation including every nation and power. The implication that the disciples' message is the drawing near of God's heavenly reign through Jesus, "God [i.e., God's reign] with us" (1:23), holds ultimate importance for both Jews and non-Jews.

This narrative of mission, even though intimating a more universal scope, is carefully set by Matthew within a more expansive story of Israel's rejection of Jesus (Matt 8–12). Israel's rejection of Jesus extends, then, to his disciples who are not above their teacher (10:24) and should expect to provoke the same rejection and persecution (10:40-42; cf. 5:10-12). Rather than silencing them or pushing them toward the margins, Israel's harsh rejection of Jesus and the mission of his followers seems to cue an expansion of his mission's scope to include non-Jews (cf. 24:9-14; 26:13; 28:18-20).

Matthew appears to carefully set this dynamic within the bounds of salvation's history, so that Jesus's messianic mission (1:21; 4:17, 23; 9:35; 15:21-24), preceded by the Baptizer (3:1-2) and followed immediately by the Twelve (10:5-7), is to the household of Israel, while the post-Easter church's mission following the risen Jesus's departure is to all the nations of earth. This same narrative movement, however, is then followed in the other three Gospels, and especially by Acts, as the normative pattern of the church's universal mission: the gospel that announces God's salvation is proclaimed to "the Jew first and also to the Greek" (Rom 1:16-17). Quite apart from its rejection motif, Matthew's plotline narrates this same missionary ideal.

Hardly another biblical passage crystallizes the dynamic tension inherent in the church's catholicity more clearly than Matthew's so-called Great Commission (28:18-20). While the different versions of the Gospel's final snapshot are typically explained as each Evangelist's editorial summary of his distinctive portrait of Jesus, each "great commission" also carries with it an implicit ecclesiology. In the first place, in addressing the future church, the risen Jesus asserts his cosmic authority (Matt 28:18; cf. Dan 7:14). The catchphrase, "in heaven and on earth," claims an authority that is coextensive with the creator's reign, which his messianic mission brought near and his spiritual presence continues to mediate to the end of the age whenever two or three disciples (i.e., the church) gather in his name (18:18-20). The tasks given to the disciples are grounded in the risen Christ's authority. The instruction of "all the nations" to comply with what Jesus taught them, the command for nations to follow the risen Jesus as they now do, and the baptism of nations into life with the triune God are all predicated on their authorization to do so. The core tasks of Matthew's Jesus, who is teacher and exemplar of God's righteousness, now become the core tasks of the church to the end of the age.

But Matthew's Jesus had no Gentile mission; his mission was to Israel and so was the initial mission of his disciples (10:5-6). What is most remarkable, then, about Jesus's parting words to the community of his disciples is its stunning catholicity. As already mentioned, Jesus repeatedly hints at the universal scope of the church's mission following his departure (cf. 24:9-14; 26:13), but here he demands it as the public marker of the church in the world.

Yet, the Lord's Great Commission also implies a conflict that plots the church's future, already predicated by Matthew's story of the crucified One. On the one hand, the scope of the church's mission is all-inclusive—it is to the nations—but, on the other hand, the church's message is exclusive: it is the instruction of Jesus that is obeyed, and it is into the triune God that the repentant are baptized. As Acts makes clear, more often than not, when the church's message that demands allegiance to a particular Lord is proclaimed to and for all the nations, the hard result is conflict, not peace. The normative ideal of the church set out by Matthew's Jesus implies that those with ears to hear the gospel message will suffer violence upon entering God's kingdom (Matt 11:12; cf. Luke 16:16).

The Gospel of Mark

Mark's insistence on Jesus's universal importance as God's Son occupies the centerpiece of his Gospel (1:1; cf. 1:11; 9:7). This truth terrifies demons who "know" Jesus (1:23-27; 5:7-13) while at the same time escaping his disciples who do not understand (4:10-13; 6:52; 7:17-18; 8:14-21; 9:10, 32) and his family who seeks to restrain him (3:21-22, 31-32). For this reason, Jesus redraws his family unit to include only "whoever does God's will" (3:33-35), which means to accept Jesus as the beloved Son in whom God's will is at work (1:11, 15; 14:36). While no other family value (ethnicity, gender, and so on) is stipulated, Mark's unrelentingly negative portrait of the community of those closest to Jesus commends the difficulty of doing God's will instantiated by Jesus. While Jesus's family stays open to new members of any sort, the demand of joining it remains difficult indeed.

Mark's version of the mission of the Twelve (6:7-13) clearly extends the tasks of Jesus's ministry to still others; they no longer remain "with him" (3:14) but are now given a share of his mission. As with Matthew, the mission of the disciples to be fishers of people (Mark 1:17) covers the same scope as Jesus who has no Gentile mission. Its initial success forms one of the Gospel's great ironies: those so hard of hearing (6:52; 7:18; 8:17-18) nonetheless are allowed to share powerfully in Jesus's messianic calling.

Israel's rejection of Jesus's mission to Israel, so prominent in Matthew and explanatory of the outward movement of the church's future mission to the nations, is missing in Mark. In part for this reason, most scholars explain Mark's so-called longer ending (16:9-20) as a conflation of other Gospel traditions (Matthew and Luke) and Acts in order to conclude this Gospel with an account of the risen Jesus's commission for the church to "go into the whole world and proclaim the good news to every creature" (16:15).[32] The

---

32. I distinguish between the "authenticity" of this ending (i.e., whether the Evangelist wrote it) and its canonicity (i.e., how it functions within scripture) in Robert W. Wall, "A Response to Thomas/Alexander, 'and the Signs Are Following' (Mark 16.9-20)," *Journal of Pentecostal Theology* 11, no. 2 (2003): 171–83.

role of Jesus's elaborate commission saying within the final form of Mark's Gospel is not only to secure the continuity between Jesus's mission and the church's future mission and membership (16:14-18) but then to attest to the ongoing presence of the risen Jesus "with them" (16:20). The catholicity of the church's global mission ("into the whole world") and its membership ("to every creature") is confirmed by the active participation of the risen Lord "with them" to confirm the gospel "word" by the "signs associated with them" (16:15, 20). The catholicity of the church is predicated on the catholicity of the risen Jesus's lordship!

The Gospel of Luke

The prophetic nature of Jesus's ministry, according to Luke (see the section on the Gospel of Luke under "The Church's Holiness according to the Fourfold Gospel"), shapes its contribution to the Gospel's conception of the church's catholicity. Luke's accounts of the mission of the Seventy (10:1-20) and of the Great Commission (24:44-53), while sharing common goods with Matthew and Mark, are different in important details and context. In the first place, quite apart from their different roles within the NT, Luke and Acts form a narrative unity; in some sense, the inchoate mission of the disciples narrated by the Gospel is read in a wider context with the narrative of the post-Pentecost church's mission in Acts. Not only do the linguistic connections between the ending of Luke and the beginning of Acts commend this reading strategy, but the movement from doubt (Luke 24:41) to worship immediately before Jesus's ascension (Luke 24:50-53) provides a theological explanation for the church's bold mission "to all nations" in Christ's absence, according to Acts (Luke 24:47).

But in the second place, the story of the disciples' mission is fitted within the Gospel's central section (Luke 9:51–19:44), which narrates Jesus's journey to Jerusalem to complete the messianic mission for which he is sent into the world: to save the world from sin and death. Unlike Matthew, which limits the mission to "the people of Israel" (Matt 10:6), Luke's Jesus instructs the Seventy as an advance team to go "to every city and place he was about to go" but does not locate these places and towns on a map (Luke 10:1). When towns are finally mentioned (10:13; Chorazin and Bethsaida), they are typological of those public places where people hear the gospel but do not then affirm its truth. Nor is Luke especially interested in describing the mission itself but rather its purpose: to demonstrate publicly God's salvation from that invisible enemy, Satan (10:17-20). If this story carries with it an implied ecclesiology, perhaps it is that the church's mission "to every city and place" (10:1) purposes to enlighten their every inhabitant that God's wisdom has triumphed over "the rulers and powers in the heavens" (Eph 3:9-10). The catholicity of the church's mission extends to the heavens but also secures its purpose: to testify to heaven's malevolent powers and principalities that they are a defeated foe.

As expected, Luke's reception of the memory of Jesus's Great Commission is reshaped by his christological commitments. In particular, the church preaches Christ to all nations as witnesses to fulfilled prophecy; Jesus therefore begins his final instructions with the prophetic formula, "this is what is written" (in the scriptures) (24:46). More critically, however, what is prophesied by Israel's scriptures and realized by Jesus's messianic mission, is "a change of heart and life for the forgiveness of sins" (24:47). Again, the most stunning example of Jesus's stretch to the marginal ones is his call for sinners to repent. If most reform movements of his day (and our own day) stressed a holiness ordered by holiness codes, Jesus's mission called sinners (not saints) to repent to receive God's forgiveness. While Luke's Jesus also demands the repentant to bear fruit in keeping with their decision to follow Jesus, his clear emphasis is to reach out to the poor and powerless, the lost and last to invite them into fellowship with God. Hence, Jesus announces his prophetic mission is to the poor, whether the financially or spiritually marginal of his world. His commission, then, is for the church to do likewise.

The other distinctive element of Luke's prophetic vision of Jesus's commission is the implication of the Spirit as the power source behind the church's mission to sinners. By comparing the two stories of the mission, the reader detects that the fall of Satan that Jesus earlier envisions has here been replaced by the filling of the Spirit. The coordination of these two events, especially when juxtaposed with the exaltation of the risen Jesus so reminiscent of Revelation's vision of Satan's heavenly defeat (Rev 12:1-12), predicts another kind of tension than the one provoked when the church proclaims a particular messiah in and for all the nations. In this case, the cosmic cast of the church's global mission instantiates a spiritual slugfest that pits the defeated but outraged Satan (see Rev 12:12; cf. Luke 10:17-20) against the powerful Spirit of the victorious Lord. We know how this struggle ends, but, in the meanwhile, perhaps the mark of the church catholic includes this deeply spiritual conflict occasioned whenever it takes the gospel of forgiveness into all the nations.

The Gospel of John

The sectarian nature of the church implied by the fourth Gospel supplies a different but necessary element of catholicity to the fourfold Gospel. On the one hand, the all-inclusive embrace of the nations, clearly articulated by the Synoptic Gospels, is not found in John. While the risen Jesus gives his disciples the Holy Spirit with the authority to "forgive *anyone's* sins" (20:22-23; emphasis added), his subsequent exchange with Peter that clarifies the costly demand to "follow me" (21:19; cf. 1:43) makes it clear that the self-sacrificial tasks involved in doing so concern the nurture of God's people (21:15-17) and not just "anyone." Even as the Spirit is given by Jesus to send the disciples out into the world to forgive sins, his earlier teaching of the Spirit defines its role in securing the risen One's continuing presence with his disciples until his return for them (14:1-5). The church's catholic mission to love even enemies demanded by the Synoptic Gospels' Jesus is circumscribed more narrowly by John's Jesus to love other believers (13:34; 15:12, 17).

Moreover, no other Gospel more sharply distinguishes the community of disciples from the hostile "world" that surrounds them than John. While God loves the world (John 3:16), Jesus does not pray for the world (17:9), since by rejecting his name those who populate the "world" belong to the realm of evil whereas Jesus abides "with" or "in" the community of disciples who do not belong to the world. Yes, they go out into the world but as a sanctified people—set apart from nonbelievers, living in the world but in no way integral to the evils that populate it (17:9-19). The church catholic witnesses to the world but in an indirect and implicit manner: they love and forgive one another and by doing so bear witness in the world of God's truth (17:20-23).

The question we must ask, then, is this: What role does John's more sectarian impulse perform in shaping the full Gospel's witness to the mission of the church catholic? Any answer to this question from a canonical perspective cannot be reduced to the old patristic notion that John's is a more "spiritual," inward Gospel and for this reason is less concerned with the practices or scope of the church's mission; nor should our response turn on the Evangelist's use of different sources, which only detaches the Gospels from each other on historical grounds.

A better response begins with the final shape of the Gospel itself. John's conception of a sectarian community is distinctive but not definitive, singular but integral to the fourfold whole. In some sense, the fourth Gospel glosses the first three in a way that resists appropriating the Gospel's witness to the church as though only the synoptic notion of catholicity, which stipulates the church's international, inclusive mission and membership counts. The church is also called to a mission of primary care for all believers—catholicity from within—without which the world remains ignorant of God's international, inclusive love.

Likewise, the synoptic definition of catholicity seems necessary when the sectarian impulse of the community shuts itself off to the outsider, even to other Christians who do not believe or vote the same way. Love for one's own can become incestuous and self-centered to the point where the Spirit is given no wiggle room to breathe fresh air into the community's life. When this happens, John's conception of a community's witness that is based upon its love for other believers will lose its persuasive power.

The Church's Apostolicity according to the Fourfold Gospel

The Creed marks out God's people as an apostolic community. Unfortunately, the Magisterial Reformation focused apostolicity upon questions of authorship, which is still the case today. Reading the Gospel with the Creed, however, makes one more alert to the theological importance of the narrative's characterization of those who would become the church's apostles. Of course, within the Gospel's narrative world the Twelve are first of all disciples of Jesus who freely respond to his call by repentance and faith. Yet even after they receive special apostolic appointments (Luke 6:12-16; cf. Matt 10:1-4), the apostles often are depicted as spiritual failures, unable to anticipate their future leading role of God's people in Jesus's absence.

In fact, even though the risen Jesus was worshipped, the apostles still doubted him following his resurrection (Matt 28:17; Mark 16:14; Luke 24:38; John 20:24-29). The Lord's prediction of his death and departure were inconceivable to his starry-eyed followers; even after the fact, they did not fully understand the risen One they had witnessed and now worshipped. Unlike Acts or the Letters in which the apostles are lifted up as personal examples to imitate and provide authoritative instructions that shape the future of the church, the fourfold Gospel mostly depicts Jesus defining the terms of their future apostleship for his unwitting successors.

The Gospel of Matthew

Peter is singled out in the Synoptic Gospels as the first apostle among equals, especially in Matthew where his theological importance has long been recognized. Even though his importance is often generalized to include all disciples—he is the first called, the first to follow (4:18)—Matthew's Peter is important not so much as an exemplary disciple but as the church's apostle. For this reason, the two mentions of "church" in Matthew (16:18; 18:17), and only here in the Gospel, are in settings in which Jesus's relationship with Peter is highlighted (cf. 16:13-20; 18:21-22). Matthew's Jesus interprets the origins of Peter's prior confession of him as the messiah (16:16), which he shares with all of Jesus's followers, as privileged information that God reveals to him in particular as an action of divine blessing (16:17) and his future promise for the church (16:18-19).

Even prior to this climactic moment, Matthew reshapes the tradition of Jesus walking on the water by inserting a story of Peter's bold but failed attempt to join Jesus before he calms the stormy sea (Matt 14:28-31; cf. Mark 6:45-52; John 6:16-21). The consensus understands the theological import of Peter's story as paradigmatic of God's salvation, which does not promise freedom from deadly threat or doubt (cf. Matt 28:17) that makes for "weak faith" (14:31; cf. 8:26; 16:8; 17:20) but rather promises the calming presence of God in the midst of that threat and doubt. But we should understand the stunning exchange between Peter and Jesus, prior to the Lord's act of saving him, as indicative of apostleship. In a boat full of terrorized disciples, Peter alone asks Jesus to order him to do the impossible: to walk on water—an act of faith that moves mountains (see 17:20 in context). Jesus orders Peter to "Come!" in response, and his command hides the condition of his future apostleship: acts of real faith that can transform impossible circumstances into real (although hard) possibilities (17:20).

It would be difficult to exaggerate the importance of the history of interpreting Matthew 16:17-19 within the church and academy.[33] Although this passage should not be used as the basis for a distinctively Petrine office within the church, it does present Jesus's definition of the Petrine apostolate, which may then be true of other apostolic successors.

(1) In the first place, the opening beatitude targets only Peter, even if the Lord's blessing elsewhere in Matthew is more generally applied (5:3-11; 11:6, 25-30; 13:6). The elaboration of his name underscores the fact that Peter is blessed by God in a special and personal way. More important, he is special because he is the recipient of divine

---

33. See Ulrich Luz, *Matthew 8–20: A Commentary on the Gospel of Matthew.* Hermeneia (Grand Rapids: Fortress, 2001), 353–77.

revelation. The Pauline tradition understands apostolic authority in a similar way. In Galatians, Paul similarly claims that the origins of his apostleship credentials are not human but by revelation of Jesus Christ (Gal 1:12). Apostles are appointed carriers of divine revelation (cf. Titus 1:3); their authority is based on their accomplishment of this task.

(2) The singularity of Peter's importance takes the form of a promise that "you are Peter" (*sy ei Petros*) and "on this rock" (*epi tautē tē petra*) "I'll build my church" (Matt 16:18). Peter personifies the metaphor, "rock," which implies that his role will be to provide Christ's church with its stable foundation unthreatened by "the gates of the underworld [i.e., death]." Jesus does not elaborate on what he means when he states that Peter is the foundation's gatekeeper who prevents death from subverting Jesus's promise of life wherever two or three disciples gather in his name (18:19-20) until "the end of this present age" (28:20). What seems clear, however, is that Peter's apostolic role is to help secure the continuing presence of the risen Jesus in his absence. Surely, Acts picks up this point to narrate, in part, how Peter realizes this promise.

(3) The metaphor, "keys of the kingdom of heaven," is also cryptic of Peter's apostolic calling (Matt 16:19). He is told that these keys will enable him to regulate the traffic (of some unspecific sort) between heaven and earth, since "binding/loosing" language is widely thought a scribal idiom, which in Matthew's setting mostly concerns the interpretation of Israel's scripture. Although the meaning of this image is contested, I suspect Jesus has in mind Peter's scribal role in biblical interpretation. That is, Peter is granted special authority to declare God's word in scripture, not only to teach the church but also to correct those who get it wrong.

The Gospel of Mark

The story of Jesus appointing the Twelve is differently placed in the four Gospel narratives, and the choice of verbal ideas differs somewhat as well. Matthew, for example, first refers to the Twelve as "disciples" before adding a formal list of their names as "apostles" (Matt 10:1-4, and only here in the

Gospel). In context, Jesus "calls" and authorizes them to engage in a mission to the "people of Israel" (10:6). Mark first uses "apostles" in a similar context but parenthetically (3:14).[34] What is important to note is that Mark's sparse narrative more decisively links the origins of the church's apostolic office in Jesus's call to share in his messianic mission "with him." The repetition of the verbal idea of a divine appointment (*poieō*; Mark 3:14, 16), which Matthew does not include, underscores their special role. Moreover, the two *hina* clauses concentrate on the essential apostolic tasks that Acts will elaborate: apostles are partners with Jesus—"with him" in the sense of continuing what he says and does—and they are, like him, sent out (*apostellein*) to preach "God's good news" (Mark 1:14).

The only other mention of "apostles" in Mark (6:30) trades on the first. The Twelve "returned to Jesus" to participate with him in the feeding of the five thousand (6:30-44). Hardly a better illustration of the nature of apostleship exists in the Gospel tradition. In the first place, the Twelve tell Jesus everything "they had done and taught" (6:30), which the reader assumes continues what Jesus had begun to do and to say (cf. Acts 1:1). This is what apostles are appointed and sent out to do (see Acts 1:2). But apostleship is also an exercise of power in that they are authorized by Jesus both to do what he does and also to share in its powerful result. Hence, Jesus gives "the disciples" (i.e., the Twelve) food to distribute among the people, and the Twelve gather the leftovers, one basket per disciple. To the extent that the church's apostolicity turns on the nature of apostleship itself, then one should conclude that according to Mark, a community whose witness follows the lead of its apostolate is authorized to continue to do and say what Jesus did according to the Gospel witness in the confidence that it shares in the power of his Spirit.

The Gospel of Luke

Scholars often note that the more expansive use of "apostle" language in Luke anticipates the portrait of the apostles in Acts. I agree. But my present interest is to suggest Luke's unique contribution to the Gospel's understanding of the nature of the church's apostolicity. Luke more clearly distinguishes between the Twelve and the other disciples of Jesus; in fact, the six mentions of *apostolos* appear to always refer to the Twelve but perhaps should be understood as a theological metaphor of the church's apostolic office.

---

34. The manuscript evidence favors including the use of "apostles" here, especially since the primary Alexandrian manuscripts, which generally favor shorter readings, include the comment.

For example, Luke's Jesus first convenes the entire community of his disciples and then chooses the Twelve "from among them" (6:13); only Luke uses the verbal idea of election (*eklegomai*), which, especially following Jesus's prayer, "draws attention to the divine impetus for the selection of the twelve to serve as 'apostles.'"[35] The Gospel's division of an apostolic mission (9:1-17) from the Seventy-two (10:1-20), even though probably drawing upon a common tradition, also has the effect of more clearly distinguishing the twelve "apostles" from other "disciples" in developing a particular portrait of apostleship.

In my mind, nowhere in the Gospel is this portrait (and so the nature of apostleship) more powerfully developed than in the Last Supper setting (22:14-38). Luke alone purposefully places the apostles with Jesus at this Passover meal so that he can instruct them "before I suffer," not only to provide them with a normative commentary on his suffering but then also to prepare them for their future ministry following his departure from Jerusalem (cf. 9:31). What follows is a catalogue of fragments from this story that pertain to the nature of apostleship, which concerns the role of Jesus's successors in leading and forming the messianic community in the absence of its risen Lord.

> (1) Jesus passes the first cup to his disciples, instructing them to "share it among yourselves" (22:17). That is, not only does apostleship share in the Lord's authority, but also it is a shared authority, deeply rooted in fellowship and mission.

> (2) Jesus personifies the bread and cup as his body "given for you" and as "the new covenant by my blood," which is received not simply in memory of his death but also as a reminder of his continuing presence as the risen One (cf. 24:44). Hidden in this Passover liturgy, which becomes the church's Eucharist, is the essence of the gospel that is proclaimed by the apostles by which an apostolic community takes its shape under the direction of the Spirit. It is by the messiah's death "given *for you* . . . poured out *for you*" and witnessed by the apostles that the new covenant promised by Jeremiah is realized.

> (3) The intramural contest over who is greatest, found also in Matthew 18 and Mark 10, is placed at the Supper to define apostolic authority

---

35. Joel B. Green, *The Gospel of Luke.* New International Commentary on the New Testament (Grand Rapids: Eerdmans, 1997), 258.

in missional ways: apostles exemplify Jesus for others to see, especially in table fellowship, by serving others (22:24-27). Extending this to the church, its apostolicity is publicly marked out by its acts of humble service toward others.

(4) Jesus's farewell address, set within the bounds of the Last Supper tradition, is a distinctive addition to this Gospel (22:24-38). Only in Luke does Jesus confer his "royal power" upon the Twelve, thereby authorizing them to judge and lead a restored Israel (22:29-30), a succession of leadership that is realized at great cost according to the narrative plotted by Acts 1–7. The language of "judgment" implies that the apostles have the legal authority to decide who belongs to Israel, which is effectively brokered by the conduct and in the presence of the apostles (cf. Acts 5:1-16).

(5) The abrupt shift to a singular "you" in 22:32 following Jesus's repeated address of "Simon" in 22:31 directs the reader's attention to Luke's portrait of Peter. Much like Matthew's Peter, Luke pays attention to his special, future role. In this case, however, a rehabilitated Peter's exemplary role, forged by spiritual testing and failure, is to "strengthen your brothers and sisters" (22:32), presumably during times of their own spiritual failures and congregational conflicts (cf. John 21:15-17). Certainly, Acts portrays Peter in this kind of role.

(6) The curious comment about exchanging clothes for swords (22:36), which leads to a misunderstanding and correction (22:38), certainly suggests that the apostolic ministry will provoke the very same kind of conflict occasioned by the messiah's ministry. Perhaps this also explains Jesus's prior rhetorical question regarding whether they lacked anything (22:35). What should interest us is what is sandwiched between: Jesus's use of what scholars call "the *dei* of divine necessity" to instruct his apostles: "scripture must [*dei*] be fulfilled in relation to me" (22:37). That is, even as Jesus's narrative follows or "fulfills" biblical "script," so also will the narrative that plots the mission of the apostles after him. In this sense, apostolicity is providential. By this I mean that God's act of electing the apostles, mediated by Jesus, purposes to preserve what God already has put into play by scriptural promise: salvation from sin and death. In this sense, the church's vocation as an apostolic community is to preserve and transmit the good

news that God has fulfilled the salvation that scripture has promised because of the suffering of Jesus (cf. 22:14-20).

The Gospel of John

Unlike Luke, the fourth Gospel has very little interest in characterizing the Twelve as a discrete group within the larger community of disciples (see only John 6:66-70). A discussion of apostolicity in John turns on its unique portrait of the anonymous disciple, "the one whom Jesus loved" (13:23; 19:26; 20:2; 21:7, 20). Although this discussion of his identity is detached from the historian's questions of the Gospel's authorship, its sources, or the historical accuracy of his portrait—all contested concerns of modern criticism—the final mention of the disciple in 21:20 is linked to his writing of "these things" (21:24). He is called a "witness" to the "many other things" Jesus did (21:25), and the act of writing this Gospel is therefore a "testimony" of what is true. Here, then, is an essential theological element of this ecclesial mark: apostolicity is the church's assignment of truth to what an eyewitness of Jesus has written down in a canonical Gospel. Moreover, the purpose of this Gospel, which is the cultivation of the belief that Jesus is the messiah, the Son of God, and that believing this about Jesus is the condition of having "life in his name" (see 20:31), is made more relevant to the reader by the narrator's confirmation that what is written about Jesus is by an eyewitness and can be trusted as true.

John's portrait of the beloved disciples is a study of the qualities that make for a trusted witness. The seating of the disciple "at Jesus' side" in a place of honor for the Last Supper (John 13:23) not only gives evidence of personal intimacy, itself an important quality, but also strategically locates the beloved disciple as an eyewitness to observe and hear Jesus close at hand at this pivotal moment in his relationship with the disciples. While John routinely uses family and friendship metaphors to cast Jesus's relations with his disciples, most significantly in his Last Supper discourse, the level of trust he has for the beloved disciple is indicated by the seat given him at the table. Again, the function of this typology of trust is to help secure the church's confidence in the disciple's written witness of Jesus and the manner of faith in him that his Gospel forms.

Once again, the placement of the disciple at Jesus's passion (John 19:26) serves a theological function to underwrite his exceptionalism that extends, by implication, to his eyewitness of Jesus (which includes John's elaborate and distinctive narrative of his death). Unlike the accounts of the other Gospels, which tell of the disciples' betrayal and abandonment of Jesus (cf. 16:32), John alone includes the beloved disciple with the Marys at the cross. But as with his placement at the table, Jesus's implied command that the disciple take his mother home with him treats him as an intimate equal to his own brother. Furthermore, the disciple's obedience to Jesus's command and his evident love for another (i.e., Mary) are exemplary of friendship with Jesus (see 15:9-17) and thereby add another layer to his personal integrity as a witness to Jesus.

The disciple's relationship with Peter, who is more prominent in the other Gospels, especially Matthew (see the section on the Gospel of Mark under "The Church's Catholicity according to the Fourfold Gospel"), is thematic of John's narrative of the resurrection (John 20:1-9). Once again, the Gospel's telling of the story centers upon the characterization of the disciple's witness of the empty tomb. What are we to make of this curious footrace and the narrator's repeated report that the disciple ran faster and bested Peter to the tomb (20:4, 8)? Is it a playground typology of the winning disciple's personal superiority or the superiority of the apostolic tradition he represents? Maybe. Surely the narrator's repetition of this detail intends to make a point, and it seems like a point, missing from the other canonical Gospels, that only an eyewitness could score.

Even though Mary is the first to find the tomb empty—she thought it had been robbed (John 20:2-3)—and also first to witness the risen Jesus (20:10-18), this story does grant the beloved disciple priority not only for reaching the tomb before Peter but also for exemplifying the proper response (thus correcting Mary) when finding it empty: "He saw and believed" (20:8). Most commentators maintain that the action of the story centers upon Peter, following the Synoptic Gospels' lead; after all, he is the first to enter the tomb and confirm that Jesus is missing. More important, however, is the disciple's personal testimony and how this shapes the reader's interpretation of the narrator's final comments about the quality of the disciple's witness that informs what he has written. The act of believing in particular is important in John, especially since this is the intended effect of reading it (20:31). It fulfills Jesus's implied prediction that witnessing his resurrection (i.e., only if he is resurrected will he depart and come back again) will produce faith (14:28). Nothing need be said about Peter's faith (or lack thereof); this narrative is shaped by a commitment to secure the quality of the apostolic tradition that produces this Gospel (and by implication all apostolic writings, including Petrine).

The priority of the beloved disciple's witness is again demonstrated at the risen Jesus's third and final appearance to his disciples by the Sea of Tiberias (John 21:1-14), again with Peter as his narrative foil. At first, Jesus remains hidden from his disciples: even though he stood on the beach and exchanged fishing tips with them, his disciples did not know that it was he (21:4). The disciple enters the narrative at this point to reveal Jesus to them (21:7), which Peter then seeks to confirm. The disciple's testimony, "It's the Lord," and Peter's immediate response to it, subsequently glossed by Jesus's rehabilitation and commission of him (21:15-17), is paradigmatic of the church's response to its apostolic testimony. That is, the disciple's witness to the things that Jesus did is revelatory (i.e., true) of who the risen Lord is, and the church's immediate response to it should be to follow him (see 21:19).

Summary

The fourfold Gospel tradition of the historical Jesus, especially its narrative of his relations with the disciples, provides the implicit ecclesiology that frames the narrative of the church's founding in Acts and the church's instructions for life and faith that follow in the canonical Letters and Apocalypse. A careful study of the Gospel's pluriformed narrative of Jesus, then, should strike the reader as foundational, not incidental as some insist, for answering this book's leading question: Why the church?

The Gospel's witness to the church's oneness is reflected by the single requirement for following Jesus: to confess him as the messiah. Membership in the community of his disciples, in turn, shapes a common life based upon a singular coherence to the teaching and example of Jesus, God's only Son and Israel's only messiah. The fourth Gospel extends this essential insight by grounding the solidarity between Jesus and his disciples in the unity of Father and Son and their "abiding" presence in the community that enables believers to resist the hateful world, know truth, and love one another.

Similarly, readers find that the fourfold Gospel tradition targets a holiness instantiated in Jesus: holiness is to be like Jesus, to follow him—not in the manner unique to his messianic office but in the manner of his relations with others. While the elites of his social world pressed for a more conventional holiness based on case law and political practices, the pattern of personal holiness (or righteousness) exemplified by a prophetic Jesus is the collective norm for his disciples. Moreover, this demanding holiness is a real possibility because the one who calls and convenes them is "God's holy one" (John 6:69).

The church's catholicity takes shape in obedience to the risen Lord's final instructions: "Go and make disciples of all nations" (Matt 28:19). The fourfold Gospel witnesses to the variety of ways in which the church fulfills its vocation to make disciples of the nations, whether by prophetic preaching or by loving one another. The church can be nothing else but an international, global community of disciples. Magi, lowly shepherds who seek after lost sheep, poor beggars, ill children, outcast women, outlaws, and Pharisees who come under the cover of night—this unlikely company that the Gospel narrative gathers together to follow Christ bears an unmistakable witness to the universal scope of his mission to save the world from death.

The Gospel depicts the community's apostolicity primarily by Jesus's relations with an uncomprehending, often mistaken Twelve before they understood their future role in leading the church after the risen One's departure. The array of connections between the Gospel and Acts demonstrates that the Twelve not only would continue the messiah's mission in the world but also would share both his Spirit-filled power and the conflict in his name that occasioned his rejection and suffering. Indeed, the church's vocation as an apostolic community is to preserve and transmit the good news that God has fulfilled the salvation that scripture has promised because of the suffering of Jesus.

Chapter Three

The Acts of the Apostles

The importance of the contribution that Acts makes to a biblical theology of the church is difficult to exaggerate. Not only does Acts help readers negotiate between the NT canonical collections and their various theologies of the church, but Acts also provides an interpretive strategy for how the church should read Israel's scripture as God's word. The Gospel's implicit ecclesiology, shaped by the phenomenology of a messianic movement, is given institutional bones by stories of the church's Spirit-led mission and resurrection practices in Acts. This is easily noted by the narrative's repeated use of *ekklēsia*, after being mentioned only twice in the fourfold Gospel (both times in Matthew; see the section on the Gospel of Matthew under "The Church's Oneness according to the Fourfold Gospel" in the previous chapter). The surfeit of stories about the "*ekklēsia* of God" in Acts is then elaborated and thickened by detailed and practical instructions found in the Pauline and Catholic letter collections, which target Christian congregations whose social and spiritual crises and an ever-widening mission require an expanded understanding of the church.

The capacity of Acts to handle this mediating role, which even the ancient church recognized, should come as no surprise to the reader. The church's foundational narrative of its Spirit-filled beginnings at Pentecost, according to God's promise and Jesus's prophecy, when read in its canonical setting,

71

recalls the Exodus story of Sinai. Both are epochal narratives that feature the founding of God's covenant communities linked together as cotexts by their linguistic and thematic parallels. Pentecost continues Sinai for the messianic era, which Peter's commentary of Joel's prophecy of Pentecost calls "the last days" of salvation's history (Acts 2:17; cf. Joel 3:1-5 LXX).

The narrative's prefatory sentence (Acts 1:1-2) provides two crucial insights that will guide this study of the one, holy, catholic, and apostolic church according to Acts. First, its story unfolds as the continuation of the former account about "everything Jesus did and taught from the beginning, right up to the day when he was taken up into heaven" (1:1-2a). Luke's opening is not so much a tip about literary genre or theological goods as it is a claim about religious authority: Acts plots a story that will continue the Gospel's witness of the now departed but risen Jesus.

Second, the Evangelist's literary cue, "former account" (Acts 1:1 NET), when read in canonical context, does not regard this plotline as the mere sequel only to his story of Jesus (Luke) but of the entire four Gospels collection. This interpretive move resists the modern study of Acts, at least since Henry Cadbury, which studies Luke-Acts as a single narrative whose literary unity is guaranteed by the narrator's theological grammar, pastoral calling, and historical circumstance.[1] In this case, the "former account" is reduced to the third of the four canonical Gospels—an exclusive pairing that tends to shortchange the pivotal role that Acts itself performs within the NT canon. While we must not dismiss the importance of reading Luke with Acts to receive this Evangelist's distinctive witness to God's people, a canonical approach examines the role and theology of a stand-alone Acts to retrieve its distinctive contribution to the study of the church.

The title given, "The Acts of the Apostles," probably by Irenaeus, who pioneered the book's reception as scripture, supports a second implication for a canonical approach to its theology of church. Naming the narrative "Acts" recognizes the role it performs as Christian scripture, which is similar to the role performed by a literary "acts," a genre of narrative literature used in antiquity (and even today) to underwrite the importance of famous individuals

---

1. For a more expansive explanation of these introductory comments, see Robert W. Wall, "A Canonical Approach to the Unity of Acts and Luke's Gospel," in *Rethinking the Unity and Reception of Luke and Acts*, ed. Andrew F. Gregory and C. Kavin Rowe (Columbia: University of South Carolina Press, 2010), 172–91. There is no evidence that Acts was combined with Luke as a single narrative at any time during the canonical process. Acts traveled a separate route from Luke into the NT canon, while the final form of Luke found its way to the Gospels collection sometime during the second century. By the time Acts was received as scripture a generation or two later, the church's authorized Gospel narrative of "everything Jesus did and taught from the beginning" (Acts 1:1) had been fixed in a fourfold form.

for a community's identity by remembering/narrating their great acts and inspiring speeches.[2] While also providing historical narratives, the primary value of employing this genre is more aesthetic: to remember certain individuals for a particular community as its trusted exemplars. A community's appeal to its founding mothers and fathers is a powerful tool in preserving its unity and shared commitments. In this case, Acts is a story about what the apostles did (e.g., signs and wonders) and said (e.g., missionary speeches) that confirm that they are indeed the "chosen" successors of the risen messiah who are given orders "in the power of the Holy Spirit" to build a community that continues to bear witness to the historical Jesus during his absence (Acts 1:2b).

The purposeful placement of Acts within the NT canon confirms what is implied by Luke's prefatory sentence: Acts continues the Gospel's story, not only because its sequence suggests an apostolic succession but also because it narrates the ongoing results of Jesus's resurrection at garden level. Moreover, the Gospels provide materials that fill in the gaps of the apostolic kerygma. This dialogue between the Gospel and Acts vocalizes an expansive use of messianic typologies to frame the narrative of the community's mission. Every contribution to our discussion of the church's four marks in Acts implicates its dialogue with the fourfold Gospel: the risen Lord who calls his disciples and forms them into community is succeeded by his chosen apostles who continue to provide Spirit-filled leadership as this messianic community is formed into the church.

Nonetheless, the history of the church's use of Acts as scripture (more or less followed by the critical reception of Acts within the modern academy) suggests that its most important role is to provide theological introductions to the canonical apostles and thus to introduce the church's reading of their NT Letters. The story's central characters are the same authors (e.g., Peter, Paul, and James) and audiences/sources (e.g., Jerusalem, Timothy, Corinth, Ephesus, and Rome) referenced or alluded to in the subsequent NT Letters.

---

2.   Richard A. Burridge, "The Genre of Acts—Revisited," in *Reading Acts Today: Essays in Honour of Loveday C. A. Alexander*, ed. Steve Walton, Thomas E. Phillips, Lloyd Keith Pietersen, and F. Scott Spencer, Library of New Testament Studies 427 (New York: T&T Clark, 2011), 3–28. Burridge's fine study attempts to reconstruct the author's communicative intentions based upon a study of an ancient genre, "acts." While useful for our purpose, the church's titling of Acts is not an attempt to retrieve what may have been Luke's purpose for writing it nor necessarily Aristotle's conception of the genre, "acts," as a biography of a person that narrates his heroic deeds. The title's function within scripture is to guide the church's continuing use of a sacred writing that will produce spiritual wisdom and maturity (see 2 Tim 3:15-17). Almost surely, then, the purpose of the title "Acts of the Apostles" is to transform the narrative into an apologia of apostolic authority that would secure both the "gospels of the apostles" and their epistolary writings.

Readers have always associated the two, noting as well a common concern for important themes of Christian community (e.g., sharing of goods, purity, suffering, missionary practices, and unity). With good reason, then, during the canonical process, Acts came to supply a narrative introduction for both Pauline and Catholic letter collections. The letters are read with the orienting concerns of Acts in mind, and in light of its story, Acts makes readers more wakeful when negotiating between the NT's two different but complementary letter collections (Pauline and Catholic).

We will begin to tease out this important point more fully in chapter 4, but keep it in mind when working through this one on Acts since the canonization of the NT has already forged this relationship. For this chapter, let me put the matter sharply: Acts makes its own distinctive and decisive contribution to the biblical canon's understanding of the Creed's ecclesial markers. This contribution consists mostly of patterns of church practice that effectively make the implied ecclesiology of the fourfold Gospel more concrete. In this sense, the ministry that Jesus began by calling out and forming a community of repentant disciples continues in his absence under the leadership of his Spirit-filled apostolic successors.

But this same narrative, when read in its canonical setting, also authorizes the church's self-understanding found elaborated in the following two letter collections, Pauline and Catholic. The "acts" of these apostles, then, not only underwrite the succession of particular persons who maintain and even extend what Jesus began but also grant authority to the apostolic traditions that produced the biblical writings we continue to receive in their name. In this sense, then, whenever the church picks up a Pauline or Petrine Letter to use in worship or catechesis, its reading is not only contextualized by the modern historian's reconstruction of the historical Paul or Peter (if this is even possible) but, more importantly, by their authorized biographies in Acts. I will return to this point when I introduce chapter 4 on the Pauline Letters.

The Church's Oneness according to Acts

The question of church unity turns on retrieving those positive ideas and images of Christian community whose members gather together with one heart and soul and whose peculiarity in the world is noted by the one God it worships and by the resurrection practices that witness to their one baptism and salvation. At the same time, Acts's formulation of this mark invites readers to also take note of intramural conflicts that threaten to divide God's people whether because of divisive practices or wrong beliefs. Congregational oneness often results from the hard and messy work of reconciling disagreeable members.

In this regard, the most useful passages in Acts on the church's oneness remain those narrative summaries repeated across the entire narrative (2:42-47; 5:12-16; 6:7; 9:31; 12:24-25; 15:12; 16:5; 19:20; 28:30-31). Although almost surely idealized accounts, they catalogue the formation of crucial elements of church unity and uniqueness. Critically, each summary concludes longer narrative units plotted by a conflict that threatens the community's internal solidarity and distinctive mission in the world. The elements that come to characterize the community of Acts, then, are shaped by active responses to real conflicts, both internal and external, and their resolution not only restores community solidarity but also provides material witness to the word of God.

The initial summary (Acts 2:42-47) concludes the story of the church's Pentecostal beginnings and is programmatic. Each narrative summary thereafter mostly repeats and elaborates this one, indicating both the material and existential progress of the church's life together under the Spirit's direction. Four decisive practices of church unity are listed (2:42) that characterize the internal life of the repentant community. To these is added the apostolic practice of "wonders and signs" (2:43), which Joel prophesizes are "pour[ed] out" upon all people with the Spirit's arrival on Pentecost (2:18-19) and that characterize the community's ministry to outsiders. Since its membership is devoutly Jewish (cf. 2:5), these practices continue from the synagogue. The priority placed on the apostles' teaching, however, indicates that all of these practices are shaped and secured by eyewitness testimony of the historical Jesus—of all that "Jesus did and taught" (1:1) and of his resurrection (1:3, 21-22; 2:32). That is, these practices are not distinctive in their expression but in their christological content. The community's internal solidarity and external witness, resulting in "God's goodness to everyone" (2:47), are predicated upon this common curriculum.

The use of *fellowship* (*koinōnia*), an important topos for friendship in Greek philosophy, is used only in this summary passage of Acts. Its strategic use here captures nicely the wholesale effect that the Spirit's reception has upon the church's formation. Baptism initiates members into a fellowship of friends who gladly gather to care for one another's spiritual and physical well-being. Similar to the Jewish community at Qumran, which tied its rituals of purification to this same ideal of friendship, the church of Acts recalls 1 Peter's exhortation that "set[ting] yourselves apart by your obedience to the truth" results in "genuine affection for your fellow believers" thanks to Jesus's

75

death. The effect of real repentance according to Acts (2:37-41) should form a community of friends (cf. 1 Pet 1:19-22).[3]

The resurrection practices of the community of goods are thematic in Acts. New believers provide evidence of their repentance by selling "pieces of property and possessions" and "distribut[ing] the proceeds to everyone who needed them" (Acts 2:44-45). Popular sentiment may well have led Luke to emphasize more traditional elements of public piety—the contented soul of Stoic thought or the civility of Platonic theory. While no doubt the narrator knew these popular philosophical notions of true friendship, the ideals that shape the community of goods are more biblical. The prophetic typology of Jubilee (cf. Lev 25:10)—Isaiah's "year of the LORD's favor" (Isa 61:2a; cf. Luke 4:19)—that had previously shaped the Gospel's narratives of Jesus's ministry among the poor (esp. Luke 4:16-21; 6:20-36; 12:22-34; 15:1–16:31; 17:20–18:4; 19:1-10; and so on) becomes the social pattern of the community's life together. Jesus's teaching his disciples to pray for "daily bread" is the expectation that God's favorable response is mediated through the gift of the Holy Spirit, who enables every disciple to give generously even as the caring parent gives without pause to the child (cf. Luke 11:1-13). While such economic practice is exemplary of Jewish piety (cf. Matt 6:1-4) and thus apropos of those who "every day . . . met together in the temple" (Acts 2:46), the community of goods of Acts is indicative of those economic practices of the restored Israel of God.

Luke's reference to temple observance (Acts 2:46) is not a supersessionist bid to take over Jewish worship practices for a "true" Israel. Rather, his point is that worship is a resurrection practice of repentant Israel whose joyful practice of eating "in their homes" and "shar[ing] food with gladness and simplicity" is evidence of life in the Spirit. This is a reference not to the Lord's Supper but to the practice of families who worship together also eating together. Sharing meals and worship is symbolic of a people's social and spiritual solidarity.

Finally, the community's oneness is formed and informed by worship that is characterized by praising God (Acts 2:47a; see 3:8). The community has no material needs, no intramural conflicts, and no broken hearts for which to petition God for tender mercy. This will come soon enough. At the beginning of its mission, there are only success stories and a community of friends filled with gladness.

This first summary of the church's mission in Jerusalem concludes with another head count of those "who were being saved," echoing Joel's prophecy

---

3. Luke Timothy Johnson, *The Acts of the Apostles*, Sacra Pagina, ed. Daniel J. Harrington (Collegeville, MN: Liturgical Press, 1992), 58–59.

that "everyone who calls on the name of the Lord will be saved" (see Acts 2:21). The reader's lingering impression of the daily rhythm of this community of the uncommon life is that it is growing "day by day" and worshipping in the Temple "day by day." Indeed, the formation and practices of this community of goods testify to God's commitment to Israel's restoration.

The second narrative summary follows the tragic story of Ananias and Sapphira (Acts 4:32–5:11), in which sharing possessions and apostolic authority as hallmarks of the church's life together (4:32a) are given sharper if not also an arresting exposition. Both the powerful testimony of the apostolic witness to the resurrection and the sharing of possessions provide the conditions for the "abundance of grace . . . at work among them all" (4:32b-33).

The repetition of "signs and wonders" (Acts 5:12; cf. 2:43) concentrates the reader's attention even more keenly on the Twelve, their prophetic powers, and their growing influence among the people (i.e., Israel) who now stretch beyond the city limits of Jerusalem (5:16). The apostles, through whom the Spirit's "signs and wonders" are performed in Jerusalem, are God's end-time prophets who are called and empowered to gather Israel together for the day of their salvation.

For this reason, this summary elaborates the public's response to the apostolic witness, which is only briefly mentioned in the first narrative (Acts 2:43, 46a, 47). What is crucial to note is that the community's priority of apostolic testimony, in this case in the form of healing and other extraordinary acts, generates a choice in the public square. On the one hand, there is unity of purpose on the church's part: they meet together in a particular place by common consent (5:12b) and work in solidarity with Peter so that "everyone was healed" (5:16). On the other hand, the "trepidation and dread" that gripped all those who heard about the fate of Ananias and Sapphira generates an apprehension (perhaps misapprehension) of the apostles' power (5:11, 13), which perhaps explains their growing conflict with Jewish authorities in the narrative that follows. The increasing pressure from this external conflict and the persecution that follows surely threaten the community's internal unity.

Surprisingly, the next narrative summary (Acts 6:7) follows yet another story of internal conflict over sharing possessions. In this case, however, the pressure point is the growing tensions between different ethnic groups within the church, exacerbated by its success and its growing membership (6:1). The controversy between Greek-speaking and Hebrew-speaking disciples, which probably extends to their different neighborhoods in Jerusalem, is a practical one: the breakdown in the apparatus that moves goods from the apostles to the needy threatens to subvert the community's principal hallmark as God's restored people.

The resolution to this conflict is guided by the four internal practices set out as community norms in Acts 2:42. Whatever new apparatus is installed to facilitate a community of goods, the priority of apostolic teaching is non-negotiable (6:2-4). The manner in which the seven-member *diakonia* is selected evinces fellowship and prayer as well (6:5-6). How the conflict, only briefly sketched, gets resolved stands at the epicenter of this story. In Acts, the church's oneness is managed as a practical matter and is forged in the face of internal tension by the application of its normative practices: apostolic teaching, fellowship, sharing goods, and worship—all empowered by the Spirit's presence.

An element of this practice of congregational unity to which Acts pays careful attention is a result that confirms divine favor (cf. Acts 2:47; 4:33). The reader has come to expect growth in the church's membership as evidence of God's approval. Two other results are mentioned: God's word grows, and the number of repentant Jews includes "a large group" from the priestly class (6:7). The "growth" of God's word may trade on Jesus's parable of the sower for whom the seed sown is "God's word" (Luke 8:11; cf. Matt 13:18-23; Mark 4:13-20), with the many converts indicative of the "good soil" on which the word fell.

The addition of "priests [who] embraced the faith" (Acts 6:7 = repentant; cf. 12:13) sounds a resounding note of victory within this narrative world, since priests are generally viewed as hostile to Jesus. Perhaps their mention in this summary sounds a loud amen to the narrative of the church's mission to Israel with the idealism that the reconciliation of once hostile opponents is the desired effect of the church's gospel ministry.

Saul's conversion (Acts 9:1-9) and commissioning (9:15-16) introduce God's intentions to extend the church's mission beyond Israel to the nations. The next narrative summary (9:31) provides an update of the church's status on the cusp of its mission to the nonproselyte Gentiles, initiated by Peter (Acts 10–11). Two indicative statements describe the situation; it is a situation of extraordinary unity both geographically, since the singular "church" is being "strengthened" in all of the provinces of Roman Palestine (Judea, Samaria, and Galilee; 9:31; cf. 1:8), and spiritually, since this same "church" increases in a membership that has "reverence for the Lord" and is "encouraged by the Holy Spirit" (9:31). The linking participle's passive voice, *oikodomoumenai* ("being built"), suggests the church's oneness is a mark dependent upon God, who builds up a covenant-keeping community that has "reverence for the Lord" and experiences the blessings of peace and increased numbers as a result.

The transition of the church's mission from Jerusalem, led by Peter, to Antioch in preparation for Paul and Barnabas's mission to the nations once again notes the triumph of God's word. In contrast to Herod's horrible end (Acts 12:20-23), "God's word continued to grow and increase" (12:24; see 6:7). In this summary of Acts, the word of God flourishes in the face of hostile opposition in its irrepressible advance to the end of the earth. Moreover, in contrast to the failure of Herod's approach to food distribution, "Barnabas and Saul returned to Antioch from Jerusalem" having completed their relief mission in service of the Judean church and according to the practice of the community of goods (12:25; see 11:27-30). The successful completion of their mission complements the advance of the gospel in the region and serves, on this basis, to validate Paul's mission that is soon to commence. Even as it moves into a second generation of leadership, the Lord's appointed apostles now retreating into the narrative's background with the execution of James (12:2) and the departure of Peter (12:17), the church's oneness continues to be marked out by its ministry of the word and its sharing of goods with the needy.

Often overlooked in the pivotal narrative of the second Jerusalem Council is a verse that effectively summarizes the first half of Acts if read as a narrative commentary of Joel's prophecy of Pentecost.[4] The assembly's "quiet" is not due so much to their unspoken agreement with Peter's words, which James soon will challenge, but rather to redirect the reader's attention to what is said next and to listen more carefully "to Barnabas and Paul describe all the signs and wonders God did among the Gentiles through their activity" (Acts 15:12). In effect, their final mission report of what "God did," not only summarizes the theme of Peter's speech (15:6-11) in response to the Pharisees' probing question about Gentile inclusion (15:5) but also provides divine authorization to the inclusion of repentant Gentiles in congregational fellowship. Peter's witness to Cornelius's Spirit baptism, and by implication to God's purification of his heart, is here applied generally to Paul and Barnabas's mission among the Gentiles.

The final use in Acts of the catchphrase, "signs and wonders" (15:12), which identifies the Spirit's outpouring according to Joel's prophecy (2:18-19), is important because the Spirit's last stop is among pagans that Paul and Barnabas had earlier encountered (14:3), which confirms their inclusion

---

4. See Robert W. Wall, "The Acts of the Apostles," in *The New Interpreter's Bible*, ed. Leander E. Keck (Nashville: Abingdon, 2002), 10:62-65.

in eschatological Israel. This narrative summary is also important because it implicates Paul's programmatic mission, narrated in Acts 13–14, both as the fulfillment of the Lord's commission (9:15-16) and as principal witness to the Lord's apostles. Paul's ministry succeeds the Twelve even as they had succeeded Jesus. The church, whose one heart and mind is formed by the core practices of the apostles (i.e., 2:42-43), continues to be so formed by the next generation of leaders. In this sense, the succession of the apostolate is an element of the church's oneness, according to Acts.

The next narrative summary (Acts 16:5) revisits familiar territory: the congregations are strengthened by Paul's house calls, and their membership numbers increase. The location of this statement, however, is critical because it follows the decree rendered by the prior Jerusalem Council, which had been made into church "dogma" (see "regulations," *dogmata*, 16:4) to both confirm and regulate Paul's mission to the nations. Paul's circumcision of Timothy (16:3) must be understood in this wider narrative setting. Paul's motive seems prompted by the practice needed to restore Timothy's Jewish identity in order to maintain good working relations in the congregations of the diaspora between repentant Jews and Gentiles.

Paul's circumcision of Timothy and his institution of church dogma agree with James and will serve Paul when he is later accused by James of preventing the children of Jews (= Timothy) from being circumcised (see Acts 21:21). The Paul of Acts is as committed as James is to keeping the Jewish heritage of the faith alive and well. His act of restoring Timothy's Jewish identity agrees with James's reading of scripture and with the Holy Spirit (see 15:28) and therefore is in accordance with God's purposes. The church's oneness is surely not subject to a supersessionist move to rid itself of its Jewish roots.

The summary of Paul's seminal Ephesians mission (Acts 19:18-22) is striking for several reasons. Most important, it concentrates the readers' attention on the repentance of *believers* (19:18) who had converted from pagan religion (e.g., magic practices). Much like Synoptic Gospel accounts of repentance that sometimes pay a financial dividend (cf. Luke 19:8), Paul watches "fifty thousand silver drachmen" worth of magic books (= pagan scriptures) tossed into a public bonfire and incinerated. This is an enormous expense, probably equal to "one hundred sixty-five years" of wages (19:18); it is the fruit of real repentance and symbolizes a congregation's resolve to turn from pagan scripture to Israel's scripture and from demonic charlatans to Paul's instruction. God's power is not appropriated as another commodity, but only through "the Lord's word [which] grew abundantly and strengthened [the congregation] powerfully [*ischuō*]" (19:20; see 4:4;

14:25; 16:6; 17:11). Here, then, is another story of a community's repair that results from right instruction.

With the amelioration of various impediments (e.g., John's baptism, magic, demon possession, sickness, and pretenders to Paul's authority), a community built around and up by the Lord's word is now formed in pagan Ephesus. Paul begins to make travel plans to return to Macedonia and Achaia before "return[ing] to Jerusalem" (Acts 19:21a). These plans are commensurate with his missionary strategy of returning to those parishes planted during earlier missions to fortify their spiritual resolve and theological understanding (see 14:21-23; 18:23; 20:2). Paul's priestly tasks, as much as his prophetic tasks, are an exercise of his religious authority within the church. Toward this end, then, he plans to follow the same route he paved in Acts 16–18. The reader suspects that his plans to visit the holy city reflect his commitments to his ancestral religion and that he will travel there as a pious pilgrim (see 20:1).

What is unexpected is his resolve that he "must [*dei*] visit Rome as well" (19:21b). The shift within the overarching geographic structure of Paul's mission in Acts from Palestine (Antioch/Jerusalem) to Rome is here noted for the first time. While Paul himself tells us that he desires to see Rome (Rom 1:10; 15:24), Luke's use of the "*dei* of divine necessity" implies that his travel plans include Rome because God has disclosed it to him as the city of his destiny—whether by vision or another's prophecy Acts does not tell us. In fact, Paul leaves Ephesus for Macedonia in relative calm (see 20:1); he is not forced to leave in a hurry, as is more typically the case.

An element of Paul's collaboration with God is careful planning. Toward the end of a successful trip, then, he dispatches "two of his assistants, Timothy and Erastus, to Macedonia, while he remained awhile in the province of Asia [= Ephesus]" (19:22). Another of Paul's colleagues, Erastus, is dropped into the narrative in this summary, never to be mentioned again. The impression he makes is as another of Paul's delegates who, as Timothy's colleague, travels ahead of Paul to prepare the way for the Lord's word. These, too, are images of a congregation's solidarity: careful planning that combines priestly and prophetic ministries, all of which cultivate the soil for the sowing of God's word.

The final narrative summary is the concluding sentence of Acts (28:30-31). Its subject matter is clear enough: citizen Paul spends two years in Rome confined to a rented flat while awaiting an audience with the emperor and entertains all who visit him by boldly preaching "God's kingdom" and teaching them about Christ (28:31). The puzzlement that this passage has provoked during the history of its interpretation stems from its haunting silence about

Paul's fate. Commentators, ancient and modern, speculate that the narrator did not write more because he did not know the details of what happened to Paul or because he knew, but considered them either too tragic or irrelevant to his plotline to tell. Given that nothing is known of the reception history of Acts prior to Irenaeus, some speculate that other versions of Acts may have included details of Paul's trial and alleged martyrdom but then were erased by a final editor (for any number of plausible reasons).

No one knows what the text does not say. What may be surmised from the narrative context is that this final sentence is a summary, not a narrative climax, of Paul's mission to the end of the earth (i.e., Rome), and so it is he who fulfills Jesus's prophecy that the church's witness to his resurrection will travel from Jerusalem to the earth's end (1:8). Acts ends with Paul being Paul: bearing witness of Jesus to all who have ears to hear.

As a narrative summary, the question readers should ask is how the story's ending deepens their lingering impression of the church's oneness. Since there is no next stage in telling the church's story according to Acts, its role is to facilitate the transition from the Bible's narrative to our own. The parting image of the Paul in Acts lingers on to exemplify the normative practice of the church being the church. The church's imitation of Paul being Paul commends that it hospitably welcomes every seeker into its company (cf. 28:30), boldly proclaiming to all with ears to hear the promise of God's kingdom and teaching them that God's promises are fulfilled because of the risen Christ. The solidarity of the global church in every age is based upon its engagement of these common missionary practices.

The Church's Holiness according to Acts

The vocabulary of holiness is not thematic of the church's story in Acts. Everywhere, however, there are indications that the various outsiders who populate Luke's narrative world recognize that there is something disruptive about this messianic community that separates it from, and even problematizes the existence of, other groups. Perhaps there is no better illustration of this than the various responses to Paul's Ephesians mission according to Acts 19, mentioned in the previous section, "The Church's Oneness according to Acts." Practitioners of magic repent publicly and turn to the Lord's word instead (see the previous section, "The Church's Oneness according to Acts"); evil spirits recognize (!) the difference between Paul and other missionaries, and the city's public square is turned upside down by the response of religious and civic leaders to Paul's mission, which is only calmed by silencing

Paul. Ephesus is one of those pagan places rubbed raw by the friction created when the gospel about Jesus collides with its economic, religious, and political systems. The church's witness to a holy God, which challenges the city's idolatries, provokes this kind of response.

This more public, disruptive kind of holy living bears witness to, in C. Kavin Rowe's apt phrase, "God's apocalypse of salvation," which challenges the sensibilities of those who would define a holy church in more quiet ways, by an inward purity of the heart rather than by public practices of holy living that commend the church as a counterculture.[5] In this section, I want to drill down once again on the critical story of the second Jerusalem Council (Acts 15) to illustrate this point.

The plotline of Paul's mission in Acts 16–28 is shaped as a response to the concern expressed first by members of James's Jerusalem congregation: whether repentant but uncircumcised Gentiles should practice Torah purity according to Jewish tradition (Acts 15:5). Interpreters of Acts commonly depict those from "among the Pharisees" as troublemakers and then presume the impropriety of their claim upon repentant Gentiles. But there is nothing in the text itself that indicates this. In fact, Luke's use of the "*dei* of divine necessity" in 15:5 ("the Gentiles *must* [*dei*] be circumcised"; emphasis added) implies that their question is perfectly reasonable since circumcision is stipulated by divine revelation—the biblical Torah (Gen 17)—and subsequent tradition as a covenant-keeping practice.

Moreover, in contrast to the agitators in Antioch who question whether nonproselyte Gentiles are even saved (see 15:1-2), the Pharisees' apparent concern is for a purity that allows congregational unity, especially now for a mission in the diaspora where heterogeneous congregations of repentant Jews and Gentiles will be formed (cf. 15:21). The Pharisees pose a question, then, that concerns the whole of Acts: in addition to the resurrection practices in play from the very beginning of the church (2:42), what practices of repentant Gentiles are required that will continue to evince our unity as a people belonging to God (2:44-47)? The inclusion of unclean, untrained pagans into a covenant-keeping community requires a response.

Peter's initial response is to reform the synagogue's traditional *halakhah*. In the narrator's programmatic telling of Cornelius's conversion story in Acts 10, the central conflict between him and Peter is defined by the heavenly

---

5. See C. Kavin Rowe, *World Upside Down: Reading Acts in the Graeco-Roman Age* (New York: Oxford University Press, 2010). Rowe writes that "God's apocalypse shapes ecclesiology: theological truth claims and the pattern of life that sustains them—the core practices of Christian communities—are inextricably bound together" (4).

audition, "Never consider unclean what God has made pure [*ekatharisen*]" (10:15). Peter interprets this subsequently in traditional Jewish terms of table fellowship: "it is forbidden for a Jew to associate or visit with outsiders" (10:28). Thus, when Peter rehearses that story for this "council," his decisive commentary is that God no longer requires repentant Gentiles to put on "a burden" of the law (15:10) because God has "purified [*katharisas*] their deepest thoughts and desires through faith" (15:9b). When Peter's commentary in Acts 15 is glossed by the earlier narrative, the concept of purity is here a synecdoche not of inward sanctification but of social propriety. The baptism of the Spirit indicates that God "made no distinction between us and them" (15:9a) and not that God had forgiven their sins—even though this is surely implied (cf. 2:38). For this reason, in the first telling of Cornelius's conversion, Peter's response to the stunning "Gentile Pentecost" is to baptize Cornelius and his household by water in order to initiate them into the church's membership (cf. 10:47-48). If read "intratextually," then the fuller meaning of Peter's comment at the Jerusalem Council is made clearer: because God has purified the hearts of unclean (i.e., nonproselyte) Gentiles, they need not undergo traditional Jewish rites of purification before table fellowship/friendship with repentant Jews.

But Peter's is not the last word! James's subsequent speech both confirms and corrects Peter. While God has purified the hearts of repentant Gentiles who call upon the risen Jesus for their salvation, the more urgent issue is ecclesiological, not soteriological, and more sociological than spiritual. Repentant Gentiles whose hearts are purified by faith in Jesus—which puts them to rights with God—must also conform to the rudimentary demands of Jewish life as members of a covenant-keeping community.[6] Especially given the testimony of Barnabas and Paul regarding what "God did among the Gentiles through their activity" (Acts 15:12), James's reading of Amos regards the purity of uncircumcised but repentant Gentiles in the diaspora congregations where Moses is read every Sabbath (15:20-21, 29; cf. 21:25).

Following others, I take it that the catalogue of purity practices introduced by James in Acts 15:20, and repeated twice again (15:29; 21:25), is based upon the so-called holiness code found in Leviticus 17–18. This code, then, is shorthand for a range of instructions that regulate the social discourse between Israel and non-Jews, including both religious and relational activi-

---

6. The particular *halakhic* matter that James may have in mind when commenting upon the Amos prophecy is the levitical concern for the effect of "the practices of the nations" upon Jewish purity or when "resident aliens" mingle with faithful Jews (Lev 17–18 AT); cf. Richard Bauckham, "James and the Gentiles (Acts 15.13-21)," in *History, Literature, and Society in the Book of Acts*, ed. Ben Witherington III (New York: Cambridge University Press, 1996), 154–84.

ties. James's commentary contemporizes levitical holiness for "the last days" (cf. Acts 2:17), when every Jew and Gentile who calls upon the Lord's name forms eschatological Israel. In any case, James expands Peter's original definition of inward purity to include both social and religious practices of purity. His expanded definition is the interpretive key in reading the second half of Acts.

When Paul returns to Jerusalem following his farewell tour through Roman Asia (Acts 21:17-26), he finds that he is still the straw that stirs the drink of controversy among other Jewish believers. The elders of the Jerusalem church led by James are no longer interested in the religious practices of uncircumcised Gentile converts as before; they are now distressed over reports that Paul's mission has subverted important religious traditions among his Jewish converts who live and worship among Gentiles in the diaspora (21:21). Significantly, then, the middle narrative of Paul's three missions that make up the second half of Acts following Jerusalem's apostolic decree (15:30–18:17, 18:18–21:26, 21:27–28:16) is bracketed by acts of ritual purification that characterize him as an exemplar of Jewish holiness (i.e., a Nazirite; 18:18-21; 21:26; cf. Num 6:1-11). In this capacity, he defends his Jewishness before the Roman governor, Felix, by providing the court with an official accounting of his ritual and personal purity (his opponents find no impurity [*adikēma*] in him; 24:20; cf. 18:14), claiming that it is motivated by his hope in the resurrection of the dead (24:15-18). If the relevant issue is whether Paul is guilty of "gentilizing" repentant Jews, the testimony of Paul's holiness wins the day.

The prophecy from Amos frames the second half of Acts in a manner similar to the prophecy from Joel in the first half: the narrator's repetition of the prophecy's language and ideas reminds the reader that "the events that have been fulfilled among us" (Luke 1:1) bring to realization God's plan of salvation. At its surface level, the Amos prophecy continues the theme of Israel's restoration and its mission to the nations: as Joel predicts that "everyone who *calls* on the *name* of the Lord will be saved" (Acts 2:21; emphasis added), so Amos prophesies in similar fashion that following the rebuilding of Israel, God would find a place for "even all the Gentiles who belong to *me*" (15:17; emphasis added). The repetition of these central symbols of "belong" (i.e., membership in the covenant community) and "me" (i.e., its risen Lord) confirms at the midpoint of Acts that Joel's prophecy is fulfilled: the "rebuilding" of repentant Israel and the inclusion of the nations in its salvation has taken place through the Spirit-filled mission of the church. The rest of Acts unfolds from Amos's prophecy against the backdrop of this eschatological horizon, as

85

Paul's mission gathers more and more believers while moving toward Rome at "the end of the earth" (1:8).

One rightly wonders what historical circumstances in Luke's world might prompt the concern for the "gentilizing" of Jewish believers. Two obvious clues are found within Acts from which we may infer the narrator's motive: the rousing success of Paul's urban mission in the diaspora among God-fearing Gentiles and a relative lack of his success among God-fearing Jews, who remain a divided house in their response to the risen Jesus (Acts 28:16-28). These data, when coupled with the destruction of the Jerusalem temple (fulfilling the Lord's prediction), the return of Palestine to Roman rule (rather than the reverse as predicted by scripture), and the virtual cessation of the Jerusalem church by the end of the first century, may have led some believers to argue that the relevant symbols of covenant renewal between God and a "true" Israel no longer include more traditional expressions of Jewish holiness. Sharply put, Christianity has superseded Judaism and need not retain anything Jewish in order to have the identity or vocation as God's people.

The response of Acts to this crisis cannot thoroughly disguise the tension within the early church or the anxiety felt by Jewish believers because of the sudden influx of Gentiles into their fellowship. However, the narrator's interest in protecting the Jewish heritage of Christian faith is not wholly expected and must be viewed as somewhat radical. Even as God does not require uncircumcised pagan converts to follow conventional Jewish practices for Christian fellowship with Jewish believers, neither does God require repentant Jews to forsake their ancestral traditions out of loyalty to the messiah. On this basis, the lesson that Acts teaches today's church is that a fully biblical conception of a holy church trades upon a fully biblical conception of a holy Israel. To reduce holiness to an inward cleansing of the heart based upon faith in Jesus alone comes dangerously close to the very problem that the James of Acts seeks to correct and the Paul of Acts seeks to exemplify.

The Church's Catholicity according to Acts

The book of Acts is a rich depository of images and ideas that address the nature of the church's global reach in mission and membership. The inclusion of the marginal within the covenant-keeping community helps plot the narrative of God's grace from its beginning. In fact, according to Jesus's prophecy (Acts 1:8), what begins as a messianic movement within Palestinian Judaism unfolds within the Roman world to embrace all kinds of people. When this messianic movement grows into its second generation and is better organized under Paul's leadership, it reaches the prophesied "end of the earth" (1:8) in downtown Rome (Acts 28). Whether needy Greek-speaking widows (Acts 6), uncircumcised but repentant Gentiles (Acts 10–15) and diaspora Jews (Acts 16), poor widows (Acts 9) and middle-class business-women (Acts 16, 18), beggars (Acts 3) and prominent citizens (Acts 13), Roman officials (Acts 13, 14) and soldiers (Acts 10, 16, 27), or Greek intellectuals (Acts 17), their conversion to Jesus and the conflicts this provokes within and outside the church (especially with unrepentant Jews) plot much of the action of this story.[7] The gospel's universal appeal to Jews first and then also to non-Jews follows, of course, scripture's prophesied way of salvation according to Acts.

Accepting these narrative accents as illustrative of the church's catholic mark, the theological goods deposited in the commission statements in Acts, which follow from the commission statements of the fourfold Gospel (see chapter 2, pp. 61–62), are especially rich veins to mine (Acts 1:8; 9:15-16; 15:27-30). To these three commission texts one might add once again the ending of Acts (28:30-31), now reread as an implicit commission to readers who seek to follow Paul's lead in their own neighborhoods. This move seems especially important if the ending of Acts is glossed by 28:28, which takes Paul's response to a divided Israel as a case of Jewish exclusion. If Paul's retort, that God's salvation is sent (*apostellō*) to Gentiles because they will listen, is tantamount to his saying that God's salvation is no longer sent to Jews because they won't listen, then the catholicity of the church's mission could be questioned. I take it, however, that this is an element of Paul being Paul (see the previous section, "The Church's Holiness according to Acts"), since it is the third such response to an audience of divided Jews (13:44-47; 18:6) and never before deterred him from taking his mission into the Jewish neighborhood of a different Roman city. Moreover, in the prior narrative Paul clearly has only the local Jewish community in mind, since in the next narrative panels, we find him once again engaged in a mission to both Jews and Gentiles.

---

7. Although there are obvious connections between this discussion of a catholic church and the arguments made from Acts a generation ago to support what Ernst Käsemann and others before him called, "early catholicism," I find their conclusions overdetermined. If by "catholicism" one has in mind a move from a Spirit-led charismatic community to an elder-led institutionalized church, perhaps prompted by the loss of expectation for Christ's imminent return or a "parting of the ways" with Judaism, it would be difficult to make this case from Acts alone. In particular, changes in the organization of the church of Acts seem prompted by changes in location and audience rather than ecclesial dispositions. The highly structured church order, the sacramentalism, and the formulation of theological doctrine into an apostolic rule of faith—all of which are prompted as the marks of "early catholicism"—are simply not prevalent in Acts. Yes, one might allow the storyteller to put the best face on the divisions within the earliest community, but to say Luke edited them out and romanticized the portraits of the apostles goes beyond the evidence or fails to consider more plausible explanations.

This is, after all, the scope of the mission that the Lord has given him (cf. 9:15-16). In this case, then, the ending of Acts finds Paul engaged in ministry to all who come, which logically includes both Jews and Gentiles. Following the apostle's lead, then, the church continues to proclaim God's kingdom to "everyone who came" (28:30-31; cf. 1:3).

The First Commission Statement, Acts 1:8

The first commission statement in Acts (1:8) is preceded by a brief summary of what Jesus does and says over the forty days between his resurrection and ascension (1:3). What the reader finds here recapitulates the conclusion to Jesus's messianic mission according to the third Gospel (cf. Luke 24:36-53), recalling, in particular, those memories that will be elaborated in Luke's second book. Here are the Lord's final instructions to his apostles that function as his last will and testament and that lend authority to the future work of his chosen successors.

The Lord instructs his apostolic successors about "God's kingdom" (Acts 1:3), which is a central idiom of Jesus's preaching ministry. While not as prominent in the speeches of Acts, it is used in the book's beginning (1:3) and ending (28:31) to form a literary *inclusio*. The reader is put on notice that the triumph of God's reign is the subtext of the entire narrative sandwiched between. The critical problem we must face, however, is that nowhere is the reader supplied with a normative definition of God's "kingdom." Elements of its definition are perhaps best inferred from its uses in the fourfold Gospel—a narrative whose central character is one God who alone reigns and is the divine choreographer of creation's history. God is not detached from this history but is powerfully present to heal and restore those who trust in God. Humanity's only hope, then, is predicated on God's providential care for all creation, and, in this context, God promises to bless all nations through the mission of a restored Israel (see 1:8). One may allow, especially from the missionary speeches to pagans (14:15-18; 17:22-31), that God is the creator and that God's reign is coextensive with creation.

This inspired conception of reality is concentrated in the prophecy of God's Spirit (Acts 1:4-5), whose arrival in the holy city portends the restoration of Israel (1:6) and the empowered mission of the church as witness of the risen One (1:7-8). According to Acts, the hope of Israel's restoration and the mission of the church are integral features of "the last days" of salvation's history inaugurated by God's Spirit at Pentecost (see 2:1-4) as cued by biblical prophecy (see 2:17-21).

The departure of the glorified Jesus into the heavens (Acts 1:9) concludes his messianic mission but also creates the circumstance that requires an apostolic succession. But the succession from messiah to his apostles is not without problems. The messianic community left behind gathers for prayer (1:14) to wait for God to act on the Lord's promise of the Spirit. Yet we note that it includes only *eleven* apostles (1:13). Will God's salvation go forward without the requisite twelve who "will sit on thrones judging [*krinō*] the twelve tribes of Israel" (see Luke 22:30 NRSV)? Time will tell.

The subtext of the apostles' question of Jesus (Acts 1:6) asks whether the Spirit-promised arrival fulfills the biblical promise that God's kingdom will be restored to Israel. Jesus's vague response to their query in 1:7 is not "an indirect denial that it is Israel to whom the Kingdom will be given."[8] Nor does it point to "the rule of God over human hearts,"[9] since Acts steadfastly refuses to substitute a distinctively Christian or spiritualized meaning for the more traditional Jewish hope of Israel's restoration.[10] The apparent intention of Jesus's answer is not to set aside the implicit connection between Pentecost and the promise of Israel's restoration but rather to clarify the terms of its fulfillment by the events of Pentecost (i.e., Acts 2).

Having sounded an initial cautionary note about any human attempt to time Israel's restoration, Jesus sets out, in a paradigmatic way, the vocation of his apostolic successors and, by implication, the community they will lead in his absence. He says, "You will receive power when the Holy Spirit has come upon you" (Acts 1:8)—words that loudly echo Isaiah's prophecy of the pouring out of the Spirit to empower Israel's renewal (see Isa 32:15). Jesus therefore redirects the earlier question to develop an understanding that God's faithfulness to promises made is worked out through the community's steady mission from Israel (Jerusalem) to the nations (Rome).

The word Jesus uses for "power" is *dynamis*—a "dynamic" life-force at work within the community's history and hearts in demonstrative ways to bring about the realization of God's promise. Power in this context does not indicate that the Spirit of prophecy confers a political authority upon the apostles but rather pertains to the practical competency of performing those missional tasks given the apostles, whether by their Spirit-inspired words or Spirit-empowered signs and wonders (see Acts 2:42-47; 4:32-35).

Jesus emphatically states that the renewing power of Israel's Spirit will come upon them in order to "be my witnesses . . . to the end of the earth"

---

8. See Robert Maddox, *The Purpose of Luke-Acts* (Edinburgh, Scotland: T&T Clark, 1982), 106.

9. Luke Timothy Johnson, *The Acts of the Apostles*, 29.

10. Jacob Jervell, *The Theology of the Acts of the Apostles*, New Testament Theology (New York: Cambridge University Press, 1996), 18–43.

(Acts 1:8). Their vocation is here defined as prophetic witnesses to the eschatological importance of Jesus's resurrection to the Jew first and also to the Greek. When Jesus turns the expectation of Israel's restoration toward the apostles' mission—from the "when" of Israel's restoration toward its "how"—the theological subtext of Acts is established. The story that Acts tells follows the mission of the church according to the Lord's prophecy, beginning "in Jerusalem [see Acts 2–7], in all Judea and Samaria [see Acts 8], and to the end of the earth[11] [see Acts 9–28]." More important, however, this same narrative scripts the fulfillment of scripture's prophecy of Israel's restoration: the church's mission beginning in Jerusalem and moving into Roman Palestine is the means by which God first calls repentant Jews into a restored Israel. Even so, Israel's restoration according to Acts aims at "the end of the earth," where repentant Jews form a missionary community to function as "a light to the nations" so that even the nations might be able to share in the blessings of Israel's salvation (see 3:19-26).

The church's catholicity, then, is defined not only by the geographic (and by implication, ethnic) scope of its witness to the Jew first ("in Jerusalem, in all Judea and Samaria") and also to the Greek ("to the end of the earth"), since God rules over all and offers salvation to all, but also by the Spirit who empowers that catholicity and the gospel of the risen One that funds it. While the Spirit of Acts is not universally received, since it is given as a gift to those who repent (2:38), the Spirit is a necessary agent of divine power that guides and empowers the church to engage in its universal mission.

The Second Commission Statement, Acts 9:15-16

The second commissioning statement is particular to Paul (Acts 9:15-16). The rhetorical importance of this text for telling Paul's story in Acts has long

---

11.   Significantly, the final phrase, *heōs eschatou tēs gēs*, is singular, "the end of the earth" and probably echoes Isa 49:6 and its prophecy of Israel's identity as a "light to the nations" (cf. 13:47!); see Jacques Dupont, *The Salvation of the Gentiles: Essays on the Acts of the Apostles* (New York: Paulist, 1979), 17–19. Others, such as, Hans Conzelmann (*Acts of the Apostles: A Commentary on the Acts of the Apostles*, ed. Eldon Jay Epp and C. R. Matthews, trans. James Limburg, A. Thomas Kraabel, and Donald H. Juel, Hermeneia [Minneapolis: Fortress, 1987], 7), find the phrase's referent in the narrative itself, quite possibly to Rome and therefore as an element of the story's *inclusio*: even as Jesus teaches the kingdom of God to his apostles at its beginning (Acts 1:3), so also Paul continues his teaching of the kingdom of God in Rome at its conclusion (28:31). In this sense, Jesus's commission is finally carried out (and on) by Paul and is an essential feature, then, of the story's Pauline apologia. Robert C. Tannehill, in *The Acts of the Apostles*, vol. 2 of *The Narrative Unity of Luke–Acts: A Literary Interpretation* (Minneapolis: Fortress, 1994), 102–12, argues that the Ethiopian eunuch (8:26-39) represents those at the "end of the earth," formally bringing to conclusion the narrative of the Lord's apostolic successors indexed by Acts 1:8 and preparing the reader for the story of Paul beginning in Acts 9.

been recognized. The repetition of its terms in Paul's subsequent speeches makes this clear (cf. 13:46-47; 20:18-35; 22:14-15; 26:16-18).[12] These same terms also underscore the continuity of what Paul will do with what the apostles have already done in witness to Jesus. In this regard, the most important term is the first: "This man is the agent I have chosen [*eklogēs*]." Even as the Lord has chosen (*eklegomai*) Israel (cf. 13:17), the Twelve (see 1:2), and then the Seven (see 6:5) as instruments of salvation, so now he has chosen Saul to continue this witness to God's salvation. In particular, the Lord has chosen Saul "to carry my name before Gentiles, kings, and Israelites" (9:15). For the first time in Acts, the international scope of the church's witness is made perfectly clear in the formulation of Saul's prophetic vocation.

The order of "Gentiles and kings"[13] before "people of Israel" reverses the pattern of Paul's urban mission in Acts, which is typically to Jews first and then to the Gentiles connected to the Jewish synagogue. In fact, Acts never depicts Paul's mission as exclusively to the Gentiles or Jews; it is an international mission because God promises an international salvation: "*everyone who calls on the name of the Lord will be saved*" (see Acts 2:21; emphasis added). The order here, then, intends to posit theological emphasis rather than to dictate a missional pattern.

The second part of the Lord's prophecy about Saul makes the connection between his suffering and witness, and thereby continues a primary theme of Acts. Importantly, it is stipulated here of Saul as a divine necessity: "I will show him how much he must [*dei*] suffer" (Acts 9:16; see 1:16, 22; 3:21; 4:12). Not only does the prospect of rejection and hardship place Saul in a continuum within Israel's history that includes the messiah and his successors, but it also profoundly qualifies the entire narrative of Paul in Acts. It forces the kind of "gut check" that turns the reader from a fixation on the heroic and invincible Paul of Christian legend to a suffering prophet like Jesus whose successes are hard won. The *dei*—the "must"—of Saul's suffering reminds the reader that this, too, is an element of God's plan of salvation: Saul suffers in the fulfillment of what God has promised Israel according to the scriptures. The repetition of "my name" in both parts of this commissioning prophecy helps to make Luke's point. The phrase recalls Joel's prophecy that

---

12. See Tannehill, *The Acts of the Apostles*, 118–20.

13. The prophecy that Paul would carry Christ's name to a plurality of "kings" is fulfilled in his speech to King Agrippa (cf. 25:23–26:29) and in anticipation of his audience with the Roman Caesar (cf. 27:24). Joseph A. Fitzmyer's argument for combining "Gentiles and kings" as a discrete audience and different from Paul's second audience, "the people of Israel" seems correct to me; see Fitzmyer, *The Acts of the Apostles*, Anchor Bible (New York: Doubleday, 1998), 429. The punctuation of this phrase is better as "before Gentiles and kings, and before the people of Israel."

in the last days "everyone who calls on the *name* of the Lord will be saved" (2:21; emphasis added). Both Saul's witness and his suffering will witness to God's faithfulness to the prophesied plan of salvation.

The Third Commission Statement, Acts 15:27-30

Interestingly, the third commissioning statement in Acts (15:27-30) also reads back into the previous narrative and fills in gaps with added details. The result is a more fully nuanced account of important moments that clarify God's purposes and the motives of those with whom God participates in the church's prophetic mission, the members of the delegation that James sends to Antioch to convey the decision made in Jerusalem. Repentant (but not proselyte) non-Jews are now included in Christian fellowship (cf. 15:19-21) and are given credentials apropos to the task to which they are commissioned. They are charged to be of one mind as "dear friends" (15:25), are instructed to risk their lives for the Lord's sake (15:26), and are commanded to live with the personal integrity to confirm orally the validity of what is written (15:27). In other words, they are representatives of the ideal church catholic. More important than these character qualifications, however, what is written and carried to Antioch has been "led" by the Holy Spirit (15:28). The content of James's reading of scripture agrees with the intentions of its author, the Holy Spirit (see 1:16). Any interpretation of scripture that is a word on target must enjoy a consensus that includes God's Spirit. The implied response to such an interpretation is obedience.

The exhortation that "you will do well to avoid such things" (15:29b) underscores the importance of reciprocity in any covenant relationship. Its conditionality commends the importance of human accountability to God's purposes, discerned by James from scripture. This is not a pointless formality—a polite way of saying good-bye to friends. There will be other disputes within emergent Christianity that will require turning back to James's reading of Amos for support and clarity in moving the word of God forward. In opening "a door of faith for the Gentiles" (14:27), a set of other concerns has also been let in that will require constant cooperation between the faith community and the Holy Spirit.

Reading the letter occasioned delight "with its encouraging message" (15:31) among the community's membership. The word *strengthened* (15:32) denotes fortifying believers to resist threats to their faith, usually through instruction and comfort (Luke 22:32; Rom 1:11; 1 Thess 3:2, 13; 1 Pet 5:10). This text is paradigmatic of follow-up ministry, a catholicizing practice of the church where mature leadership stands with inexperienced converts in working through the implications of new teaching. The note of "peace" sounded at the return of Silas and Judas to the elders and apostles of the Jerusalem church is a familiar idealism that always serves Luke's larger theological purpose: the intention of James's speech is Christian solidarity for the sake of the gospel.[14] That is, the universalism that marks out this missionary movement is of a piece with its desire for Christian unity. There is no functional catholicity without it.

The optimism of this narrative panel concludes with Paul and Barnabas together in ministry where it all began for them: "in Antioch, where, . . . they taught and proclaimed the good news of the Lord's word" (Acts 15:35; see 11:25-26; cf. 4:31; 6:7). But this partnership will suddenly end with only passing comment, and a new chapter in the story of Paul sans Barnabas will begin, still under the aegis of the Spirit and still on the road that will lead him to "the end of the earth."

I want to return to the ending of Acts since this passage is an implicit commission for readers of this canonical story to continue the mission of Paul, now in his absence but with his story in Acts in mind (see an earlier section, "The Church's Oneness according to Acts"). In teasing out the implications of this text for understanding the church's catholicity, we should note again that Paul "welcomed everyone [*pas*] who came to see him" (Acts 28:30). The Western version of Acts (which some think is the version Irenaeus received) rightly adds the appositional phrase, "all Jews and Gentiles," to *pas*. That is, Paul's earlier retort to the departing Jewish leadership team visiting with him (see 28:24-28) should not be read as his rejection of a Jewish mission or of a Gentile particularism at the expense of interested Jews. Even as the promise of God's salvation is for all creation (see 3:19-26) and Paul's commission is to extend the gospel of God to all people (see 9:15) to help realize Joel's prophecy that "everyone [*pas*] who calls on the Lord shall be saved" (2:21), so these are the very terms on which Acts ends. Paul's steadfast obedience to his vocation envisages the hope and promise of God's salvation for all people and exemplifies the ongoing witness for readers of Acts.

The two features of Paul's prophetic ministry are "to preach God's kingdom" and "to teach about the Lord Jesus Christ" (Acts 28:31). These two tasks are boldly executed by inspiration of the Spirit of prophecy (see 4:13, 29-31) and are "unhindered"—a phrase placed in the emphatic position not merely to characterize Paul's personal freedom but as a theological idiom to characterize the "unhindered" and unstoppable spread of God's gospel. The

---

14. Some manuscripts add a verse 34, "Silas decided to stay there," and edit Silas out of verse 33 to keep him in Antioch with Paul until their departure in 15:40.

implied desideratum of Acts is that the church's catholicity is guaranteed by the gospel's unhindered engagement of all seekers, without which the church simply cannot be the church catholic.

The Church's Apostolicity according to Acts

One of the most important roles that Acts performs within the biblical canon is to provide the church with a normative definition of apostolicity: an "apostle" is a witness of the historical Jesus (cf. Acts 1:21), chosen and instructed by the risen Jesus (cf. 1:2-4), and then authorized by God to do what apostles do and say in this canonical narrative. These are complex narrative characters whose witness of Jesus is the plumb line that secures their proclamation as well as their heroic leadership and personal qualities as exemplars of the faith.

While Acts offers portraits of individual apostles, which is a first-order way in which we understand the church's apostolicity, it also extends to the congregations to which the apostles are linked. The direct involvement of the apostles in the community's theological formation, indicated by their leadership and teaching ministry, leads the reader to assume that what is true of the individual apostle is insinuated upon the entire community. That is, the community itself becomes "apostolic" by virtue of the presence of an apostle in its midst, leading and teaching them about the risen One by eyewitness and biblical witness.[15]

During the canonization of the NT, it also became important to link the individual apostles and their respective stories in Acts to the writings linked to them by tradition or authorship. Although it is wrongheaded to make a book's authority depend upon the historian's assessment of its apostolic authorship (rather than the apostolicity of its theological goods), the significance of the working relationship between the apostles of Acts and the enduring importance of the two letter collections that follow cannot be overestimated. The personal characteristics of the apostles not only attend the communities they founded but the canonical writings to which their memories are attached.

---

15. Of course, the Paul of Acts is not portrayed as one of the Twelve appointed by Jesus and filled with the Spirit to continue what Jesus said and did (1:1-2). This requires a credential that Paul does not have: an association with the historical Jesus from the beginning (1:21-22). David P. Moessner argues that the implicit apostolicity of the Paul of Acts as successor of the Twelve is underwritten by his faithful witness to them—to what they did and said; Moessner, "Luke's 'Witness of Witnesses': Paul as Definer and Defender of the Tradition of the Apostles - 'from the beginning,'" in *Paul and the Heritage of Israel: Paul's Claim upon Israel's legacy in Luke and Acts in the Light of the Pauline Letters*, Library of New Testament Studies 452, ed. David P. Moessner, Daniel Marguerat, Mikeal C. Parsons, and Michael Wolter (New York: T&T Clark, 2012), 117–47.

The Apostles' Speeches

Among the many narrative elements that guide the study of the church in Acts, the apostles' *speeches* are especially important for the reader to note.[16] They make up roughly one-third of the composition and often provide apt summaries of the narrative's core theological commitments. Arguably, the most important of these speeches serve the church's missionary ends. Peter's Pentecost sermon (see 2:14-41), the inaugural sermon of Paul's mission to the nations at Pisidian Antioch (see 13:16-41), and Paul's sharply stated Socratic retort at the Athenian Areopagus (see 17:22-31) are good examples of missionary discourse that have provided models for the church's proclamation throughout its history.

Still other speeches, however, are important to the concept of apostolicity in Acts. For example, Stephen's apologia as a prophet like Jesus stipulates the nature of the prophetic vocation that glosses, in particular, the conflict between Christian preaching and Jewish tradition (see 7:1-53). Paul's so-called farewell speech defines the sort of person that best serves an orderly succession of future leaders in the fledging church his mission has founded (see 20:18-35). Finally, the various defense speeches of the Paul of Acts at the book's end (see 22:1-21; 24:10-21; 26:2-23; 28:17-20) serve to defend his spiritual authority within a Christianity that may have thought (and still does) his witness either too radical (i.e., insufficiently like Jesus or observant of Jewish traditions) or too irrelevant.

Even though reflecting different rhetorical conventions to serve different narrative settings, the speeches of Acts draw upon a common pool of images and ideas.[17] The result is a profound sense of continuity in the content of Christian proclamation from the risen Jesus (see Acts 1:3) to the imprisoned Paul (see 28:30-31) and in the vocation of a messianic community filled by the Holy Spirit to perform competently, faithfully, and boldly all of the tasks of the prophet like Jesus. Thus, every speech in Acts, whether missionary, apologetic, or edifying, is centered by the nonnegotiable content of God's saving word: Jesus performs signs and wonders as God's messiah; he then suffers and is crucified; and finally he is resurrected and exalted by God to confirm that "no other name has been given among humans through which

---

16. See Marion L. Soards, *The Speeches in Acts: Their Content, Context, and Concerns* (Louisville: Westminster John Knox, 1994).

17. The implications of the rhetorical shaping of the speeches of Acts will be considered in some detail when commenting upon specific passages. For a useful introduction to this literary element, especially as it relates to ancient models of public speaking, see the relevant essays gathered together in Bruce Winter and Andrew D. Clarke, eds., *The Book of Acts in Its Ancient Literary Setting*, vol. 1 of *The Book of Acts in Its First Century Setting* (Grand Rapids: Eerdmans, 1993).

we must be saved" (4:12). As such, these speeches provide an important retrospective on previous events as well as a christological reminder that prepares the church for its future.

Paul's speech to the Ephesian elders at Miletus (Acts 20:18-35) serves nicely to illustrate these various points. Because it is his only speech addressed to believers, it carries paradigmatic value for the church: faithful readers may imagine that Paul's speech to the Ephesian elders sounds like a message that Paul would bring to any fledgling Christian congregation. Especially his sermon topics concerning Christian leadership and character, in which the Paul of Acts is exemplary, are relevant themes for the church today.

Moreover, in contrast to Paul's missionary speeches or legal briefs, this one addresses a pastoral setting similar to his letters, many of which convey similar concerns and interests.[18] For this reason, an analysis of this speech may prove to have special importance in understanding the relationship between the Paul of Acts and the Pauline Letters.[19] While the majority of modern commentators remain uncertain as to whether Luke reports what he hears, this speech conveys the portrait of a canonical Paul that is formative of Christian mission well into the future.[20] This is the essential meaning of the church's apostolicity: that its core beliefs and practices are received from those appointed and authorized as the Lord's successors and his principal interpreters.

Finally, Paul's speech targets those who are responsible for transmitting and interpreting his legacy to others in his absence. His previous mission in Ephesus has laid a foundation and his gospel has defined its theological boundaries; yet this deposit of God's grace is under constant threat, and spiritual vigilance is required of those who are custodians of it. By extension, if the Pauline Letters are the textual precipitate of Paul's legacy, then the church's apostolicity depends upon its faithful interpreters to imitate his testimony to God's grace and faithful service to God's calling. The responsibility of interpreting Paul for the next generation of believers is no longer a matter of casting lots or of holding ecclesial office but a matter of good character and orthodox beliefs in faithful imitation of Paul.

The first half of Paul's speech (Acts 20:18-27) concentrates on the nature of his legacy. In a single sentence, Paul defends his Asian mission, centered in Ephesus, in two integral movements. He first appeals to the entire body of

---

18. This intracanonical relationship is especially true with the so-called Pastoral Epistles (1–2 Timothy and Titus), in which the canonical Paul addresses a similar problem that faces the Paul of Acts in Miletus: the continuation of the Pauline legacy in a post-Pauline setting through his appointed delegates.

19. See Wall, *1 & 2 Timothy and Titus*, 36–40.

20. Cf. Childs, *The New Testament as Canon*, 225–27.

evidence of "how I lived among you" (20:18; cf. 1 Thess 2:1-2; 5:10-11; Phil 4:15)—a life characterized by his humble service to the Lord and by his costly endurance of "trials that came upon me because of the Jews' schemes" (20:19; cf. 2 Cor 1:3-11). While testimony of his "humility" reflects Paul's commentary on his inward affections (20:19; cf. 2 Cor 10:1; 11:7; 1 Thess 2:6), the appeal to consider his suffering that resulted from various "schemes" against him is more empirical and invites his auditors to evaluate the hard evidence in his favor.[21] The reader, too, can participate in this review by recalling the narrative of his Ephesian mission in consideration of Paul's struggles there (see 19:8-10; 20:3; cf. 20:33-34).

The second broad movement concerns the disposition of his pastoral obligations to the Ephesian church. Paul's description of prophetic tasks performed is exemplary of Christian leadership that will secure the church's future. Paul later recalls these same images as characteristic of the ministry that would continue his legacy in his absence. He asserts that he "held back nothing [*hypostellō*] that would be helpful" to believers (20:20). In his speech, Paul uses a word (*hypostellō*) that connotes apostasy (20:20, 27). On the one hand, he has not retreated from his missionary calling in order to form congregations of new converts "in your homes" (20:20; see also 15:16-17; Rom 16:5; Phlm 21)—unlike Judas, for example, whose betrayal of Jesus was a repudiation of his divine appointment to care for the messianic community (Acts 1:16b-17). On the other hand, Paul "held back nothing" from the message that he publicly proclaimed "to both Jews and Greeks that they must change their hearts and lives as they turn to God and have faith in our Lord Jesus" (20:20-21; cf. Rom 10:8-13). Not only does the Paul of Acts refuse to disavow Jesus's calling by faithfully engaging in urban mission but he also refuses to cease proclaiming the gospel, which he summarizes by the familiar catchwords *repentance* and *faith*. The storyteller need not remind readers of those places or of that biblical protocol that Paul has routinely followed, whether as a philosopher in downtown Athens (Acts 17) or as a prophet in Jewish synagogues (Acts 13), where he faithfully argues the gospel's case in different idioms for different audiences (cf. 20:24).

---

21. The importance of "humility" in Paul's retrospective is intensified by its rarity. It is used only here in Acts, infrequently in the NT, and not at all in the LXX. Significantly, its NT use is mostly Pauline and posited in the virtue catalogues of Ephesians (4:2) and Colossians (2:18, 23; 3:12)—writings whose Pauline traditions are closely associated with those that fund the Paul of Acts. Steve Walton suggests that it has Christian currency—a "coin word" of the earliest church that expressed an affection prompted by the Spirit at odds with well-known vices such as excessive personal ambition or a sense of rivalry; cf. Walton, *Leadership and Lifestyle: The Portrait of Paul in the Miletus Speech and 1 Thessalonians*, Society for the New Testament Studies Monograph Series 108 (New York: Cambridge University Press, 2000), 75–76.

The shift from apologia (retrospect) to prophecy (prospect) is signaled by an evocative conjunction, "Now . . . I" (Acts 20:22). Even as Paul's faithfulness is evinced by his costly devotion to prophetic tasks, he remains faithful to or "compelled" (20:22) by what the "Holy Spirit testifies to me from city to city that prisons and troubles await me" (20:23). Details of a particular revelation from the Spirit to Paul go unmentioned. Only Paul and the readers of Acts know that he will make it to Rome, with a protracted and difficult layover in Jerusalem, where Paul will be "completing my mission," which is "the ministry I received from the Lord Jesus" (20:24; cf. 1 Cor 9:24; Phil 3:8-13).

Paul concludes his personal reminiscence by again declaring that "I held back nothing" nor apostatized from his prophetic obligations in proclaiming the gospel in Ephesus (Acts 20:27; see 20:20). The striking declaration that he is "not responsible for anyone's fate" (20:26; cf. 1 Thess 2:10) recalls his earlier indictment of unrepentant Jews in Corinth (see 18:6), which presumed that they no longer could excuse their rejection of God's gospel on grounds of their ignorance of its claims and scripture's warrants: Paul's preaching ministry has clarified God's script of salvation's history, and so to refuse his message is to refuse God's invitation. In this new setting in which Paul addresses believers, the issue is not the salvation of his auditors but their succession of Paul's mission in Ephesus. Whether or not the foundation he has laid in that city continues to be built up is no longer in his hands; his departure signals the official beginning of their own ministry in his absence.

The addition of a final summary of Paul's gospel, "the entire plan of God" (Acts 20:27; cf. Eph 1:11), delineates the theological boundaries of that ecclesial foundation. Elsewhere in Acts, God's "counsel" denotes God's sovereign purpose that is worked out in the messiah's mission (see 2:22-23) and now in the church's mission by the Lord's appointed apostles under the aegis of the Holy Spirit (see 4:28; 5:38; 13:36; cf. Gal 1:4; Eph 1:9, 11). There is no Pauline teaching that deviates from God's *boulē* and therefore Pauline teaching is "canonical" in congregations founded by it. The implication is that *God* views any deviation from his catechesis apostasy, and such apostasy would subvert God's scripted plans for salvation's progress into the future of Ephesus.

The second half of Paul's speech (Acts 20:28-35) shifts from a description of his past and prophecy of his future to consideration of his succession in Ephesus by the elders of the church. His rehearsal of the dangers that will face the church following his departure is enclosed by his charge for its leaders to "watch [*prosechete*] yourselves and the whole flock" (20:28; see 5:35b) and to "stay alert" (*grēgoreite*) to his pastoral example (20:31). The image of a shepherd watching over his flock is a familiar biblical metaphor of the leader's provident care over Israel (cf. Exod 10:28; Deut 4:9; Ezek 14:11-12; Jer 23:2; Hos 5:1; Mic 5:4; John 10:11-16; 21:16-17) of which the Paul of Acts is exemplary. He presumes their competence to do so because "the Holy Spirit has placed you as supervisors," which suggests not only the mediation of the Spirit's power for ministry (20:28; see 1:8) but also the Spirit's authorizing "mark" in their lives that others have recognized (see 6:3-4).

Two potential dangers are noted: false teachers will come as "savage wolves" from the outside (Acts 20:29) and even from "some of your own people" inside the flock of God (20:30). The catchphrase echoes the Lord's reference to "savage wolves" (cf. Matt 7:15; 10:16; Luke 10:3; John 10:12), which connotes, in his use, "false prophets" within Israel—teachers of Israel who reject his messianic word. The phrase has a similar meaning in Paul's speech, except that now it is his proclamation about God's kingdom that establishes a rule of faith which measures doctrinal purity within the church: the "savage wolf" is any teacher who does not stop "twisting the straight ways of the Lord" presented in Pauline teaching (Acts 13:10; cf. Phil 2:15).

Paul's warning of false teaching within the church is unusual in Acts. The repetition and variety of references to Paul's teaching in this speech underscore the importance of theological purity in maintaining and transmitting the Pauline legacy to the next generation of believers. Furthermore, Paul calls upon the elders to "remember that for three years I constantly and tearfully warned each one of you. I never stopped warning you" (Acts 20:31; cf. 2 Cor 2:4). Luke's characteristic use of hyperbole again underscores the value of Paul's personal example, which also carries canonical status within the ongoing community.

The final lines of the speech combine blessing (Acts 20:32) and exhortation (20:33-35) similar to the benedictions of the Pauline Letters. The main thread of Paul's speech remains fixed on his message (= *logos*) of God's grace (see 20:24; 14:3; 5:32). The edifying connection of Paul's gospel with the building up (*epoikodomeō*) of his successors (20:32; cf. Rom 14:19; 15:2; 1 Cor 3:9; 8:1; 10:23; 14:3-5, 12, 17, 26; 2 Cor 10:8; 12:19; 13:10; 1 Thess 5:11) for their future "inheritance" (cf. Rom 15:16; 1 Cor 6:9-11; Gal 3:18; 4:30; 5:21; Titus 3:7) reflect Pauline themes even if in Luke's vocabulary. As with the content of what is taught, these moral norms are in imitation of Paul and are obedient to the Lord's command "It is more blessed to give than to receive."[22] The purpose of appealing to Jesus is to underscore the practical

---

22. As is well-known, this wisdom saying is not found in the Gospel tradition (cf. Sir 4:31; *Did.* 1:5; 4:5; Luke 1:45), although in essence, this is the Lord's teaching, (see Luke 6:35-38, paraphrased) and, in any case, it has generic value recognized by all civilized cultures. Hence, Hans Conzelmann argues that this

truth that the community's solidarity is only as strong as its commitment to its own "weak" (see Acts 4:32-35; 6:1-7).[23] Finally, it is not because of his example but because of the command of Jesus that Paul can also say that "we must [*dei*]"—a divine necessity—help the poor and powerless. This practice remains the social mark of the community of goods in whose life the kingdom of God has been restored by God's grace.

Summary

The portrait of the apostles in Acts points readers forward to their appropriation of the two canonical collections of apostolic letters. At a rhetorical level, biblical narratives read with the Spirit within a congregation of the faithful have the capacity to evoke powerful impressions that influence how we approach related, more discursive literature such as the Pauline Letters. Acts tells us something of the apostles' personae, circumstances, vocations, and religious motives that enable the interpreter of their letters to fill in the gaps imaginatively and in agreement with the traditions of the apostles.

Yet, Acts is not only an evocative narrative; it is also a theological narrative that gives its own witness to God's gospel. The interpreter's interest in the relationship between Acts and the canonical letters is also motivated by theological understanding: How does Acts illumine the theological contribution of each witness to form a fuller understanding of the living testimony in which the church apostolic is rooted?

The pivotal role that Acts performs within the biblical canon intensifies the distinctive contribution it makes to NT ecclesiology. As a narrative that continues to plot "everything Jesus did and taught from the beginning" (Acts 1:1), the patterns of church practice that unfold in Acts make more concrete the implied ecclesiology of the fourfold Gospel. In this sense, the ministry that Jesus began by calling out and forming a community of repentant disciples continues in his absence under the leadership of his Spirit-filled apostolic successors. The open ending of Acts reminds today's readers that this biblical story is their story too.

In Acts, the church's oneness is forged in the face of internal tension by the application of apostolic teaching, fellowship, sharing goods, and worship—all empowered by the Spirit's presence. With Saul's conversion and

---

is a Greek proverb rehabilitated by Luke "with a slight Christian touch, namely, the selection of 'blessed'"; see Conzelmann, *Acts of the Apostles*, 176.

23.   Cf. Ernst Haenchen, *The Acts of the Apostles: A Commentary*, trans. Bernard Noble and Gerald Shinn (Philadelphia: Westminster, 1971), 594.

commissioning, God's intentions are made known to extend the church's mission beyond Israel to the nations.

Although the vocabulary of holiness is not thematic of the church's story in Acts, there was something disruptive about this messianic community that separated it from other groups, including its expansion beyond the Jews. Now, Peter and other apostles confirm, while God does not require uncircumcised pagan converts to follow conventional Jewish practices, he also does not require Jews to forsake their ancestral traditions. James expands Peter's original definition of inward purity to include social and religious practices of purity, and his expanded definition is the interpretive key in reading the second half of Acts.

As the messianic movement grows, Acts illustrates the church's global reach and catholicity in its mission and membership. What begins as a messianic movement in Palestinian Judaism pushes into the Roman world according to Jesus's prophecy to embrace all kinds of people, including repentant Gentiles, diaspora Jews, poor widows, Roman officials and soldiers, and Greek intellectuals, but not without a cost. Those like Paul who are called to carry the gospel are also called to suffer for Christ's sake. Acts reminds us that there is no mission without sacrifice; the Lord's way is cruciform. The universalism of the gospel's witness is illustrative of the church's catholic mark, which includes not only the work of evangelism to the Jew first and also the Greek but also the importance of circling back to walk alongside new believers, securing their fragile faith while integrating them into the whole community.

The narrative genre of "acts" serves readers by lifting up particular individuals as canonical exemplars; the portraits of these apostles postulate that through their leadership and instruction the community itself becomes "apostolic." When Paul warns believers about false teaching within the church, he underscores the importance of theological purity as the next generation of the church continues to proclaim God's kingdom. Likewise, the portrait of the apostles in Acts directs congregations of the faithful on how to approach related, discursive literature such as the Pauline and Catholic collections of letters and even the dramatic symbolism of the Apocalypse.

Chapter Four

The Pauline Letters Collection

Atheological study of the church according to the Pauline Letters, if cued by a canonical perspective, is indexed by the prior story of Paul in Acts. While the historical accuracy and theological purpose of Luke's portrayal of Paul and his urban mission remain contested among scholars, our approach, rather, turns on the church's canonization of Acts to provide a narrative context for readers of the Pauline Letters collection.[1] At the very least, we should allow that the long history of interpreting Acts from Irenaeus forward recognizes the strategic relationship between Acts and the Pauline Letters.[2] Acts supplies a canonical narrative that not only helps to contextualize

---

1. The distinction sometimes made between the historical (or "real") Paul and the Paul who shows up in Acts is typically overdetermined by modern scholarship. The traditions of Paul received and used by Luke to tell his story in Acts for his post-Pauline audience are, in fact, traditions of the *historical* Paul. That is, Luke's Paul is not a fictional figure but a theologian's interpretation of Paul, preserved in memories of his ministry and persona that he has received even if this Paul does not agree with the various reconstructed Pauls of historical criticism. My larger point, however, is that the storyteller's creative reshaping of this legacy in Acts is ultimately what the church canonizes for an emergent second Testament by the end of the second century to frame its reading of an extant Pauline canon already being used as scripture within the church catholic; see Robert W. Wall, *1 & 2 Timothy and Titus*, Two Horizons New Testament Commentary (Grand Rapids: Eerdmans, 2012), 36–40. My use of an "implied" or postulated author is borrowed (if vaguely so) from Wayne C. Booth's *The Rhetoric of Fiction*, 2nd ed. (Chicago: University of Chicago Press, 1983). I would argue that the church's acceptance of Pauline authorship is not based upon the judgment of modern historians but is mostly a theo- logical construction from the raw materials of Acts and the biographies of his letters, especially the Pastorals.

2. As is well-known, the earliest manuscripts of Acts place it with a collection of Pauline letters and

the church's ongoing use of its Pauline witness but also legitimizes its interest in doing so: that is, Acts testifies that there is hardly another figure from the church's past who is more important for its future than Paul, whose pattern of ministry and exemplary fidelity to "the Way" of the risen Lord shape the church's identity in, and mission for, the world.

In the first place, Acts provides a biographical sketch of Paul suitable for framing his canonical letters. According to Acts, Paul is a covenant-keeping Pharisee from the diaspora who, as a persecutor of Christians, converts to the risen Jesus and then is called by him to make his name known to both Jews and non-Jews (Acts 9:15-16). As predicted by Jesus, he suffers because of his faithfulness but perseveres in his urban mission to the Roman world to found Christian congregations of repentant Jews and non-Jews according to Jerusalem's decree (cf. Acts 15:19-21, 22-29). The Acts narrative of his missions in various Roman cities not only provides normative patterns for being a one, holy, catholic, and apostolic community (see chapter 3), but it also contextualizes the church's reading of the two collections of canonical letters, which are either addressed to these same congregations (Pauline) or written by these same apostolic figures (Catholic). Even as these letters begin with Paul addressing Roman believers, so also Acts famously concludes with a snapshot of Paul's mission in downtown Rome where, although under house arrest, he continues to preach God's reign from his rented flat at the "end of the earth" in fulfillment of Jesus's orienting prophecy (Acts 1:8).

The arresting conclusion to Acts (28:30-31) supplies a sense of ending apropos to the beginning of the Pauline collection, which also addresses Roman believers (Rom 1:1-15). The implication forged by this canonical seam seems clear: the exemplary Paul of Acts, faithful to his calling to the bitter end, is the implied author of the first collection of NT letters. In the opening to Romans, the reader is immediately made aware of the apostle's missionary calling to preach God's gospel to all comers, which has forged his distinctive understanding of God's gospel (cf. Rom 1:5, 9; see also 2:16; 16:25). The catechesis of a Pauline congregation initiates believers not only into the core beliefs of his gospel but also into a keen sense that the church's oneness, holiness, catholicity, and apostolicity is formed by participating in Paul's missionary vocation.

Acts also anticipates the issues and conflicts that may well occasion the church's reading of the Pauline Letters. The story's constant images of the

---

still other manuscripts with the so-called *Apostolos* in which Acts is placed with the collection of the Catholic Epistles. I would allow that the canonical perspective that relates Acts and Paul also relates Acts and the Pillars of the Jerusalem Apostolate, including James, Peter, and John, in a similar way.

community's solidarity in the face of internal pressures and external hostility anticipate Paul's unyielding concern for church unity in his letters. James's dramatic turn at the Jerusalem Council and his subsequent letter, which spells out a concern for the church's purity practices, provide the orienting concern of the NT's holiness teaching: God not only purifies the heart by faith but also sends the Spirit, who empowers a repentant community, to engage in a manner of public life that testifies to the community's faith in Christ. The church's catholicity is clearly expressed geographically by plotting a mission that follows the gospel from downtown Jerusalem, the epicenter of God's sacred universe, to downtown Rome, the epicenter of the world's pagan universe. Even more clearly, Acts testifies to the acts of the apostles which confirm them as the Spirit-filled successors of the risen Jesus who are appointed by God to lead the disciples—the Israel of God (cf. Luke 22:28-30)—following his departure. The letters that follow Acts are apostolic writings, the enduring testimony of those God appointed to continue what Jesus had begun to say and do (cf. Acts 1:1-2).

A canonical perspective also considers the Pauline Letters as a collected whole. The practices of modern criticism tend to drill down on individual books or even specific passages within those books for an in-depth analysis of the various historical circumstances and literary specifics that occasioned the composition of each. This important work often prevents readers from claiming that a text says something when it clearly doesn't. Nonetheless, the methodological interests of modern criticism tend to read a collection piecemeal rather than as a coherent whole, which is how the church has preserved its Pauline legacy for future generations of believers.

Far more debilitating is the modern practice of dividing the Pauline whole into discrete parts, mostly according to the historian's verdict of authorship and date of composition. Current textbooks routinely cut and divide the Pauline collection into subcollections that distinguish the "authentic" (those probably authored by Paul) from pseudepigraphic letters (those probably written after Paul's death), which are diminished in importance or dismissed entirely from a study of Pauline theology. The fallacy of this historical criticism is to presuppose that scripture's theological goods are somehow decided by the historian's judgment of authorship rather than by the church's recognition of an inspired text's capacity to communicate the words of the risen Christ to his disciples.

In this regard, a canonical perspective shifts the interpreter's attention from an author's composition of a letter as the point of its origins to its postbiblical canonization as the church's scripture. At that moment when scripture originated as scripture, the church congregated individual compositions into whole collections with a precise size and shape for subsequent generations to use *as the church's scripture* (rather than as occasional writings that target a particular congregation of ancient auditors-readers). Today's readers, then, pick up an individual Pauline letter only as an integral member of a canonical collection of thirteen, which provides a discrete intertextual and theological context that continues to guide its interpretation and use *as the church's scripture.*[3]

A Pauline Theology of Church

A pair of metaphors for the church is especially important when constructing a Pauline theology of church: body and household. The interplay between them and what each implies for marking out the church in the world will be the focus of this discussion. Each represents different ways of covenant keeping according to which a faithful community lives for God in the world. As such, a body or a household helps the reader imagine different but complementary ways in which God's people might negotiate between its different members.

In the Pauline use, both metaphors correspond directly between the material reality (i.e., a human body or a family household) and its implied meaning (i.e., a congregation of believers).[4] For example, Paul uses "body" generally to speak of human existence in terms of one's physical or bodily presence, while at the same time including what a person consists of inwardly, spiritually. The "body" is the whole person. To speak of a person's "bodily" or creaturely existence recognizes the capacity for a range of social relationships

---

3. According to Harry Y. Gamble's assessment, the early history of Paul's letters and the gradual process by which they were collected are obscure ("The New Testament Canon: Recent Research and the Status Quaestionis," in *The Canon Debate*, ed. Lee Martin McDonald and James A. Sanders [Peabody, MA: Hendrickson, 2002], 282–87); We know, however, that the ancient church circulated various versions of the Pauline letter canon, differently formed and arranged according to theological, stichometric, and chronological principles. We also have the Pauline testimony of 2 Timothy, whoever its author, forged by memories of his apostolic persona and mission as well as "faithful sayings" (e.g., 1 Tim 1:15; 3:1; 4:9; 2 Tim 2:11; Titus 3:8) and summaries of his core beliefs that fashion a Pauline rule of faith (e.g., 1 Tim 2:4-6; 3:16; 2 Tim 1:9-10; Titus 2:11-14; 3:4-7). Second Timothy describes the apostle as a Christian saint and martyr (cf. 2 Tim 1:8-12; 3:11-12; 4:6-8) whose unrivaled authority within the church insinuates the claims of his gospel as normative and prescriptive of a truly Christian life and witness. This is the raw disposition of a community's canon consciousness that gathers together the letters of the venerated apostle to "fix" his enduring testimony.

4. The reasons why Paul would select these metaphors is, of course, never stated in the letters. Common sense would suggest that he uses them because they are familiar to his readers in a way that allows him to define the church's identity in understandable ways.

and cooperation with other "bodies" and also for an inward life shaped by an individual's peculiar existence and experience of the world and Spirit. Critical in this regard is the body's capacity for spiritual transformation based on one's life with God. What is true of the individual is analogous to the entire community.

Perhaps the best illustration of the correspondence that Paul makes between human body parts and the church's diverse membership is his essay on spiritual gifts (1 Cor 12:12-27; cf. Rom 12:4-8). The healthy congregation is like a human body in that each body part has an indispensable role to perform in a healthy body in a way that corresponds to the practice of each spiritual gift within the spiritually healthy congregation. More creatively, Paul also describes the community baptized into Christ's body as a "mortal body" (Rom 6:12) with the transformed capacity for resisting sin to use in covenant-keeping acts of moral rectitude (Rom 6:13-14). This figuration of a charismatic church stands at the center of Paul's most radical definition of divine grace, according to which the internal body of believers bears witness to God's victory over sin.

This use of the metaphor allows Paul to embrace the diversity between individual believers while enclosing them all within a single "body" or congregation—different gifts, then, but the same Spirit who guides their use to a common end of loving and nurturing one another as, for example, different gender and social groups who make the same confession of faith in one God and work together in common mission for Christ's sake.

The most powerful use of the "body" metaphor in the Pauline Letters relates the church to the human body of Jesus. Jesus secures God's promised salvation for the church by various bodily acts: crucifixion and resurrection, which anticipate his bodily *parousia*. The messiah's human body is the pivotal point in the history of God's salvation; therefore, the move to speak of the church's salvation in bodily terms seems logical, which explains Paul's otherwise cryptic exhortation in 1 Corinthians 6:20, which concludes his essay on sexual (or embodied) ethics: "You have been bought and paid for [by Christ's body], so honor God with your body."

In a letter responding to conflict between the different Christian congregations of Greater Corinth, Paul makes this point most decisively when concluding 1 Corinthians. Here he rehearses the relevant parts of his christological tradition about Jesus's bodily acts in saving the church (15:3-4). This defense becomes in turn his prologue to a stunning discourse on the eschatology of the human body and the church's hope in Christ (15:35-58). If a

106

community confesses its common belief in Jesus's bodily resurrection, even while admitting it is counterintuitive to believe so (15:12-34), then it is reasonable to anticipate a bodily resurrection of all those in Christ at day's end. Indeed, "death has been swallowed up by a victory" (15:54, citing Isa 25:8). The realism that underwrites this figuration is provided by the participatory Christology of Romans 6, which asserts that the "person that we used to be" is "crucified with [Christ] in order to get rid of the corpse . . . controlled by sin" (Rom 6:6).

The strategic role of Ephesians within the Pauline corpus has long been recognized.[5] Not only does the letter summarize the content of Pauline instructions, but also its encyclical genre suggests a catechetical role that intends to unify the growing variety of Pauline congregations. The depiction of Paul's apostolic ministry as the global norm (Eph 3:2-13) is of a piece with this role and signals a development in Pauline ecclesiology. Here the metaphor of the church as a body reaches its most mature, even mythical expression, so that the two, church and body, are placed in appositional (rather than analogical) relationship: the church is no longer *like* Christ's body; it *is* the body of Christ in which his "fullness" fully dwells (Eph 1:23).

All that this practically implies is up for interpretive grabs, but the letter subsequently stipulates that "being" Christ's cruciform body in and for the world takes the shape of an ecclesial body of reconciled ethnic groups (Eph 2:14-16; cf. Col 1:22). No longer is the church a local body of diverse believers; because of Paul's influence, the church is now universalized, and its influence is expanded on earth. While a diversity of spiritual gifts is given to "each one of us" (Eph 4:7a) for the entire congregation's edification (Eph 4:12-16), the leaders of the messianic community continue the Lord's mission on earth following his ascension by their special gifts (4:11) apportioned by differing measures of divine grace (4:7b). The catalogue of these gifts of God's grace is not in order of importance to a particular congregation (as in 1 Cor 12) but rather in an order of their application to Christ's body in a way that facilitates the globalization of its ministry of reconciliation between Jews and Gentiles. In this regard, then, the church's "foundation" is set by "apostles and prophets" (Eph 2:20), whose ministry of God's word is succeeded by the church's evangelists, whose ministry to outsiders produces new converts to Christ, who then require shepherding into a mature faith by gifted "pastors and teachers." In this orderly exercise of diverse gifts, the church maintains its "unity of the Spirit" (Eph 4:3), which includes the dispositions of one

---

5. Most prominently by Edgar J. Goodspeed, "The Place of Ephesians in the First Pauline Collection," *Anglican Theological Review* 12 (1930): 189–212.

believer toward another—a unity that ties all together in love and peace (4:1-2) as well as the community's confession of faith in a Godhead who is three in one (Eph 4:4-6).

The Pastoral Epistles, whose late addition to the corpus completed the Pauline canon, add a second crucial typology of church: "God's household . . . is the church of the living God" (1 Tim 3:15). Uncharacteristically, "church" is used only three times in these three letters, all in 1 Timothy (3:5, 15; 5:16), and nowhere is "body" used of the church; so this statement about the church placed at the epicenter of the first Pastoral Epistle is decisive to all three.

Scholars agree that the Pauline use of "household" trades on the manners and mechanisms of the Roman family house, arguably the Empire's most important social institution.[6] The Pauline issue at stake is not the family values of today but the use of the family household to reimagine the church's place within a wider secular culture. The role of urban households especially was to reinforce social status and distinguish between the complementary roles of household members. Households helped solidify connections between members of an extended family and the public square, so that social manners and hospitable relations with outsiders were high values in maintaining an honorable reputation within the community and in conducting the family business. Moreover, the quality of life within the family was an important concern, but this was defined by the practices or roles performed by different family members. Especially important was the moral leadership of household heads, which more than anything produced unity within the family and good relations with outsiders.

Roman households also took charge of the welfare of the extended family unit, which included the marriage and education of its members as well as their material provisions of its widows or other members in times of need and sickness. Issues of gender roles (and status within the family) were more clearly defined as a matter of keeping house order and facilitating the transition from one generation to the next. In all of these matters, the public reputation and internal continuity of the extended family were paramount; its principal role was to safeguard the complex web of working relationships, internal and external, for the good of the social order. And so, too, is the Christian household, which is society's microcosm of God's way of ordering the real world, God's eternal kingdom.

The practical instructions found in these letters are mostly funded by a wide consensus of those conventions and practices that order the Roman

---

6. See, for instance, Carolyn Osiek and David L. Balch, *Families in the New Testament World: Households and House Churches*, The Family, Religion, and Culture (Louisville: Westminster John Knox, 1997).

household. They mostly address the leaders of congregations in transition, left in place without the departed Paul's apostolic leadership (cf. 1 Tim 1:3) and therefore without the certainty of whether his legacy would even make it to the next generation of Christians (cf. 2 Tim 2:1-2). Timothy and Titus are the implied delegates of Paul's apostolate, appointed with the responsibility of preserving his moral and theological traditions for the church's next generation (cf. 1 Tim 6:20-21; 2 Tim 1:13-14; see also Acts 20:17-35). The mission of their "household" of believers is therefore more institutional—that is, the instructions of the Pastorals intend to preserve an apostolic "brand" of Christianity for the public square (cf. 1 Tim 1:4-5).

The contrast between God's household and Christ's charismatic body as types of Pauline congregations seems clear and may reflect Pauline responses to differing circumstances or cultures. How does a community of kindred spirits, who reject their social status to live and worship together as the "body of Christ" under the Spirit's direction in expectation of the Lord's soon arrival (cf. 1 Cor 7:29; Rom 11:25), dialogue with the extended household of believers ordered from top to bottom by apostolic instruction that is motivated by what outsiders might think? Good question!

The canonical response to this question, however, does not begin with an explanation of these two Pauline ecclesiologies chronologically as though one replaced the other in a political response to Paul's departure. Nor is the Pauline household metaphor easily reduced to a mundane matter of naming God's church after its customary meeting place. The Pastorals reimagine God's people in the familiar terms of a Roman (i.e., pagan!) household precisely because it enables readers to understand why and for what ends a congregation and its leadership are organized in the manner envisaged by these instructions.

Both ecclesial households and bodies are integral parts of a Pauline whole and should be studied together. To reimagine the church as God's family household brings to clarity certain aspects of being the church that complete the conception of the church as Christ's body. In particular, the hierarchal organization of a household privileges those in charge. In a household that no longer has access to Paul's apostolic charisma, this "charge" is ordered by the memory of Paul's message and mission. It all begins there. The Pastorals' use of the "household" image is underwritten by an expanded résumé of the Apostle Paul included in these three letters. For example, even a cursory comparison between the Pauline greeting of Titus and the equally lengthy one of Romans notes that the one (Romans) concerns Paul's core beliefs whereas the other (Titus) regards Paul himself, who takes responsibility for the salvation of God's elect. It is not the risen Christ that sets out the terms of the gospel as in Romans but God's word delivered directly to Paul "at the appropriate time" (Titus 1:3). On this basis, "knowledge of the truth" is now delivered to fashion the faith of God's elect so that God's promise to them, made in ages past, might now be fulfilled (Titus 1:1). Paul is now front and center in the outworking of God's promised salvation.

Consider also the evocative claim that Paul is appointed as "a teacher of the Gentiles in faith and truth" (1 Tim 2:7). No other apostle need be mentioned (and isn't). What the canonical Paul of the Pastorals once taught is now compressed into canonical sayings spread across the Pastoral Epistles (1 Tim 1:15; 2:15–3:1a; 4:9; 2 Tim 2:11-13; Titus 3:4-8) as well as in dense theological formulas (e.g., 1 Tim 3:16) and memorable one-liners. These texts are less useful for catechesis as they are the kind of sound bites that summon the community's teachers to a curriculum for instruction organized around these big ideas.

If God's household is a community of believers whose public life is guided and secured by apostolic testimony, then any discussion of the church's oneness, holiness, and even its catholicity must in some sense be linked to the apostolicity of Paul. If the marks of the church as body moved forward from the sense of its organic oneness, then these same marks viewed as a household move backward from its apostolicity. Whatever else may be said about the other marks is funded by the memories of the dramatic conversion (e.g., 1 Tim 1:12-17), the faithful mission (e.g., 2 Tim 1:8-14; 2:8-13), the personal struggles and suffering (e.g., 2 Tim 3:10-13), and especially the instruction (e.g., 1 Tim 1:4-7) of the canonical Paul of the Pastorals (and Acts). This biblical portrait of his enduring legacy underwrites the importance of a Pauline understanding of the church as God's household.

The Bodily Marks of a Pauline Congregation

The Church Is One

The dimension of the church's oneness captured by the "body" metaphor emphasizes its charismatic and diverse character: its membership is united and its witness unique according to the Spirit's will, who gifts every member of the congregation differently for a common end: spiritual formation. This is mostly internal work; outsiders are excluded both from the reception of the Spirit's charismata and from their edifying effect (see 1 Cor 14:13-25).

No Pauline letter explores this idea of unity more thoroughly than does 1 Corinthians. The crisis to which this letter responds is a church divided (cf. 1:10-17; 11:18-19). The reasons for its internal divisions regard a number of complex issues both sociological and theological. Paul employs the interplay of two "body types"—Christ's body and the congregation's body of believers—to call a congregation of "those who have been made holy" (1:2) to make its testimony of Christ by its life together (1:4-9).

No passage in this letter makes this point clearer than 1 Corinthian 12's theological essay on spiritual gifts. Already, Paul alerts his readers of his concern for a congregation divided along socioeconomic lines (11:17-20), which subverts its reception of the Lord's body in the Supper (11:24-29). The diversity of social class per se is not at issue, but rather that when that diversity becomes division between believers, the congregation's witness to Christ's death is compromised (11:26).

Paul begins a new essay on spiritual gifts with a similar threat in view: a diversity of gifts, which the Spirit intends for the common good, can be corrupted by self-interest into internal division that privileges certain gifts over others. The opening statement sets out Paul's working principle: God's Spirit (and not some pagan religious exercise) prompts the repentant community's hallmark profession that "Jesus is Lord" (1 Cor 12:3; cf. Rom 10:9). This profession of faith, which is only prompted by the Spirit, is what distinguishes the church from all other social institutions and religious practices (cf. 1 Cor 12:2).

The professing community, even though characterized by a variety of charismata, serves and works together in the realm of this same Spirit (1 Cor 12:4-5), who produces them (lit. "works them out") in every one (12:6) for the common good (12:7). These various Spirit-productions, which are evidently catalogued according to congregational need (12:8-10; cf. Rom 12:4-8; Eph 4:11), are individually apportioned according to the will of God's Spirit (1 Cor 12:11). The Spirit's choices are planned; they are not arbitrary or incidental, but intentional and purposeful according to the Spirit's (not human) will. The subtext of this idea is Paul's keen emphasis on the *diversity* of the membership's charismata. This diversity, however, is also a potential source of internal division. This may explain why he inserts the famous poem on love as the enduring virtue and "even better way" (1 Cor 12:31) of Christian fellowship (1 Cor 13) in the middle of his essay on spiritual gifts (1 Cor 12–14).

For this same reason, Paul introduces his body metaphor at this point of his essay by a straightforward analogy: even as a single human has many body parts, so also does the body of Christ (1 Cor 12:12). The body of Christ, like the human body, maintains its oneness (unity and uniqueness) through the work of God's Spirit. Repentant individuals are baptized into (*eis*) Christ's body (cf. Rom 6:3-4; Acts 1:5; 11:16) upon the profession that "Jesus is Lord," which is only by the Spirit (1 Cor 12:3); in turn they are "given one Spirit to drink" (12:13; cf. "drink" imagery in 3:2-8) who distributes many charismata according to its singular will and for the common good.

The implication is clear enough. The Spirit convenes the diverse membership of a charismatic community, whether counted by religious background (1 Cor 8–10), social status (1:26; 11:2-34), or spiritual gifts (1 Cor 12). This same Spirit also assumes responsibility for the internal integrity of Christ's body. This is the practical force of Paul's concluding exhortation; believers "are the body of Christ and parts of each other" (12:27; cf. Rom 12:5). The congregation's ministry and worship, its liturgy and catechesis (as well as its finances!) are oriented by this essential way of thinking about its membership and about the agency of God's Spirit that produces it.

The Church Is Holy

Paul routinely addresses congregations of his readers-auditors, sometimes with tongue in cheek, as "saints" (*hagioi*; Rom 1:7 AT; 1 Cor 1:2; 2 Cor 1:1; Eph 1:1; Col 1:2). He does so, not because he assumes their exemplary life, but because they have been "made holy to God [*hagiazō*] in Christ Jesus" (1 Cor 1:2). Paul's odd take on a holy congregation whose internal life is rife with moral laziness and theological confusion trades on God's shocking calling of wayward Israel as a "kingdom of priests for me and a holy nation" on Mount Sinai (Exod 19:6). Sainthood is the sacred vocation of God's people conferred by God as a lavish response of divine mercy, not in just recognition of human merit. The community need not work hard to be holy; its holiness is the effect of entering into covenant with Christ by faith.

Nonetheless, its sanctification by and for God's sake both enables and obliges holy works that extend to every nook and cranny of its bodily existence. No passage better expresses this Pauline conception of church than Romans 6. Even though marked out by a merciful God as a community of holy ones, Paul insists that every believer respond to baptism into Christ by a bodily existence of moral purity. Although routinely overlooked in commentaries, the relevant text for our purposes is 6:12-14, a moment of transition in Paul's argument about the destiny of humanity's sinfulness when it bumps heads with divine grace.

The transition is noted by the shift from verbal indicatives to imperatives, which links together Paul's prior description of the bodily effect that baptism into the crucified Christ has on sin—"our [plural] sinful body has been abolished" (Rom 6:6 AT)—with the following exhortation: "Don't let sin rule your [plural] body" (6:12). Paul uses *sōma* in Romans mostly as a metaphor (synecdoche) of human existence as a whole (see, however, 7:4; 12:5). For example, the human "body" whose hearts desire impurity will engage in impure acts (cf. 1:24). Conversely, the Spirit enlivens the human "body" of God's children who have died to sin (8:13-14) while this "body" awaits its future and final redemption (8:23).

Clearly, however, Christian existence according to Romans 6 is a union with Christ's body: the people baptized into Christ and united with him (6:4-5). The redemptive results of his bodily death and resurrection are the embodied marks of a new way of "walking" (i.e., living) in the world (6:4b; cf. Eph 4:17–5:20). While Paul recognizes (as did Jesus) that Christian existence is "mortal" and that sin is still possible, the congregational body parts ("members," Rom 6:13; cf. use of *melos* in 1 Cor 12:12-27) are still "in Christ Jesus" (Rom 6:11) and as such offer (*paristēmi*; cf. Rom 12:1) their bodies to God even as Christ did as an act of righteousness (i.e., faithfulness).

Critically, Paul goes on to conclude that the community's embodied works of righteousness are the *res* of their sanctification (Rom 6:19), the end of which is eternal life (6:22; cf. 2:7). Considered from this perspective, works of righteousness (or moral rectitude) are sharply contrasted with works of moral impurity (6:20). Bodily existence united with the crucified and risen Christ is marked out by its moral purity, which is a keen emphasis in Pauline ethics (cf. 1 Thess 3:13–4:12; 2 Cor 7:1). In this sense, the church's confession of its holiness never assumes that this is only a status due to its shared presence with a holy God; it also expresses the church's intention to live a life of moral purity that embodies the faithfulness of its cruciform Lord.

The Church Is Catholic

The catholicity of the church is figured by Colossians 1:15-20, which confesses Christ as "the head of the body, the church" (1:18). The Christology of this passage has been a storm center of Pauline criticism, at first in trying to locate its sources in antiquity and more recently to fit its core idea of a cosmic Christ within the trajectory of the Pauline witness; neither will concern us here. The initial claim that this passage makes about the preexistent Christ's relationship with the created order—"all things" were created in, through,

113

and for him (1:16) and in him "all things" are held together (1:17)—frames the ecclesial assertion that this Christ is "head of the body, the church" (1:18).

Parallel to this statement about Christ's relationship with the created order is a second statement about his role in God's redemption of creation (Col 1:19-20), which climaxes with the distinctively Pauline assertion that God reconciled "all things" to Godself through Christ's death and resurrection to inaugurate creation's new beginning and the hope for its dramatically different ending (see 1:21-23).

The question for us to consider is the effect of mentioning the church as a body with Christ as its head and then to locate this puzzling metaphor in a puzzling place between these two stanzas that affirm Christ's role at the beginnings of both creation and a new creation. How does Christ, as the head, relate to the church as the body? And what does this suggest about the church's providential role in the history of creation? Any response to these hard questions is complex and contested. Some scholars argue that the reference to the "church," which seems to intrude upon the christological point scored by this passage, is added to a preformed Pauline hymn by either the letter's author or a later editor. The logic concerns the use of "body," which routinely was used of the cosmos in antiquity. The cosmos congregates all kinds of celestial members—"all things"—in the same way a human body consists of a range of body parts. If "headship" is taken as a political metaphor of executive authority, this passage plainly allows that the preexistent Christ is the "head" of the cosmic body, since "all things were created by him . . . and all things are held together in him" (Col 1:16-17). In this reading of a speculated "original" hymn, the antecedent of "the body" is "all things": Christ has executive authority over all things.

But the addition of "church" to the lyric would repurpose the sense of this stanza in its final canonical form. That is, the antecedent of "the body" is no longer the cosmos but the church; Christ has executive authority over the church as its risen Lord. But this quintessentially Pauline idea is transformed by its placement at the pivotal point of this hymn in at least two different ways. In some sense, the church is a microcosm that embodies Christ's lordship over all things. At the very least, this means that the scope of a congregation's witness—of every local body of believers—is coextensive with the created order. If the church's head is Christ (an idea more fully developed in Ephesians), who is also head of creation, then these two bodies over which Christ exercises executive authority must be viewed as interpenetrating. Thus, the very nature of the church, if cast in the image of its creator, must include a global mission and diverse membership equal to creation's scope. If Christ is for all and in all (Col 1:16-17), then his ecclesial body must include "Greeks and Jews, circumcised and uncircumcised, barbarian, Scythian, slave and free" (3:11) and all those others we might add to this list today.

More significantly, this passage goes on to declare that creation's head, so then also the church's, is the *risen* Christ whose death reconciled all things to God in order to present the church blameless before God (Col 1:19-22). The church's every practice and its gospel, if a microcosm of this new order, embody and herald this hope (1:23). If it is the earthly body in which the new creation has dawned, then the church is entrusted with the message and ministry of the reconciliation of all things (see Col 1:16-21).

The Church Is Apostolic

Paul's interpretation of his apostolic calling is picked up in the follow-ing passage in Colossians (Col 1:23b–2:5). What Paul says of his apostolic ministry marks out, at least in part, the nature of the church's own ministry as an "apostolic" community. This may be implied by the cryptic comment that introduces his testimony that he suffers "in my flesh [*sarx*]" (AT) what is lacking of Christ's tribulation on behalf of "his body, which is the church" (1:24). Personal suffering is characteristic of Paul's apostolic ministry accord-ing to Acts (cf. 9:14-15; 20:19, 23-24) and his letters (cf. 1 Cor 4:9-13; 2 Cor 11:23-27; Gal 6:17; 2 Tim 2:1-7; 3:10-14), but no other Pauline text elaborates it to this extent.

Paul accepts his suffering for the sake of Christ's body, the church (Col 1:24). But he does so believing that he is continuing "Christ's suffering" in order to "complet[e] what is missing" (1:24)—a rhetorically powerful expres-sion of Paul's participatory Christology. He can rejoice "now" in his suffering knowing that this is the "physical" mark that testifies to his solidarity with Christ in realizing God's eschatological purpose to reconcile and redeem all things. The mention of the church in the same breath sustains the earlier sense that the church is a microcosm of Paul's apostolic ministry. Even as he continues as a servant of the church (*diakonos*; 1:23b, 25), facing the same kind of tribulation Christ faced in his service to God (cf. Isa 53), so also must the apostolic church, which is Christ's suffering body.

Paul speaks of his service to the Colossian congregation as God-given according to God's economy of salvation (*oikonomia*; Col 1:25; cf. 1 Tim 1:4). Neither he nor they have anything to do with it; his is an apostolic task obediently done in order to make the age-old mysteries of God's word known right "now" to his audiences (Col 1:24-26). What are these mysteries? That the church of saints now includes repentant, reconciled Gentiles who hope for glory, "which is Christ living in you" (1:27; cf. Rom 16:25-26; Eph 3:3-6). This divine word, which issues both warning and wisdom to every auditor, proclaims nothing less than an apocalypse of God's salvation because of Christ's faithfulness.

The church's apostolic mark, if an imitation of Paul, is deeply rooted in a participatory Christology that not only anticipates sharing in the bodily suffering of Christ—as long as a ministry of reconciliation is necessary—but also suffers because of its vocational faithfulness (2 Tim 2:1-13). At the same time, such bodily toil also expects the presence of the risen One who is "in you" (Col 1:27) not only to stir hope of God's final victory but also to inspire the energy necessary for an effective witness.

The Pauline Congregation as God's Household

The Church Is Apostolic

Let me begin with the apostolic mark, which is pivotal in a Pauline conception of the church as a household. Similar to the Pauline use of "body" as a type of church, the use of "household" is not incidental to its subject matter. The congregation's membership and the necessary tasks that build up a faithful congregation are roughly analogous to those of the extended family household of the Roman world. First Timothy can even ask the rhetorical question of potential supervisors, "If they don't know how to manage their own household, how can they take care of God's church?" (3:5). Indeed! Management style (3:2-7, 8-13), maintaining proper boundaries between different members of the household (5:1–6:2), fostering good relations with other households (2:1-2; 3:6-7) within the wider culture (2:8-15), proper use of money (6:3-10, 18-20), inculcating a memory and a sense of legacy in the next generation (1:10-19a), and a proper succession of family leadership (3:14-16; 4:6-16; cf. 2 Tim 2:2) are all keen interests in maintaining a stable household, whether ecclesial, political, or familial.

Urban family households in antiquity were hierarchal. Management took care of everyday business, but the paterfamilias was in charge. While God is surely in charge of God's household, the church, Titus's epistolary greeting makes it clear that at this particular moment in the history of God's salvation, God has authorized the Apostle Paul to make God's message of eternal life known to the "chosen people" (Titus 1:1-3). In practical terms, the delegated paterfamilias of God's current household is the apostle.

It is commonplace these days for scholars to suggest that the expanded résumé of the Apostle Paul in the Pastoral Epistles serves as a post-Pauline apologia to support his legitimacy as the church's exemplar and apostle. Perhaps so, but at the very moment the Pastoral Epistles were added to complete the Pauline canon long after their composition, the Pastorals' portrait of a canonical Paul was used to settle a heated intramural debate over Paul's legacy for subsequent generations of believers.[7]

And so it serves the church today: the Pastorals' portrait of the canonical Paul defines his enduring importance for the future of God's people. The goods that sketch Paul's biography include his experience of conversion (cf. 1 Tim 1:12-16), his apostolic calling (cf. 1 Tim 1:12-16; 2 Tim 1:8-12; Titus 1:1-3), his reception of God's word at a *kairos* moment in salvation's history (Titus 1:3; cf. 1 Tim 1:10-11), and his distinctive appointment by the risen Christ as teacher of the nations (1 Tim 2:7; cf. Acts 13:47). This extraordinary résumé is extended to include his exemplary missionary experiences (e.g., 2 Tim 3:10-13) and a roster of personal opponents and supporters (1 Tim 1:20; 2 Tim 1:15-18; 2:17; 4:9-21; Titus 3:12-14). One may even allow that the eternal destiny of these (and so any) individuals is related to their relationship with Paul—not unlike the frightened sailors on the ship in stormy seas narrated in Acts 27, whose safe haven is wherever Paul is found. The church is the curator of this canonical Paul and so is a safe haven for the destiny of God's people. For this reason, the church's Pauline legacy is passed on from one leader to another, with the Spirit's help, to safeguard and transmit it for the next generation (1 Tim 6:20; 2 Tim 1:13-14; 2:1-2).

The Church Is One

Paul's extraordinary comment that Timothy (not the church) is his congregation's "backbone and support of the truth" (1 Tim 3:15b) has important implications for his marking of the church's oneness.[8] The church's ongoing stewardship of God's truth depends upon the presence and performance of those congregational leaders delegated to secure this legacy in Paul's absence. Timothy is the custodian of a *particular* apostle's rule of faith; he leads by teaching, interpreting, and adapting a distinctively Pauline assessment of "the

---

7. See Wall, *1 & 2 Timothy and Titus*, 15–40.

8. For my argument why this phrase refers to Timothy rather than the church, see Wall, *1 & 2 Timothy and Titus*, 111–14.

truth" about Christ (3:15-16) as the congregation's norm when receiving the theological goods of God's saving word. This idea agrees with Ephesians, which claims that God's household is "built on the foundation of the apostles and prophets" (Eph 2:20; cf. Rom 15:20-21).

Each family member has a different household chore to perform. Unlike the diversity of spiritual gifts, which are equally important and that all serve the Spirit's appointed purpose, some household members are delegated more responsibility (and so status) than others by reason of their virtue. The church's vocation is hardly introspective and intramural but, according to Ephesians, does battle on earth with the "rulers, authorities, forces of cosmic darkness, and spiritual powers of evil in the heavens" (6:12), which continue to obscure the gospel's truth and frustrate the church's obedience to its exalted Lord.

Naturally, the Lord's most important agent is his invincible apostle whose achievement to enlighten everyone (especially Gentiles) about God's plan to reconcile all things to Godself has been faithfully realized, if at considerable cost (cf. 2 Tim 4:5-8; Acts 9:14-15; 20:19-24). Paul's mission makes it possible that "through the church" the victory of God is disclosed to the hostile heavenly "powers" that continue to wage war on earth against all that God has accomplished because of Christ (Eph 3:1-13; cf. 6:10-20).

The clearest evidence of God's victory is the oneness of Jew and Gentile to form the distinctive membership of God's household. In particular, those hopeless Gentiles excluded from God's covenant with Israel are now "brought near" to Jews to form a community of shalom (Eph 2:11-22). The household's load-bearing "wall of partition" that had once separated Jewish insiders from Gentile outsiders is demolished back to the studs as the reconciling effect of Christ's death. The newly remodeled structure not only provides space for repentant/reconciled Gentiles to coexist with repentant/reconciled Jews in peace but also is constructed with a christological cornerstone and a foundation of apostles and prophets (2:19-20). Like Gaudi's magnificent *Sagrada Familia* in Barcelona, which has been under constant construction for decades, God's household created by Christ's body continues to grow into the fullness of Christ's body to provide a sacred place (a "temple") for the Spirit to dwell and work (2:19-22).

The Church Is Holy

The development of Paul's conception of the church from Christ's body of individual believers to God's sacred (and more public) household of "one new person" (Eph 2:15) results in a different implication of the church's one-ness than found in his description of a charismatic community. Rather than a principal focus on the internal workings of a local congregation, whose diverse members are fitted together into a single body by the Spirit to enable the loving ministry of one gifted believer to other insiders, the unity of God's household regards its mixed character as a whole. Now a common ground of beliefs and practices shared by both Jewish and Gentile believers not only testifies publicly to God's eternal purpose (3:11) to reconcile outsiders (Gen-tiles) but also sounds a transcendent note of triumph as well to the "rulers, authorities, forces of cosmic darkness, and spiritual powers of evil" (6:12), who are the ultimate outsiders to God's eternal purpose.

The catalogues of credentials needed by aspiring congregational leaders found in 1 Timothy 3 and Titus 1 do not list spiritual gifts but well-known qualities of public morality. Today's American churches, which are often pre-occupied with legal rights and denominational slights, too easily dismiss these catalogues of human virtues as yet another reflection of a strange world and reject that world as irrelevant for our own. What goes missing, however, is the underlying theological principle that household leaders qualify by their holy character rather than by their personal charisma.

Within the charismatic community of the Corinthian correspondence, where the Spirit is Lord (cf. 2 Cor 3:17), who alone determines church or-der by its distribution of spiritual gifts (1 Cor 12:11), the Timothy corre-spondence commends a process of selection based on human virtue that is recognized, perhaps even confirmed by, outsiders (1 Tim 3:7a). While every relationship within God's household is conducted "with appropriate respect" (*hagneia*; 5:2), this attentiveness to outsiders extends to a definition of leaders who must meet and greet outsiders on behalf of the congregation. They must, then, be "without fault" (3:2) and "have a good reputation with those outside the church" (3:7). Moreover, the delegate of Paul's apostolic authority is the church's "backbone and support of the truth" (3:15). The competence neces-sary to perform this critical role requires God's sanctification that readies the leader to engage in God's good work (2 Tim 2:21). The contrasting catalogues of purity and profanity found in 2 Timothy 2:22-26 (cf. Titus 3:1-7, 8-11) suggest that God sanctifies (*hagiazō*) the Lord's servants for this good work on the condition that they first cleanse themselves (*ekkathairō*) of bad theology (cf. 2:8-19) and immoral behavior (cf. 2:21). Only then are they vessels fit for noble use since the source of their productive practices is a "clean heart" (2:22, *ek katharas kardias*), which also enables them to avoid the "devil's trap" (2:26).

119

This same basic conception of holiness may also cue an elevated interest in personal virtue that adorns all of the leaders of God's household, including its supervisor (1 Tim 3:2-7) and servant staff (3:8-13). The shift from a charismatic community ruled over by the Spirit to a household church ruled over by competent leaders anticipates this concern. What is crucial to note as well is that this move in leadership registers an "institutional" concern in public appearances: How do God's people "appear" to outsiders? There is a close connection between Paul's decisive sense of apostolic calling (2:7) and the prudent manner by which Christian women, especially those with a public profile, conduct their daily business (2:8-12). Strikingly, the salvation of women is conditioned upon the practice of holiness (*hagiasmos*), which is considered a prudent choice for just this reason (2:15).[9]

The Church Is Catholic

The contribution of the Pastorals' use of the household metaphor to a discussion of the church's catholicity is doubtless mined from this border area where believers meet outsiders. Paul's use of the household metaphor is theologically motivated: God's desire is to save everyone, especially the outsider (1 Tim 2:4, 7), which requires language that pays close attention to outsiders in prospect of living peacefully with them (2:2) and seeing their eventual conversion to Christianity.[10] While the Pauline use of a Spirit-ruled "body" concentrates on a congregation's internal solidarity dynamics, the Pastoral Epistles posit a much keener interest in what outsiders think and how they might respond to the gospel on the basis of what they observe of believers in the public square. Their opinion counts in a way that is simply not found in the rest of the Pauline canon. Indeed, there are two kinds of outsiders according to 1 Timothy 3:6-7. The first outsider is the ordinary citizen whose public testimony concerns whether a prospective administrator has "a good reputation" (see 3:7, *apo tōn ezōthen*). These are also subjects of God's redemptive purpose—"sinners" for whom "Christ Jesus came into the world to save" (1:15), whom God desires to save (2:3-4), and therefore about whom the church should present itself as a compelling testimony of God's mercy. But evidently there are outsiders, once of "the faith," who now pose a moral and spiritual threat to believers (cf. 4:1-2). Timothy is told to point even these people in a different doctrinal direction (1:3). There are demonic outsiders,

---

9. See Wall, *1 & 2 Timothy and Titus*, 94–98.

10. Jouette M. Bassler, *1 Timothy, 2 Timothy, Titus*, Abingdon New Testament Commentaries (Nashville: Abingdon, 1996), 106–7.

too (3:6-7; 4:1; cf. 2 Tim 2:26), who may influence believers in a negative way and are to be avoided.

Another intriguing element of this notion of community is a reference to a female order of servant leadership. The servant staff of a middle-class Roman household would typically include men and women. Qualities of female servants would necessarily mostly match those of their male equals. This is qualified, of course, by 1 Timothy 2:11-12, so that this set of instructions, which targets a particular social location, would not include women teachers. It should be pointed out, however, that there are examples of female heads of households, which on occasion extend to the political structure of the congregation (cf. Acts 16:14-15, 40).

A Brief Footnote about the "Pauline" Letter to the Hebrews

Although its anonymity, epistolary form, and vague address certainly do not seem to fit within the Pauline collection, the form of its superscription, "To the Hebrews," does. Even if the letter's earliest reception history typically considered Hebrews a part of the Pauline corpus, most recognized its discontinuity with other Pauline Letters (Ephesians and Colossians being possible exceptions). Today's consensus among scholars, reflected in every critical introduction to the NT, is that Hebrews is a non-Pauline letter (i.e., neither written by Paul nor sympathetic with a Pauline narrative of salvation). Most other bits of the historical critical prolegomena that scholars wrap around this letter—its date and location, whether social or canonical, and its occasion and intended audience—remain contested and indeterminate (or unimportant); its anonymity has become a trope of a critical ambivalence toward its earliest history.

A canonical perspective, in fact, is less interested in these issues only to push forward the question, how does Hebrews function within the biblical canon? Any response to this complex question awaits a future study. The following suggestions are programmatic of a way of thinking about the role Hebrews performs within the NT and therefore are ways of thinking about how its teaching might extend a NT theology of the church. But first this observation: there has been a relative lack of interest in this letter's formal contribution to a NT theology of the church. Those studies that show an interest are more implicit, cued by topics or interpretive problems such as the relationship between "old" and "new" covenants.

When this relationship between old and new covenants is applied to the church, however, a supersessionist view of a church triumphant often emerges (on this point, see the introduction to this book). The very idea that the church, mostly comprised of repentant pagans, has replaced Israel in the history of God's salvation certainly creates problems for a Pauline conception of one church catholic in which Jews and Gentiles, once separated, are now members of the same household (Eph 2:11-22; cf. Rom 11:16-24).

The problem of Hebrews has been taken head-on by Richard B. Hays, although not without criticism.[11] If Jeremiah's oracle of a "new" covenant (Jer 31:31-34) is read in context, the relevant issue is not that Israel is replaced, but restored. That is, Hays argues that the letter's idea of "new" covenant trades not on the prophet's promise of a brand-new relationship with God, which voids Sinai and Judaism's priestly institution cued by it, but his promise of a *renewed* one, made possible because of Christ's priestly work. In this sense, the biblical promises of God made to Israel, which are carried to fulfillment within the bounds of a covenant relationship, *continue* (not cease) to their realization because of Christ. Hays allows that this idea may not have been mainstream but housed within a marginal (and diaspora) community of messianic Jews.

From a canonical perspective, the theological problem raised by Hebrews is applied to scripture's Pauline legacy: How does this idea of a restored and continuing covenantalism interact with the rest of the Pauline canon? Any response to this question is complex and would take us far afield. Let me begin the conversation, however, by closer consideration of the ancient aesthetic that includes Hebrews, finally at the very end of the Pauline corpus.

Two possible roles are implicated by this final resting place. The first is as an appendix to the Pauline canon. If an appendix, Hebrews adds nonessential information that nonetheless clarifies scripture's presentation of Paul's gospel. The thirteen-letter Pauline corpus was deemed aesthetically complete, but the church included Hebrews to clarify Pauline teaching that would be ambiguous without it—for example, Paul's controversial claim that repentant Gentiles are grafted into God's "planting" of God's people because of their faith in Christ (Rom 11:16-24).

---

11. Richard B. Hays, "'Here We Have No Lasting City': New Covenantalism in Hebrews," in *The Epistle to the Hebrews and Christian Theology*, ed. Richard Bauckham, Daniel R. Driver, Trevor A. Hart, and Nathan MacDonald (Grand Rapids: Eerdmans, 2009), 151–73. But see Mark D. Nanos's response to Hays in the same collection, "*New* or *Renewed* Covenantalism? A Response to Richard Hays," in Bauckham et al., *The Epistle to the Hebrews and Christian Theology*, 183–88. While Nanos would like Hays to be right, he finally thinks it is wishful thinking to read Hebrews as *not* advocating that the messiah-centered church has replaced the Moses-centered synagogue.

Another possible role suggested by the final placement of Hebrews between the two-letter corpora, is that of a bridge, which facilitates a mutually informing conversation between the Pauline and Pillars (the sevenfold Catholic Epistles corpus) traditions. In this case, the thesis of Hebrews, that the atoning death of a priestly Christ renews God's covenant for a restored people, draws naturally upon Pauline Christology. The dialectic between Christology and ethics in Hebrews, however, implies that Christ's renewal of Israel's covenant with God for all who believe is demonstrated concretely in the life of a covenant-keeping community. This dialectic between faith and faithfulness, which is exemplified by Christ, nicely captures the pivotal claim of James 2:22 that confessions of faith are completed by merciful works—a claim that supplies the working theological grammar of the Catholic Epistles collection. To this collection we now turn.

Summary

Paul imagines that the nature and practices of a congregation of diverse believers are much like the parts of a well-functioning human body or the responsible members of an extended family household. These should not be read as competing metaphors, as though one is more "developed" or "genuine" than the other. From a canonical perspective, both are necessary ways by which to conceive of a Pauline theology of the church. Especially in Ephesians, the two come together as an integral whole: the church *is* the maturing body of the risen Christ, its exalted head (Eph 4:15-16), in whom all believers of every sort dwell together as the household of God (2:19-22).

According to the variety of instructions found in the so-called Pastoral Letters (1–2 Tim, Titus), the daily practices and roles that organize this same congregation's internal social life and mission to nonbelievers are similar to those of a Roman household. In this sense, believers not only have spiritual gifts to exercise but household chores to perform!

Whether its members are Jew or Gentile, female or male, rich or poor, slave or master, the congregation's unity as Christ's body is given public expression by their confession that "Jesus is Lord" (Rom 10:9). The congregation is also unified by the internal witness and work of one Spirit, whose different gifts given to individual believers serve a common purpose (spiritual formation) and are performed with a common motive (love for others). But this same diversity that is characteristic of any congregation, whether calibrated socially or spiritually, is prone to intramural conflicts that threaten to fracture the body of believers. A Spirit-led charismatic congregation, then, may be reorganized, top to bottom, into a social organism that operates more like an efficient family household managed by competent people with each member behaving rightly and doing those necessary tasks that form a right (i.e., Pauline) faith and that enables the community to engage in a global mission patterned after Paul's apostolic vocation.

Paul's assumption of a congregation's holiness trades on God's Sinaitic declaration that Israel is a "kingdom of priests for me and a holy nation" (Exod 19:6). God's people are holy because the God who elects and calls them into a covenant relationship is holy. The transformation of the church from Christ's body into God's household, however, carries with it a more active, dynamic conception of holiness. Faith in Christ baptizes every new believer into a communion of saints, where each participates with the risen Christ for holy ends (Rom 6:22). At the same time, the special responsibilities granted to the leaders of God's household to secure its internal and external relationships cue an elevated interest in their personal holiness. As a prudent matter, the congregation's leaders must embody the holy life as public testimony that God's grace promises to make God's people a "holy nation."

The catholicity of the church is aptly figured by the stockpile of metaphors found in Colossians 1:15-20. Christ, who is "first in all things" through whom "all things are reconciled," is "the head of the body, the church" (1:18-19). The church is a microcosm that embodies Christ's lordship over, and reconciliation of, all things. The very nature and calling of being a church, if reflecting the image of its Lord, is all-inclusive—extending even to nonhuman creation—and fully engaged in a ministry of reconciliation. When viewed as a household of believers, the church's witness targets outsiders whom Christ also ransomed to reveal God's interest in saving all people (1 Tim 2:4-6).

What the canonical Paul says about himself—his conversion, his suffering and self-sacrifice, his mission to the nations, and his gospel message—especially according to the Pastoral Letters and the book of Acts, marks out, in large measure, the characteristics and practices of the ongoing church's ministry as an "apostolic" community. Paul accepts his suffering for the sake of Christ's body, believing that he is continuing "Christ's tribulation" to "complete what it lacks." The church's apostolic mark, if an imitation of Paul, is deeply rooted in a participatory Christology that not only anticipates sharing in the bodily suffering of Christ but also suffers because of its vocational faithfulness. Finally, post-Pauline leaders of the church are custodians of an apostolic tradition, keenly aware of the importance of passing on to the next generation the memories and message of Paul that will help shape the future church.

124

Chapter Five

The Catholic Epistles Collection

Any claim for the theological coherence of a collection as diverse as the sevenfold Catholic Epistles (CE) corpus (James–Jude) would stun most modern scholars by its audacity! The critical orthodoxy that informs most current introductions to NT theology, no matter their methodological orientation or confessional affiliation, assumes that the real differences between the Catholic Epistles mark out their independence from each other. Nonetheless, the contention of this chapter is that the formation of these diverse letters into a single canonical collection is not arbitrary but purposed to vocalize a powerful witness to God's word by sounding a chorus of different but complementary voices. In any case, the formation of any canonical unit was not based upon the church's recognition of the theological uniformity of its collected writings.

Moreover, the placement of a collection within scripture and sometimes even the sequence of its writings are highly suggestive of a pattern that guides readers when relating different collections together to fashion edifying conversations about God's word. For example, we have already observed the logical importance of reading the story of Paul in Acts before reading the letters of Paul. Acts may also be read as introducing the implied or "canonical" authors of the Catholic Epistles, noting especially that the interests of the James of Acts bear a striking family resemblance to those of his NT letter.

Even more significant as an interpretive cue, when the CE collection reached its final shape sometime during the fourth century, the church was almost finished forming a canon of Christian writings that already included a Pauline Letters collection. The church's episcopacy had long since used this Pauline canon to catechize believers into the Christian faith, but it also noted the dangerous tendencies when this witness was used to the exclusion of all other apostolic traditions—a warning Irenaeus had already sounded in *Against Heresies*. At least in part, then, this second collection of letters was added to the biblical canon to provide an internal apparatus of apostolic checks-and-balances to make certain that the church's use of scripture was a word on target. We should suppose that this practice is still in place: Pillars providing balance to Pauline perspectives, thereby providing scripture's faithful readers with a more accurate accounting of God's full gospel.

The final sequence of this canonical collection from James to Jude is not based upon a traditional chronology of their compositional history nor is the group arranged according to length (as is the canonical edition of the Pauline collection). Some have surmised that the collection is a simple matter of convenience: they are independent letters indexed by Paul's reference to the Jerusalem "Pillars" in Galatians 2:9: "James, Cephas, and John." However sensible this explanation is, the "pillars" metaphor cannot be precisely applied to a collection that also includes Jude! The CE are rather gathered together into a particular sequence that orders the church's reading for maximal theological benefit.

The importance of this sequence of the CE is confirmed by the consistent adumbration of this same ordering in both manuscripts and canon lists from the fourth century forward. Following the internal logic of this sequence, then, we should expect that core themes introduced by James are next picked up by 1 Peter for elaboration, which is then linked to 2 Peter even as 2 Peter is linked to 1 John, epitomized by 2 John, qualified by 3 John, and concluded by Jude, as though links of a chain. The approach of this chapter in answering the question, "Why the church?" will begin by using these chain links to construct a fence around this Pillars collection of letters.[1]

The Church of the Catholic Epistles Collection

James puts into play the collection's principal conception of the church as a diaspora community, constituted by a poor and powerless membership,

---

1. For the full development of this argument, see David R. Nienhuis and Robert W. Wall, *Reading the Epistles of James, Peter, John, and Jude as Scripture: The Shaping and Shape of a Canonical Collection* (Grand Rapids: Eerdmans, 2013).

who although tested by many trials (1:2), wisely befriends God rather than the world. God has chosen these members to be rich in faith (2:5) and recipients of future blessings promised to those who demonstrably love God (1:12). The community's steady faith, when proved by spiritual testing, is formed and guided by its humble reception of God's "word that is able to save you" (1:21), which is instantiated by various prophetic exemplars, especially the Lord Jesus Christ (2:1). This word provides the compass that guides the community's covenant-keeping practices apropos to friendship with God (2:23; 1:22-27; cf. 4:4). This same compass directs the community's mission to rescue lapsed believers who have departed from God's word and whose future with God is thereby imperiled (5:19-20).

But a "world" of hostile forces resides within individuals (Jas 1:13-15; 3:7, 14-16; 4:1-5) and surrounds this powerless community (4:4; 2:2-4, 6-7; 5:1-6), generating difficult tests of faith in God's word (1:2-8). The community's covenant with God is maintained only by a firm rejection of these worldly forces, evinced by its care of needy members (1:22–2:26), its edifying speech toward each other (3:1-18), and its steady pursuit for spiritual wisdom rather than material possessions (4:1–5:6).

Although the Spirit goes unmentioned in James, the reader's intuition honed by a prior reading of the Pauline contrast between "flesh" and "Spirit" will readily recognize similar contrasts in James: for example, between an earthly and heavenly wisdom (Jas 3:13-18) and between the two rival mindsets (4:4-10). In the first contrast, the reader's intuition may suppose that heavenly wisdom is actually a "true word" (1:18) carried by God's Spirit to form a fruitful community (3:17-18; cf. Gal 5:21-23); and, in the second contrast, this same Spirit may be insinuated upon the purified community to help it resist envy and friendship with the world and rather to draw it near to God's Torah instead (Jas 4:4-12).

The opening of 1 Peter repeats and elaborates the community's address introduced by James but in a more optimistic idiom: yes, the church is a diaspora community (1 Pet 1:1), constituted by resident "immigrants and strangers" (2:11; 1:1-2) who suffer "various trials" (1:6) at the hands of a hostile public (4:4, 12-17). But this same community is made holy "through the Holy Spirit's work" "because of the faithful obedience and sacrifice of Jesus Christ" (1:2), so that members may prove their allegiance to a holy God and so secure the salvation of their souls (1:6-9; 4:14).

The community's faith and moral purity are also conceived and formed by attentiveness to God's word (1 Pet 1:23). But 1 Peter elaborates this foundational conception by rooting it in two antecedent stories: First is the story of

OT Israel by which the Spirit-led prophets witness the community's participation in the election, exodus, and exile of Israel (1:12; 2:4-10). The second
story plots the messiah Jesus's footsteps in which the community now treads
(2:21) and by whom it now experiences God's promised salvation (3:18-22).
The community's suffering, then, is a public marker of its partnership with
Christ in the salvation of the world. The hostile world that marginalizes and
ridicules this community does so because it is ignorant of God's word and the
destiny of God's people.

Second Peter repeats 1 Peter's exhortation that the community obey
God's word so that God may rescue its members from their trials (2 Pet 2:9)
and confirm their election and calling (1:10). Yet, 2 Peter understands these
trials less in terms of the community's marginal status within the world (as
per Jas and 1 Pet), and rather locates the crisis *within* the community where
teachers are denying the truth of the apostolic word. In principle, God's word,
whether given in biblical prophecy (1:20; cf. 1 Pet 1:10-12) or by apostolic
pronouncement (2 Pet 1:16-19), is received and understood in the company
of the Holy Spirit (1:21). To deny this word is to deny the powerful impress
of God's Spirit in guiding the community's formation and, indeed, its destiny
with God forever.

The "trial" faced by 2 Peter, then, is more epistemic: rival claims of the
truth confuse believers, resulting in their disaffection from the faith (2 Pet
2:1-3). This theological crisis is also of a piece with the biblical story of un-
faithful Israel, which ends in divine judgment rather than promised blessing
(2:4-22).

Not only does 2 Peter understand God's word as constitutive of the apostolic tradition, but also 1 John continues to develop this foundationalism.
As with 2 Peter, the crisis facing 1 John is the community's epistemic confusion stemming from a rival interpretation that subverts the "word of life"
received from the apostles (1 John 1:1-2). First John elaborates the dangers of
accepting a nonapostolic version of truth by calling it a lie, a deception, and
a falsehood, the effect of which is to subvert fellowship with God and each
other. In particular, without a definitive apostolic witness of Jesus that only
eyewitnesses can provide, there is no effective remedy for sin or example of
the Christian practice of loving one another.

Again, as with 2 Peter, God's Spirit is given to the community (1 John
3:24) to lead its members to discriminate between error and truth, between
false prophets and those whose teaching agrees with the apostles (4:1-6). The
members of a community, who embrace the truth (2:12-28) and experience
new birth (2:29–3:1), purify themselves of sin to practice not sinning (3:3-

10). The transformation of moral life and the formation of a confident faith herald God's victory over sin and death (2:28; 5:1-5).

The community's characteristic moral practice is self-sacrificial, active love between members who share the same gospel truth (1 John 3:11-23; 4:7-21). Second John, which epitomizes 1 John, applies this moral practice to the community's hospitable treatment of its itinerant missionaries. Third John glosses this moral norm by warning how easily this practice can devolve into a power struggle between rival leaders more interested in self-love than practicing selfless love for other believers. Faithful leaders are necessary to govern the community in a way that facilitates the teaching of truth consistent with the apostolic witness and the practice of selfless love for other believers, especially those who depend upon the community's support for the ministry of the gospel.

Jude concludes by sounding notes that nicely summarize the collection's witness to the church. The church is "loved by God the Father and kept safe by Jesus Christ" (Jude 1), and so God's Spirit keeps it company (19-20). Its membership is marked out as those who adhere to the "most holy faith" (20) "delivered once and for all to God's holy people" (3) and who practice love as God loves (22-23), pray as the Spirit leads (20), and are protected by God to keep them from falling in expectation of a future in God's glorious presence (24; cf. Jas 5:19-20).

Toward a Participatory Ecclesiology: Paul *and* Pillars

Only by trusting in God's covenant-keeping grace can the church realistically confess to a life marked out by oneness, holiness, catholicity, and apostolicity. This note is sounded loudly by Paul's canonical witness. This synthesis, if read from the perspective of the NT's formation, presents a complement to this prior witness, which clarifies (rather than confuses) the importance of the church's covenant-keeping practices as equally indispensable in forming faith and witness.

Covenants are partnerships. Although latent in each collection of letters, when both are brought together to form a complementary whole, the result is a heightened sense of what might be termed a *participatory ecclesiology*. That is, an obedient people lean into what they already are by God's election and creation to become the church—or as James puts it, "faith was made complete by his faithful actions" (2:22). The central argument of this chapter is that the theological importance of the CE collection—in fact, the primary reason for its canonization—cannot be fully discerned by studying it apart from the

Pauline collection. The two collections are meant to be read together, Pauline *and* Pillars, in order to forge a complete understanding of God's full gospel.

More practically put, if our response to the question, "Why the church?" is exclusively Pauline, history detects a tendency to respond with glib theologies of a sovereign God who alone does all the covenant keeping. The church's passive role is to sit back and trust God. Faith alone saves. But the witness of the CE collection does not allow this response to our question. Its biblical witness to God's people testifies to an activist community whose marks must be instantiated in their moral and spiritual practices for its faith to effect God's grace. These practices are necessarily covenant keeping, then, without which friendship with God is impossible to sustain. In this sense, the Pillars might explain that an obedient church is necessary since, by its works, God's saving grace is confirmed for all to see. The following exposition explores this idea according to the confessing community's four marks.

The Church Is One

The Pauline conception of the church's oneness presents different ways of negotiating the relationships within a congregation whose diverse membership threatens the unity of its common life and mission in the world. In response, the Spirit-led community is imagined to function like a healthy human body whose different body parts perform indispensable but distinctive roles, working together as a complete organism to produce a profitable life. In this case, God's Spirit as the community's ruler assumes the singular responsibility for giving each member of the congregation an indispensable and distinctive gift for their mutual use in bringing the entire congregation to spiritual maturity, its "common good" (1 Cor 12:7). God's Spirit, who is one (12:9), puts this particular body together according to its will (12:11) so that there is no division between its body parts; toward the end of unity, then, those "lesser" parts are elevated to a level of parity with those of greater honor (12:24-25). Because of God's action, distinctions among believers are obliterated so that Paul can conclude, "you are the body of Christ and parts of each other" (12:27; cf. Gal 3:28; Col 3:11). According to this teaching, the church's oneness is fashioned by the work and according to the will of one God for the church's common good.

The Pauline use of "household" reimagines this same principle of oneness in institutional form, not only to facilitate the church's more public, socially alert mission to outsiders but to stabilize and transmit the deposit of apostolic truth to the next generation (2 Tim 1:8–2:2). Orderly households are well

130

suited to this task. Moreover, because the church is God's house (1 Tim 3:15) and God is one God (2:4), a congregation's solidarity is the public expression of its confession of faith in God. Toward these various ends, then, household order is maintained by those who are competent to supervise and serve it. But it is also maintained by a certain social responsibility, especially among those with influence and affluence (2:9-12; 6:17-19). In the special case of Timothy, he leads by the charism of the Spirit and ordination of the apostle (4:14; 2 Tim 1:5-7, 13-14). Household leaders are exemplars, custodians, and transmitters of the gospel truth without which the church has no future. Their moral superiority helps to secure the household's public reputation as above the reproach of outsiders and even the salvation of the household's membership (1 Tim 4:14-16). Finally, the solidarity of God's household depends upon all members performing the chores given them (1 Tim 5:1–6:2).

Whether defined by human talent organized from top to bottom to shape the church, or by the Spirit's distribution of spiritual gifts, each equally indispensable to the whole body, a Pauline conception of the church's oneness is more concerned with what the church is by God's grace. The Pillars collection is more concerned with what the church does in response. James puts this idea into play by characterizing the church as a prophetic community befriended by God because of its ready reception of God's word (Jas 1:5-21) that guides its covenant-keeping practices toward others, especially its own "orphans and widows in their difficulties" (1:22-27; cf. 2:1-13). Its battle is not located in the world per se as much as within each believer who struggles against temptation and doubt in steady pursuit of God's wisdom. In this sense, worldly forces that seek to subvert the community's covenant with God are defeated by the wise choices each believer makes to do God's will.

First Peter expands this idea of a community's solidarity with God by casting the surrounding culture as hostile (1 Pet 4:4), so that Christians are resident aliens who suffer like Christ for doing God's will (2:11-12; 3:17-18). The opening exhortation of 2 Peter is to "make every effort to add moral excellence to your faith" as the right response to this threat (2 Pet 1:5; 1 Pet 3:13-18). But 2 Peter relocates this same threat from the border region, where the conflict between the church and hostile forces is fully engaged, to the environs of the congregation itself: the congregation's oneness is under threat by its own teachers who sneak false claims about "the master who bought them" into the catechesis of new believers (2:1-3). Unity is insured by compliance to a common apostolic witness, and yet these teachers promote a different conception of moral freedom (2:17-22) and the coming judgment (3:1-7) than those received from Jesus and inspired by God's Spirit (1:12-21).

131

The practical effects of losing this epistemic battle with false teachers is nowhere more clearly stated than in 1 John. The community's activism, which is to love one another, is subverted by any distortion of the truth as received from the incarnate Word by his apostles (1 John 1:1-3). With the truth of this witness in hand and heart, a people held captive to a lie cannot experience new birth (2:12-28; 2:29–3:1). They will not purify themselves and are unable to practice not sinning and love for one another (3:2-10; 5:18).

The community's solidarity, formed by its unwavering acceptance of the apostolic witness to God's singular truth as revealed by the incarnate Word, is practiced by hospitality toward other believers (2–3 John; cf. 1 John 4:20-21). This firm embrace of other believers requires the exclusion of those deceived ones who have rejected the community's apostolic "teaching about Christ" (2 John 7-10). This extraordinary form of hospitality is a radical demonstration of a congregation's oneness, which is formed by a modification of its moral norm to love only those who share its account of truth.

The Church Is Holy

Paul routinely addresses his readers as holy ones (*hagioi*), not because he assumes their exemplary life but because they belong to a community that has been "made holy to God [*hagiazō*] in Christ Jesus" (1 Cor 1:2). The church's holiness is one effect of God's acceptance of Christ's faithful work on our behalf. We may even suppose that the church's experience with holiness occurs orly when it rubs up against a holy God in worship. Although God's sanctification of the covenant community is by grace through faith—"not of works lest anyone boast"—the reality of it both enables and obligates holy works.

Thus, while the risen Christ has already poured out the Holy Spirit to cleanse and transform believers in waters of regeneration (Titus 3:4-6; cf. 1 Cor 6:11), the magnificent Pauline confession that claims this belief is sandwiched between an extensive virtue/vice list (Titus 3:1-3) and a reminder that "good" rather than impure works follow after an experience of saving grace (Titus 3:8; cf. Rom 6:20-22). If we are sanctified by grace through faith in Christ alone, then the practical effect of that grace in real life is to live a Christlike life that extends to every nook and cranny of our bodily existence, privately and publicly.

The crucial point to observe when reading the Pauline witness for images of a holy church is that God's sanctification is not made complete by holy actions; rather, God's preexisting sanctification of the redeemed community and God's gift of the sanctifying Spirit are confirmed by the faith community's holy practices.

As one might expect, when the pivotal metaphor for church shifts from body to household, the Pauline idea of holiness shifts from a corporate reality to a standard to which household leaders must aspire in meeting the hefty demands of their ministry (see 1 Tim 4:7b in context of 4:8-16). Nonetheless, this idea of holiness follows immediately upon the claim that even our mundane practices, such as marriage and meals, are sanctified by prayer and God's word (4:5). The repetition of "holiness" words suggests an interplay that charges Timothy's quest after personal holiness as spiritual "training" supported by a God who makes things holy by acts of worship.

A different but complementary conception of this mark found in the Catholic Epistles collection is sounded by a different vocabulary of holiness. Strikingly, the Greek word for "purify," *hagnizō*, well-known to readers of the Greek OT (cf. Exod 19:10), is not found in the Pauline Letters. But in three different Catholic Epistles, this verb is used at strategic moments in the argument of each to define actions believers must take in purifying themselves in order to maintain their communion with a holy God. Each is used as the centerpiece of instruction that examines the character of Christian existence: (1) James 4:8: "*Purify* your hearts, you double-minded" (emphasis added); (2) 1 Peter 1:22: "You have *purified* your souls by your obedience to the truth"(AT); and most dramatically, (3) 1 John 3:3: "Everyone who has this hope in [Jesus] *purifies* himself even as [Jesus] is *pure*" (emphasis added). Several features of this triad of verses are noteworthy because they help us feel the weight of this collection's impress on the church's holiness mark.

(1) Unlike the note that the Pauline witness sounds most loudly (although not exclusively), that sanctification is God's gracious work upon God's people, the verbal voice in each of these three texts is active: believers *actively* respond in obedience to a holy God.

(2) While the first two texts address the entire community, the final verse addresses the individual believer who places hope for a future with God in Christ's victory over sin. In fact, 1 John 3:3 adds the singular pronoun *eauton* (himself) to create the reflexive sense: an individual believer takes purity upon himself or herself to perform holy (i.e., loving) acts. The rite of self-purification is no less than to cease sinning in imitation of God's Son, Jesus, in whose faithful purity one hopes realistically for eternal life with God (cf. 1 John 3:4-10).

133

(3) Additionally, the passage from James depicts the start of a journey to a holy place, when pilgrims cleanse themselves of profane and dirty things that may intrude upon or interfere with their steady pilgrimage toward God. These practices that purify believers for their rendezvous with God are not performed by God upon or within the pilgrim; they are the actions required of the pilgrim in preparation for meeting with a holy God. Earlier, James 1:27 uses a pair of purity adjectives, *katharos kai amiantos* ("pure and undefiled") to describe the kind of religious practices God recognizes as law-observant (cf. *amiantos* in 1 Pet 1:4).

(4) This same dynamic is envisaged in the passage from 1 Peter, which predicates the loving solidarity of believers, wonderfully pictured as a community of pure hearts, on their prior obedience to the gospel message: "by your obedience to the truth so that you might have *genuine affection for your fellow believers*" (1:22, emphasis added). It is within such a community of friends that the "Holy Spirit's work of making you holy" can realistically target obedience to Jesus Christ (see 1:2).

Read within its canonical setting, this collection's witness complements the prior Pauline corpus and so gets readers closer to the whole truth of the matter: since God's grace has purified our hearts, transforming us into "new creatures," and since God has given us the indwelling Spirit who is holy, disciples of the living Christ are now able to embody God's holiness in their moral and spiritual practices. By stipulating that a faithful people's holy works are the condition that forms *koinōnia* with the triune God, the community's performance of good works, quite apart from but still integral to faith, is the *mutual* effect of God's sanctifying grace at work in a people who freely respond by living a holy life in a manner that heralds the coming victory of God. On that day, 2 Peter promises that a life of holiness will feel right at home because it will be set within the bounds of a new creation (2 Pet 3:11-13; 1 Thess 5:23).

From the perspective of the NT's entire witness to God's gospel, Paul's letters interpret holiness as the singular effect of God's gracious action upon the church. The Catholic Epistles collection offers a complementary witness: the community sanctified by God's grace actively responds in holy ways. That is, the NT witness to the holy life is more robust than an accounting of God's purifying grace upon the sinful heart through faith in Christ alone; it includes a description of the holy life. The community's holiness is demonstrated for all the world to see by the dynamic exchange of impure practices that contaminate fellowship with God and neighbor for a social activism of mercy and justice.

The Church Is Catholic

The pivotal piece of a Pauline conception of the church's catholicity regards its global ministry of reconciliation. The scope of this ministry is coextensive with creation, so that the church's witness to God's all-encompassing victory (on behalf of "all things") translates not only its proclamation of Paul's gospel to those nonbelievers outside of the household of God but also to the heavenly, malevolent "rulers and powers" (Eph 3:10). Naturally, the intent of the church's mission to the latter is not evangelistic, since these powers are already doomed, but merely confirmatory of their future fate.

The addition of the CE collection to the NT canon does not qualify this mission statement one bit: the church's catholicity delineates the scope of its gospel ministry, especially to those outside of Christ. But the second letter collection underscores another dimension of the community's catholic character to make scripture's witness more complete in this regard: while the collection does not deny the presence of outsiders, they are excluded from the community's primary concern to attend to its own members who are typically marginalized by others. That is, the principal ministry of the church is more sectarian and introspective, since it is a "diaspora" community (1 Pet 1:1; Jas 1:1) comprised of "immigrants and strangers" (1 Pet 1:1-2; 2:11).

The culture wrapped around the community is no longer viewed as a target of the church's global mission. In fact, the world is generally viewed as a competing, hostile entity that is off-limits to God's people. In James, the community's mission is to its former members who have departed from the way of wisdom (5:19-20). While the evil world that the community avoids is also "within" each member according to James, a social world primarily surrounds it, generally led by the rich and famous who mistreat the community's poor and powerless (2:2-4; 4:4; 5:1-6). Oddly, the catholicity of the church is marked out by the inclusion of these poor members who are God's elect (2:5), even though rejected by the world (cf. 1 Pet 1:1-2).

Even though this borderland between community and its social world is defined differently in 1 Peter, the hostility between the two is clear (1 Pet 4:4, 12-17). In fact, neither of the two biblical stories that interpret this hostility, Israel's (1:12; 2:4-10) and Christ's (3:18-22), are examples of the community's mission as they are in Paul; rather, both anticipate the community's

135

social ostracization to explain the reason for its righteous suffering for the world's salvation. Unlike the implicit hand-wringing of James, which worries that doubt and duplicity will subvert the community's application of God's wisdom to its present trials, 1 Peter considers these conflicts in the cultural borderland conducive to spiritual growth.

Nowhere is the inclusiveness of this collection's sectarian impulse better noted than in 1 John. On the one hand, while Christ's death deals with the sins of the "whole world" (2:2), its application is clearly directed to those Christians who embrace the truth of the apostles' witness of the incarnate Word (1:1-3, 5; 3:11). That is, the scope of Christ's work is universal, but its effect is limited to a particular kind of Christianity—one that has rejected the claims of "antichrist" for the claims of the apostolic tradition.

In fact, tracking 1 John's use of the word *world* makes this point clear. Even though used of both the location and the object of Christ's expiatory sacrifice (2:2; 4:9) as "savior of the world" (4:14), the world is also demonized (2:15-17; cf. 5:19) or used in a dualism that sharply contrasts God's children with those who despise them (3:13) and the "spirit of the antichrist," which rejects Jesus (4:1-5). First John concludes, then, that the church's mission is not "world" evangelism but to "defeat" the sinful preoccupations of the world by a rigorously tested faith in Jesus (5:4-5; cf. 4:4).

Nonetheless, the decisive element of the church's catholic mark, according to this collection, is its mission to safeguard the faith of its own marginal membership in a hostile environment. The endings of both James and Jude (and perhaps also 1 John) indicate the fragile character of faith when grown on the margins where the opposition party is most keenly felt; the endings of these two letters enclose the entire collection in this concern. Again, it is thematic of the church's catholicity that its membership includes and even privileges those the world has rejected or bypassed, but there are costs to consider. For this reason, James ends by encouraging the community (and perhaps its leaders in particular) to bring those who wander from truth back into the fold. Likewise, Jude asks members to "build each other up on the foundation of your most holy faith, . . . have mercy on those who doubt," and snatch some from the fire (Jude 20-23). Such a rescue mission directed at insiders is motivated by a belief that God is "the one who is able to protect you from falling" in order "to present you blameless" (Jude 24). But it is finally the church that must act to snatch its struggling members "from the fire" to realize its core belief in divine providence.

Finally, the collection's "catholic" nomenclature is apropos to this definition. While often understood as referring to the collection's general address (see 1 Pet 1:1), perhaps "catholic" is more profitably understood as characteristic of a community whose membership not only includes people that other groups reject or belittle but also those insiders that others would have long since given up on.

The Church Is Apostolic

Especially from a canonical perspective, the characteristics of the church's apostolicity are those of the *canonical* Paul—that is, the traditions of Paul received and used to draw his superlative biography in Acts and the Pastoral Letters. Simply put, the Apostle Paul personifies the apostolic church. His life and ministry, which are defined and made accessible by this biblical biography and hermeneutic of his letters collection, help supply the substance of the church's self-understanding as an apostolic community. Indeed, receiving scripture's Pauline witness protects the faith from heresy.

The résumé of this canonical Paul need not (and does not!) mention other apostles. But the Pillars collection is grounded in a particular epistemology of apostleship that trades on a different kind of experience from the one that secured Paul's apostolic office. Noteworthy are the early challenges to Paul's claim of apostolicity, which have less to do with the content of his gospel or his mission to the Gentiles, which seem to be the issue in play in Romans and perhaps 2 Corinthians. The conflict to which Paul responds in Galatians 1–2 regards the source of Paul's apostleship: What credentials can Paul show to support his office? Paul's response to this question grounds his appointment in divine revelation (Gal 1:10-12) and in his dramatic conversion (1:13), when the resurrected Jesus encounters Paul while traveling to Damascus to oppose the church's mission there. That is, Paul's apostleship is not based upon his friendship with, or eyewitness to, the historical Jesus; he was not schooled by Jesus's teaching or by imitation of an observed life.

One possible result of this highly reductionist claim of apostleship is that Pauline Christology is mostly stripped of the life of the historical Jesus, whom Paul never observed. The content of his witness derives from an encounter with Jesus, a revelation from him. As such, the Lord's messianic work is concentrated on the cross and in the resurrection. The Pillars Christology is shaped by an experience of the human Jesus, his life (1 John), teaching (James), and suffering (1 Peter). The two collections' respective ecclesiologies reflect these differences, especially if one allows that the interest in the community's responses to God's saving grace is modeled by an observed Jesus (cf. 1 Pet 2:21; 1 John 2:6).

137

Acts recognizes that the source of Paul's authority is different from that of the Twelve, who unlike Paul were eyewitnesses of the historical Jesus (see Acts 1:21-22). Paul's message about the risen Jesus and religious authority granted him is ex post facto. The consistent appeal of the CE collection to the apostolic tradition is located in a different source than the Pauline collection: an encounter/eyewitness "from the beginning" of the historical Jesus (1 John 1:1). Accordingly, the community's apostolic mark is an ipso facto experience of the historical Jesus rather than an ex post facto experience of the risen Lord.

The result is more than rhetorical: the materials gleaned from what the apostles have personally seen, heard, and handled of the real Jesus supply the gospel's theological goods and establish the rule of faith that regulates the spiritual journey of anyone who comes out of the world and into a covenant-keeping relationship with God. Moreover, the community's *koinōnia* with God hinges on a clear apprehension of the apostles' eye- and earwitness of the incarnate Word (1 John 1:3). True believers must reject any teaching that opposes what the apostles ("we") observed of the word of life "from the beginning" regarding the marks of authentic Christian discipleship.

Critically, several CE (2 Pet, 1 John, 2 John, Jude) address intramural disputes between rival Christianities. The message about Jesus continues to divide God's people, even as it did according to the fourfold Gospel and Acts. Whenever disagreements threaten to split the household of God's Israel, leaders of rival groups typically debate issues of evidence and sources, each claiming superior evidence mined from better sources to confirm their particular version of truth over the falsehoods of others. Similarly, the CE's collected response to this religious crisis provides a biblical model for today's church whenever a division within the ranks threatens to break apart the body of Christ.

But these letters exhibit little interest in defining and demonizing the teaching of rival Christian groups. First John's "antichrist" is probably not a person at all but a theological metaphor for anyone who opposes the community's apostolic message (cf. 2:18-19, 22). What seems clearer than the group's identity is the importance of an eyewitness tradition to set the boundary marker for eternal life. As such, the real crisis is once again not outward but inward: How does apostolic-led teaching clarify an identity of a communion of saints and on this basis assure them of having fellowship "with the Father and with his Son, Jesus Christ" (1 John 1:3; cf. 2 Pet 2:20-21)?

138

Summary

The sevenfold (James–Jude) Catholic Epistles provide an internal apparatus of apostolic checks and balances to ensure that the church's use of scripture is a word on target. The theological importance of the CE collection as a witness to the truth about God's church cannot be fully discerned by studying it apart from the Pauline collection. From the beginning, these two canonical collections are meant to be read together to forge a complete understanding of God's full gospel, often the one guiding the church's appropriation of the other.

In a Pauline conception of the church's oneness, the Spirit-led community is imagined to function as a healthy human "body," while the Pauline use of "household" reimagines the same principle of oneness as a human-led organization. The Pauline conception of the church's oneness is concerned with what the church is by God's grace. The Pillars collection is more concerned with what the church does in response to God's grace. In a sense, worldly forces that seek to subvert the community's covenant with God are defeated by the wise choices each believer makes.

Paul routinely addresses his readers as "holy ones" (*hagioi*) (AT), not because of their exemplary lives but because they have "been made holy to God [*hagiazō*] in Jesus Christ" (1 Cor 1:2). Rather, God's preexisting sanctification of the redeemed community and his gift of the sanctifying Spirit are confirmed by the faith community's holy practices. In the Pillars collection, a different but complementary conception of this mark of holiness is defined by actions the believers must take in purifying themselves to maintain their communion with a holy God. Since God's grace has transformed us into "new creatures," disciples of the living God are now able to embody God's holiness in their moral and spiritual practices.

A Pauline conception of the church's catholicity regards its global ministry of reconciliation. The decisive element of the church's catholic mark, according to the Pillars collection, is its mission to safeguard the welfare of its own membership from a hostile world, whether to insure the material well-being of its poor and powerless or the faith of its disaffected members. It is the responsibility of the community of believers to render well-timed grace in time of need or to "snatch" wayward members "from the fire" in order to insure they all participate in the promised salvation of God.

Scripture's profile of the canonical Paul is the very personification of the apostolic church; his exemplary life and mission to the nations supply the theological goods of the church's self-understanding as an apostolic community—a community in Paul's image. His teaching and example therefore delineate the boundaries of the community's faith and witness, beyond which is found falsehood and fraud. The epistemology of the Pillars collection is rather grounded on the apostles' personal experience of the historical Jesus; his observed life, his heard teaching, and his shared suffering provide the content of the truth. The shift is from the apostolic persona (Paul) to the historical Jesus (Pillars). In this sense, then, a truly apostolic community rejects any teaching that opposes what the apostles observed regarding the marks of authentic Christian discipleship, setting the boundary marker for eternal life. And this must also enforce a check, and necessary corrective if called for, of the manner and substance of the church's appropriation of scripture's Pauline witness.

Chapter Six

Apocalypse of John

For most of the second century, the Apocalypse circulated with a "Johannine" corpus, which included the fourth Gospel and 1–2 John.[1] The church had collected and circulated this corpus based upon their theological agreements, common vocabulary, and a shared legacy that linked these anonymous writings to Saint John's apostolate. For reasons now unknown to us, this small corpus of writings had been dismantled by the end of the third century (if not earlier): John's Gospel was placed in the fourfold canonical collection, the Epistles had found their way into a second collection of "catholic" letters, and the Apocalypse, left to fend for itself against various opponents, was finally placed at the end of the NT (although not until the eleventh century in the East after much hand-wringing).

This brief summary of a long and complex history introduces this book's final chapter to make a key point: although we can now only speculate about the bumpy route that the Apocalypse took in getting there, the church's reception of it into the biblical canon appears to be independent of other Johannine writings. That is, the role intended for it to perform within the NT, cued by its canonization, appears distinct from other Johannine writings and may be envisaged by its placement as scripture's last book.

---

1. There remains no evidence either from manuscripts or from early Christian writings that 3 John was in use during the second century. This silence can be explained in different ways, but it may indicate that 3 John was not yet a part of a widely used Johannine corpus and only later was added to it, sometime during the third century.

The reader's intuition may very well agree with the church's decision to place the Apocalypse at scripture's end since it envisions the end-times of God's redemptive plan. The rhetorical role of a book's concluding chapter, however, is not precisely the same as "the end." A conclusion need not end things once and for all but simply set out the conditions for the plotline's imagined continuation into a future still to unfold, of a story not yet told. The role that the Apocalypse performs in scripture is a conclusion, not an ending: readers are guided to envision God's victory over death and renewal of creation as conditions of life eternal, whose narrative is not yet told.

The book's odd title, The Apocalypse of John, is another property of the canonical process and not of the author's composition. The church gives the book its title to help readers recognize its authority—despite its strangeness and the controversy that swirled around it from the beginning. The first word, *apocalypse*, recognizes that this is the only biblical book so-named, thereby securing the community's sense of its distinctive role and theological character within the biblical canon. This is a stand-alone book.

The title's reference to Saint John cues the contradiction we observe in the book's opening sentence: this apocalypse does not belong to John but is rather the "apocalypse of Jesus Christ" that God gave John via angelic intercession. One must assume such an obvious contradiction in such an important place is purposeful, targeting a special authority that underwrites its reception into the biblical canon as God's authoritative word. But the predicate of John's authority is not apostolic, since nowhere does the prophet refer to himself as an apostle. Rather, his authority is due to his status as Christ's "servant" who is commissioned with the task of authoring a book of revelation "in a Spirit-inspired trance" (Rev 1:10; 4:2; 17:3; 21:10) based on visions sent him by the heavenly "Human One" (1:13-19).[2]

The deep impress of this move to wrap biblical compositions around the point of canonization helps secure the timelessness of their ecclesial address: scripture is always read in the present tense by its faithful readers. Against the emphasis of modern historical criticism, which seeks to explain the Apocalypse's visionary world against the background of antiquity (sometimes freezing its meaning there), or the emphasis of popular theological interpretation, which seeks to explain this same word as a cipher for the end of time, a canonical approach to this book follows the lead of the church's first interpreters

---

2. Other translations (e.g. NASB, AKJV, NIV, ASV, NRSV, ESV, CEV) prefer "son of man" to "the Human One." In either case, this apocalyptic figure alludes to Dan 7:13-14 where the prophet envisions the appearance of a heavenly king who arrives on earth looking like a human being with the God-given task of ruling the nations forever.

(e.g., Tyconius, Augustine, and Bede): this is a book, like every other biblical book, that seeks to disclose God's gospel to the church of every age and time zone. "If you can hear, listen to what the Spirit is saying to the churches" (Rev 2:29; 3:6, 13, 22; cf. 22:16-17).

This way of approaching the book finds support in its literary architecture. Although the genre of its composition is apocalyptic—that is, it is a book filled with otherworldly visions that reveal behind-the-scenes mysteries about how the world really operates—these visions are formatted by the prophet into a pastoral letter. The symbolic, vivid images, characteristic of apocalyptic writings, do not disguise the practical bent of its canonical shape, which is to provide pastoral comfort for the afflicted and prophesy affliction against the comfortable so that the whole church is prepared for the coming victory of God—on earth as it is in heaven.

This is a biblical book for, of, and about the church, as the opening vision makes clear. The exalted Lord appears to the prophet "in the middle of the [seven] lampstands" (Rev 1:12-13), which he subsequently interprets as the sevenfold (i.e., catholic) church (1:20). He commissions John to write down the visions he is about to receive for this same church, which the Lord is about to address (Rev 2–3). From start to finish, then, the Apocalypse is a vision about the eschatological church, past, present, and future (see the scope of John's commission, 1:19).

But the book's apocalyptic idiom is cosmic and dualistic. Its visions of the church constantly run between heaven and earth, between an old order that is passing away and ruled by an unholy trinity (= the evil one and two beasts; cf. Rev 12–13) already defeated and the promised new creation ruled over by the eternal holy Trinity that is soon to come to earth as it now is in heaven. The apocalypse of God's salvation with Christ triggers a loud collision between these two worlds, the reverberations of which are everywhere observed and experienced. John sees, feels, and hears it, mostly from a distance, but on occasion even he participates in its arresting results. What seems clear from the beginning of this pastoral letter, when the exalted Christ addresses John's seven-point parish (Rev 2–3), is that the church presently has one foot in each world. In different ways and to different degrees, today's church experiences firsthand the collision between the passing old and the coming new. This is what I mean by reading the Apocalypse in the present tense: when one holy, catholic, and apostolic church gathers on earth to worship God, its heavenly ecclesial counterpart, which is wholly one, holy, catholic, and apostolic, gathers in worship of the holy Trinity knowing that evil and death are already defeated foes. Today's church is constantly becoming by God's grace what it already is.

How does the Apocalypse's adumbration of the church's four marks conclude and so complete scripture's witness of God's people? To this discussion we now turn.

The Church Is One

Any coherent discussion of the church in the Apocalypse concentrates on the Lord's address of the sevenfold church in Revelation 2–3. The sender's greetings found in the personal letters of antiquity are typically shaped by the sender's perspective of the readers-auditors. This frames whatever else the sender writes them in the rest of the letter. In the case of this apocalyptic letter, the prophet's pastoral theology of church is shaped by the vision that elaborates his opening address of the "seven churches that are in Asia" (1:4).

The history of the church's use of these two chapters indicates that the vision's sevenfold address is routinely taken to symbolize the church's catholicity.[3] Readers often find their own congregations here; the forces and factors that threaten the oneness of John's church in Roman Asia are taken as roughly analogous to those that threaten the eschatological standing of their own congregations, even if located in a very different era.

One suspects that this interpretive track is rightly directed by the prophet's repetition of the same "thus says" formula used by OT prophets when speaking God's word to Israel: "these are the words" (2:1, 8, 12, 18; 3:1, 7, 14) of the exalted Lord to seven local congregations that define what will attract or discourage his presence and participation with his people. Like OT prophets, John casts his vision of the sevenfold church as the oracle of a prophet who both diagnoses the community's current spiritual health but then prognosticates what it must do to "overcome" evil to live with God forever. These are therefore crucial chapters in finding our theological legs in tracking down God's word for the church catholic of every age.

Moreover, John uses *ekklēsia* fifteen times in these two chapters (Rev 2–3) but then only once more in the rest of the book. The book's theology of church from the risen Lord's angle of vision is clearly concentrated here. The primary idea of church evidently targets a particular community of believers gathered together in real places for worship and witness. The canonical mailing address is the sevenfold congregation of the church catholic, but the

---

3. The symbolic value of the number seven for Christians derives from the sum of three (= holy Trinity) and four (= four corners of creation), which come together in the realization of the new creation because of Christ's life and work. This new creation, of course, has a past, present, and future that are plotted by the visions that John receives and writes down in this book.

messy mixture of local culture and Christian faith that the living Jesus found in the local congregations over which the Apostle John had oversight is the same he might find in the whole church at any given time.[4]

The prophet writes down what he sees and hears in a carefully crafted literary pattern, so that those hearing the Apocalypse read aloud (Rev 1:3) will not miss the Lord's message for them. First, his messages for each congregation follow the same outline for effective communication. Each opens with a description of the community's experience of its exalted and living Lord (2:1, 8, 12, 18; 3:1a, 7, 13), who is present in their midst and closely observant of how they conduct their spiritual and moral lives (see 1:13, 20; 2:1).

For this reason, the second part of each oracle begins with an ominous, "I know your works" (Rev 2:2, 9, 13, 19; 3:1b, 8, 15), which introduces a catalogue of accusations or commendations that evaluate the congregation's readiness to receive the Lord upon his any-moment return (2:5, 16, 25; 3:3, 11, 20) so that they are ready to participate in his final conquest over death (2:5, 10, 25-28; 3:5, 11-12, 21). The steady mention of a congregation's "works" (2:2, 5, 6, 19, 22, 23, 26; 3:1, 2, 8, 15) makes it clear that the Lord is a Lord who measures discipleship by works in keeping with his example, characterized by a loving relationship and a firm rejection of the various evils (religious and cultural) that surround and threaten their communion with God.

A final part of each oracle regards a particular congregation's responsiveness to the Lord's exhortation, "If you can hear, listen to what the Spirit is saying" (Rev 2:7, 11, 17, 29; 3:6, 13, 22). Whether or not to repent and restore a right relationship with the Lord mostly depends on that congregation's spiritual need and capacity to do so. Those who need to "repent" (i.e., to reorient themselves to a life like Christ's) and do so will "emerge victorious" at day's end and participate in God's new creation—the markers of which are everywhere mentioned in concluding each oracle (e.g., "the tree of life, which is in God's paradise," 2:7; see 22:2; "the hidden manna" and the "white stone," 2:17; see 21:5; "sit with me on my throne," 3:21; see 22:3).

How one listens to these "words of this prophecy" (1:3), whether in terror at the warnings to either repent from present sin or else face God's end-time judgment or in shalom at the exhortations to hope for the Lord's coming victory, depends on the congregation's responsiveness to the divine word. In fact, John's sevenfold oracle is precisely arranged so that the two congregations in gravest danger are those first and last mentioned (Ephesus and Laodicea), while the congregations in best shape (Smyrna and Philadelphia) are placed

---

4. The canonizing of Revelation universalizes its address, signifying that the sevenfold (= whole) church of chapters 2–3 targets the church catholic in every age and location.

after and before these two in stark contrast. The other three congregations, noteworthy because of the description of their middling spiritual life, are appropriately found smack in the middle (Pergamum, Thyatira, and Sardis)!

The contrasting pairs that begin and conclude the prophet's address have gained the most attention during the history of the Apocalypse's interpretation for good reason. The haunting images of the abandoned "love you had at first" of the Ephesian believers (2:4) or of the Lord spitting out the "lukewarm" works of the Laodiceans (3:16) remind every reader that giving up a demanding discipleship by giving in to a feel-good or secular religion undermines a community's union with Christ.

Indeed, the threats come from all directions, both within the churches, especially from teachers who have departed from the apostolic witness (e.g., Rev 2:13-15, 20-23), and from the pressures of cultural expectation. The pressure of being a patriotic citizen in Caesar's empire is no different from what Christians experience today, when being a loyal citizen invites compromise of our allegiance to God's reign (cf. 2:9-10) or when routine business practices emphasize financial profit at the expense of Christian virtue (cf. 3:17-18). God's people are responsible for God's reputation in the world and therefore must resist any practice that subverts our "love and faithfulness, . . . service and endurance" (2:19). This is a fundamental feature of the church's oneness with Christ.

Nonetheless, the centerpiece of John's address of the sevenfold church is what the Lord has to say for the congregation at Thyatira (2:18-29), and we should read this passage accordingly. There are three literary clues we should pick up in recognizing the importance of this often-neglected oracle. First, it stands at the center of an inverted parallelism or chiasm (ABCDC'B'A'), which pairs the first and seventh, second and sixth, and third and fifth members by their common form and linking words. What the careful reader finds where these two parallel lines intersect—where "X marks the spot"—is most important. Everything else funnels down to there and so intends to attract the interpreter's close attention. The Thyatira oracle is this vision's pivotal point, where "X marks the spot."

Second, this oracle is the longest and most complex address to the seven congregations. The sheer length of a biblical passage is often a cue of its importance; at least it should heighten the readers' interest so that they slow down and study it more carefully.

Finally, the use of Psalm 2 in Revelation 2:26-27 introduces one of the Apocalypse's essential co-texts (cf. 11:15, 18; 12:5; 14:1; 19:15): the entire book envisions the victory of the triune God over the rebellious nations currently under the control of an unholy trinity (= the evil one and two beasts; cf. Rev 12–13).

But the real importance of Thyatira is that its congregational profile expresses vividly the theological crisis that occasions any faithful reading of this book. This is a membership of rank-and-file believers whose everyday struggles and practical concerns are those that face congregations in every age. In this sense, this is a good concluding text for scoring the mark of oneness in the NT.

Thyatira was a city known for its trade guilds (think labor unions), membership in which would have involved idolatry. There was precious little idol-free space for urban Christians of antiquity. Their activities of daily life required decisions in business and social life that implicated one deeply in local traditions of idol worship (not unlike our own world of social media and personal technologies that preoccupy us and integrate us into a culture of self-absorption). The OT prophets speak of idolatry as a failure of attentiveness, the inability or unwillingness to focus our attention and desire upon God in the face of myriad distractions. John draws upon this prophetic criticism to frame the congregation's divided attention (2:20) by recalling a false prophet, whom he calls "Jezebel" (cf. 2 Kgs 9), because like the Jezebel of old she apparently tolerated the routines of idolatry with impunity as a way of getting ahead in business and social standing (Rev 2:20).[5] Compromise, whether theological or moral, is the essential threat of the church's oneness, which is measured by its solidarity with the risen One.

The Lord's concluding note promises himself to those who "[emerge] victorious" (i.e., repent; 3:21) and continue to keep "my practices" (2:26a, 28). Jesus is the "bright morning star" (22:16), which is yet another striking metaphor of his messianic reign (cf. Num 24:17; Isa 60:3), specifically of the "light" that dawns at the daybreak of the new creation to illumine the nations of God's victory. The remnant of believers (like those in Thyatira) who repent and do the Lord's works—by rejecting the false prophet and avoiding idols—bears witness to this bright future.

The Church Is Holy

No other passage gives readers a better expression of the holy church in the Apocalypse than the vision of the 144,000 disciples on Mount Zion, who

---

5. The specific reference to the curious phrase, the "'deep secrets' of Satan" (Rev 2:24), is uncertain. Evidently, it is a label used of Jezebel's teaching, probably mentioned here sarcastically: there is nothing "deep" about it! Its content is slim because it is satanic and will be proven false when Jesus returns (2:25).

have followed the Lamb wherever he goes and who now stand in solidarity with him (see Rev 14:1-5). But first I'll explain the context. John's flashback of God's victory over the evil one (12:10-12), already cued by the exalted Son's homecoming (12:5) and ensuing war in heaven (12:7-9), prepares readers for the terrifying vision of "What now?" We are told without much fuss or fanfare that the devil's defeat and demotion from heaven to earth have made him furious, not only because he has lost his heavenly status (and decisively so) but also because he now knows "he only has a short time" left to unsettle God's plan of salvation before God's victory is made final (12:12). The devil's current target is the woman's "children . . . who keep God's commandments and hold firmly to the witness of Jesus" (12:17)—the decisive image of a holy church in this biblical book. Holiness is not covenant being but covenant keeping.

The prophet sees the devil from a distance standing on earth's seashore (12:18), a fierce but defeated foe without anything more to lose and so ready to make a stand against God's people one last time. It is fitting that the evil one recruits his partners from the sea, since in John's apocalyptic world the sea is home to evil and so is an appropriate resource to draw allies skilled at violence and injustice. Two beasts are noted in particular, one from the sea and another from the land, to form with the devil an unholy trinity. Together they rule over earth's anti-God kingdom in which the woman's children live.

If the devil is an evil parody of the first person of the holy Trinity, the beast he recruits from the sea parodies the second person (Rev 13:1-10). As we would expect, the first two persons of this unholy trinity are one; they bear a striking family resemblance (cf. 12:3 and 13:1). John also recognizes this beast under the light of Daniel's vision of four beasts, which represent the four anti-God kingdoms of his world (cf. Dan 7:1-8). Bits and pieces of those four beasts fill out the picture of the antichrist that John draws for us, but the seven heads, the total of Daniel's beasts, now wear crowns, symbolic of kings rather than kingdoms. The prophet recognizes that kingdoms are personified by their rulers, whether Roman Caesars or American presidents; even though the structures and institutions of their nation-states shape the opposition to the practices of God's reign, these crowned (or elected) individuals are vested with "power, throne, and great authority" (13:2) to give direction that shapes the people and places under their rule. Evil rulers beget kingdoms that practice evil.

Likewise, the faithfulness of a single king, Christ Jesus, results in the triumph of God's reign (cf. Rom 5:18-21). Holiness is formed within those communities ruled by the holy Trinity who practice holiness. Perhaps for this reason, John at last recognizes the powerful beast as an "antichrist"—a parody of God's Paschal Lamb who also was "slain and killed" and whose "deadly wound was healed" (Rev 13:3; 5:6).[6] The result is the global deification of both dragon and beast (13:3b-4), adorned with "blasphemous names" given them by their worshippers (13:1). This image, of course, is full of irony since their act of worship, rooted in unbelief and ignorance of God (see 9:20-21; cf. 13:8), mistakes who really controls earth's destiny: the Almighty One who sits on heaven's Throne and the messianic Lamb—a very different kind of slain beast—who stands beside it. But it also suggests that the failure to repent and turn to God has the consequence of supporting, even worshipping, those in charge of the political/social institutions opposed to the redemptive purposes of God.

The catalogue of brutal practices that the evil beast is authorized to perform (Rev 13:5-7) offers a razor-sharp contrast to the redemptive practices of the faithful Lamb. Yet John hints at a divine purpose behind the beast's madness: the beast's lies and use of violence to bring submission to his rule of evil occasion a time of spiritual testing, when those faithful to the gospel should expect to suffer and even die (3:8-10). The present age on earth remains evil and the forces of evil, now in closer proximity with the devil thrown down to earth, seem to be in charge. The response of God's people called for by the Apocalypse is not to take up arms in retaliation but to face up to the reality of the present moment: to resist is futile (13:10) but also unnecessary since "salvation and power and kingdom of our God [not the dragon] and the authority of his Christ [not the beast] have come" (12:10).[7]

A second monster emerges from the polluted land to complete this unholy trinity. Called elsewhere "the false prophet" (Rev 16:13; 19:20; 20:10), its "priestly" role is to direct the global worship of the other beast (13:12). The idiom of its various malevolent activities (all stated in the present tense)—to exercise the authority of the first beast (13:12), to make fire to come down

---

6.   We could also take this analogy between beast and Christ more literally: the beast was slain but then resuscitated; Jesus was slain on the cross but then resurrected. The difference, of course, is that the beast's healing is temporary—a resuscitation to do more mischief for "a short time," not a resurrection to bring life eternal.

7.   Rev 13:8 speaks of names written in the "scroll of life" from "the time the earth was made." Some have embraced this text literally as a biblical justification for the doctrine of predestination. In context, however, this idea that salvation is something that God grants some people (but not others) before salvation was even needed makes nonsense of the importance that John places upon the decision to repent and turn to God. The better reading is to understand the phrases "from the time the earth was made" and the Lamb's "scroll of life" as tropes of God's faithfulness to realize the full plan of salvation written down on another scroll (see 5:1). Those who repent and follow the Lamb wherever he goes are willing participants in this salvation and on this basis they are named among the Lamb's people for life.

from heaven (13:13), to give breath that animates the beast's image (13:15)—parody the Spirit's work on Christ's behalf. The purpose of the Apocalypse's parody of God is to underscore the earlier claim that the evil one's work is to deceive the whole world (12:9). Evil works its magic by convincing people that falsehood is truth, that what is bad is really good for you, that God is not good, and that there is salvation in something other than the Lamb. Deception, especially when the beast and its henchman open their mouths to speak blasphemies against God (13:6), is the principal instrument in the devil's toolbox.

But the impression shaped by John's vision is of the effectiveness and pervasiveness of evil's reign. The unholy trinity seems in charge. Evil is winning; its deceptions are easily believed; God's ways are marginalized and even removed from the public square. This deadly pair of beasts leaves no wiggle room, so that everyone is forced to submit and be marked as belonging to the beast's people (Rev 13:16); their very survival depends upon it (13:17). If God's people are not for them, they are against them, and if God's people are against them, they are either led into exile (where their witness is no longer heard) or killed by the sword (13:10).

This terrifying vision depicts the essential struggle of the church's holy life in the present tense: living in a manner that pleases a holy God is a slugfest. It is a life that is cultivated not in a "me-and-thee" vacuum but in a world organized by institutions that are fiercely opposed to God. In such a world, covenant keeping is constantly subjected to brutal assault. An embattled holiness does not win out without suffering and even martyrdom.

The stirring vision of the 144,000 saints, now standing with the Lamb on Mount Zion (Rev 14:1), must be understood in connection with the previous vision of the oppressive regime of the two beasts. Much has been written about the numerology of 144,000 (cf. 7:1-4). Simply put, it is a large compound of twelve, the number that symbolizes God's people. John now sees the heavenly community, which he had earlier only heard (cf. 7:4). What John actually "sees," then, is the messiah's tribe: "a great crowd that no one could number"—the same crowd of folks "from every nation, tribe, people, and language" that the messianic Lamb purchased for God with his shed blood (7:9; see 5:9).

If Revelation 12:1-12 is a flashback from today that centers us on the heavenly victory of the exalted Christ, then 14:1-5 looks forward to God's final battle on earth against death and evil. This literary "sandwich" makes it perfectly clear that today's reign of terror, described between, is but for "a short time" (12:12).

Richard Bauckham understands, then, that this is a scene of holy war, each army identified by the tattoos on their foreheads (cf. Rev 13:16-17; 14:1).[8] Mount Zion, where the Lamb's forces muster for battle, is where David built Jerusalem, the holy city. It is the place where God brings to fulfillment the promises made to God's people. This is holy war that finally and fully will bring to realization God's promise to repair and restore creation on earth as the promise already has been realized in heaven.

The battle song of the messiah's forces, sung with harp accompaniment in front of heaven's Throne, is "a new song" (Rev 14:3). Its lyrics undoubtedly reprise those of the "new song" sung in heaven when the worthy Lamb took the inscrolled plan of salvation from God's hand and began to open its seven seals so to publish its glad tidings of great joy (cf. 5:9-10). It is a song of salvation sung by those "purchased from the earth" (14:3), because it is they who testify to the efficacy of the Lamb's shed blood that cleanses them from sin for service of a holy God (cf. 7:14-15).

For this moment, however, these saints are envisioned as soldiers of the Lamb's army. Saints prepare themselves for holy war by abstaining from sex (Rev 14:4; cf. 1 Sam 21:5-6)—we should assume that the "women" in this case are the Apocalypse's two evil women, Jezebel (Rev 2:20) and Babylon's prostitute (17:1-2)—and by intently following the Lamb *wherever* he goes (even to death). This verb "to follow," the key act of discipleship, is its only use outside of the Gospels and Acts. In this case, to follow Jesus includes confessing the truth about him (cf. 1 John 2:22-23; 4:15) and "blamelessly" following his righteous example.

The word *blameless* doesn't mean perfect but rather means without defect. In this context, John has in mind a manner of a holy life that is unmistakably Christlike. Some interpreters have taken this to require sexual abstinence: the 144,000 must not engage in sex in order to follow Christ wholly (cf. 1 Cor 7:1-7). Within the context of John's visionary drama, however, the point is to underscore that a people's complete faithfulness to Christ is the mark of holiness. Only this kind of company of disciples can effectively wage God's battle against evil on earth.

Readers of the Apocalypse already know the outcome of this holy war. The heavenly choir, which is informed with more inside information acquired with cosmic eyesight, already has celebrated God's victory over the destroyers of earth (cf. Rev 11:17-19; 12:10-12). But it is a victory whose full effect is not yet celebrated on earth as it is in heaven. In this sense, then, the confession

---

8. Richard Bauckham, "Revelation," in *The Oxford Bible Commentary*, ed. John Barton and John Muddiman (New York: Oxford University Press, 2001), 1298.

of a holy church, which is on earth, is profoundly hopeful, affirming God's coming victory when the heavenly company comes to earth still following the triumphant Lamb wherever he goes, now in doxology and worship.

The Church Is Catholic

The Apocalypse's narrative of God's salvation is plotted by a temporal and spatial ambivalence between what is already realized by God's people in heaven and the same that is not yet fully realized by God's people still on earth. While John's vision helps us imagine that the Lamb has already ended sin's reign, we also note that human existence remains largely unchanged and even the church's witness looks sometimes compromised because unrepentant sin still remains on earth (Rev 9:20-21). The martyrs' poignant refrain, "How long?" (6:10), is still applied to creation's continuing experience of God's past judgment of evil on the cross: When will we experience God's victory over wickedness on earth as it is in heaven? When will God make good on the prophet's promise that the apocalypse of God's salvation is "soon . . . for the time is near" (1:1, 3)?

John's response to this question in Revelation 11–12 retains a deep sense of the church's dual citizenship on earth and in heaven. Our exploration of this familiar theme seeks to extend the scope of the present church's catholicity to include both heaven and earth. That is, to confess that the church is "catholic" recognizes both its global and cosmic dimensions (see Ephesians). In this sense, the worship practices of the heavenly church envisioned by John are "words of this prophecy" (1:3) that look forward to that moment when the community of saints on earth, presently suffering and embattled (see under the previous section, "The Church Is Holy"), will join its heavenly counterpart in unending worship of the holy Trinity. In this sense the reach and witness of God's people are as inclusive and expansive as the cosmic place created by "the Almighty, maker of heaven and earth, and of all that is, seen and unseen" (Nicene Creed).

The present passage is framed by an interlude (cf. Rev 10:1–11:14) within an arresting vision of divine judgment (cf. Rev 8–11) that is brought to dramatic conclusion by a seventh trumpet fanfare (Rev 11:15-21). The final two panels of this interlude depict a civil war between God's people and God's enemies, "the nations," which takes place in and around "the temple" (11:1-2). Into this war step "two" witnesses, which Torah stipulates in making God's case against evil (cf. Deut 19:15). Who are they? If the "nations" are nonbelievers whose mission to destroy God's people takes place over a three-and-a-half-year period (i.e., half the length of time according to God's recorded plan; see 10:1-11), then the "two witnesses" likely represent God's people over this same span of time. The misery God describes to John in 11:5-13 is the effect of a global confrontation between God's people (= two witnesses) and those who refuse to repent and remain opposed to God's gospel (= nations; cf. 9:20-21).

Indeed, any definition of catholicity must include the global nature of the conflict between good and evil. Those who gloat over the bodies of martyred saints (Rev 11:7-8) and refuse them burial rights (a horrendous offense in the Jewish culture) are numbered from "the peoples, tribes, languages, and nations" (11:9-10). This snapshot of the civil war between God's people and God's enemies, and the fearful images of suffering it contains, occupies the centerpiece of the Apocalypse's pastoral message: the church bears witness to God's victory in Christ by participating in his suffering, sometimes even in his death, until he returns to realize on earth what is already so in heaven. Indeed, the "hour" of destruction that brings this second horror to an end (11:13-14) gives glory "to the God of heaven" as victor.

The final trumpet fanfare does not announce a "third horror" (Rev 11:14), which is "coming soon" (and is described in 12:1–19:10), but rather the decisiveness and finality of God's victory over "the nations" (see 11:13): "the kingdom of the world has become the kingdom of our Lord and his Christ, . . . forever and always" (11:15). The lyrics are of the triumphant chorus sung by heaven's church choir (11:15-18) in worshipful praise of the Lord God Almighty, whose rule over creation has been enforced by judgment (11:16-17). The judgment is just, since the punishment of the nations matches their malicious crimes (11:18): those who are destroyers of the earth are themselves destroyed by earth's creator Lord.

Although this is a heavenly scene, what is true in heaven is true on earth, a fact that is confirmed for all the nations to see as the Apocalypse unfolds toward its stunning conclusion: the slaughtered but exalted Lamb returns to earth to destroy the destroyers as the purifying act of the creator, who is utterly faithful to creation and to the promise of restoring it anew.

For this moment, however, the vision of the seals—a vision about the present results of Jesus's past work on the cross—happily concludes in heaven rather than on earth: John sees the temple's open door and through it he catches a glimpse of the hope chest—the ark of the covenant—that contains elements of God's promise of an enduring covenant with God's people that nothing, "not death or life, not angels or rulers, not present things or future things" (Rom 8:38), can or will threaten.

153

God's victory because of God's Christ, announced by trumpet fanfare (Rev 11:15-18), yields a salutary result in heaven where the Lord God Almighty is worshipped and God's triumph over the destroyers of earth is celebrated, but God's victory is not yet fully experienced on earth. The heavenly temple, where the ark and presence of a covenant-keeping God are fully on display (11:19), is now open for the business of salvation. Here it is where the heavenly congregation gathers to experience already what its earthly congregation has not yet but soon will.

The "then" that opens Revelation 12 marks a new beginning and cast of characters. This is a vision about the present moment of God's salvation from ground level. If the constant chants of God's victory reverberate through heaven's throne room, Christ's sacrifice for creation's salvation has a somewhat different result on earth: a spiritual war ensues between God's people and an unholy trinity that leads the opposition to God on earth.

First, there's a flashback that refocuses the reader on the climax of scripture's story of God's salvation. This passage is found at the pivotal point of the Apocalypse because it is the pivotal point of human history. John envisions the story of Christmas, which marks the real beginning of history's last days. The Gospel narratives of the messiah's birth (Matt 1–2; Luke 1–2) are plotted as a familiar conflict between the forces of evil (i.e., Herod and Rome) and God.[9] Here, too, a pregnant woman is now in labor (Rev 12:2) and about to give birth to a son (12:4-5), but she is threatened by "a great fiery red dragon" (12:3) that intends to "devour her child" (12:4).

John records this scene as heaven's way of signaling earth (Rev 12:1). The elaborate description of the pregnant woman tells nothing of her real identity. Frankly, the two most common interpretations of this woman—that she is either Mary or Eve—make little sense in this context. The personal stories of neither match the woman's characterization in 12:6, 13-16. More likely, this woman is the figuration of a community. Other entire communities, both for and against God, are personified in the Apocalypse by female characters (14:4; 17:18; 21:9-10), so here too. Even the child of a pregnant woman could symbolize a people living "within" another people, as Isaiah imagined the "deliverance" of Judah (see Isa 26:17; cf. 66:7-8). In any case, the grand entrance of this stunning woman, dressed in the sun, standing on the moon, and wearing a crown of twelve stars, would seem to suggest that she stands for

---

9. The salvation myths of several cultures tell this same story of a cosmic battle between the forces of good and evil. In each case, the myth is personified by the particular history of that culture in large part to assure people that their origins did not come without a fight won by their gods! See Robert W. Wall, *Revelation*, Understanding the Bible Commentary Series (Peabody, MA: Hendrickson, 1991), 158–59.

God's faithful people (Israel and the church; see Rev 12:17), which birthed and then nurtured God's messiah for the salvation of the world.[10]

The agony she experiences giving birth may represent the heroic suffering of Israel's faithful remnant that carried God's promises forward from the exile (Mic 5:3; cf. Heb 11:29-40) as well as the earliest community of Christ's followers (for whom John writes), many of whom were martyred for their faithfulness (cf. Rev 2:8-11; 3:7-13; 6:9-11; 14:1-5). The Apocalypse has already made clear that faithfulness to God's redemptive purposes comes at a steep price; however, the wider Johannine tradition, which includes the letters of John, makes it equally clear that ultimately "the evil one cannot touch" "the ones born from God" (1 John 5:18).

This is an incredible promise since the portrait of the evil one presents a dreadful figure: a serpent of a fiery-red "power" color, seven heads each with a crown, and a vast tail that takes down a third of the sky's stars. This dragon has other names: "the old snake, who is called the devil and Satan, the deceiver of the whole world" (Rev 12:9). Its parody of God suggests its role as God's archrival who seemingly offers stiff competition for determining creation's destiny. For this reason, the clipped way in which John reports the woman "gave birth to a son" who "was snatched up to God" (12:5) creates an impression that underscores the gospel's theme: evil, no matter how imposing and powerful it may be, does not accomplish its malevolent purpose.[11] God has won the battle and, so it would seem, without much fuss or foment on God's part. The messiah is born to rule the nations (see 11:15), the dragon doesn't devour the child, and once finished with salvation's work, the child is snatched back to God. One and done.

The woman's flight to the desert place God has prepared for her allows her (i.e., God's people) to take refuge for the forty-two months allotted God's enemies—under the first beast's earthly rule (see Rev 13:5)—to trample down the redemptive prospects of the unbelieving community (see 11:1-2). Christ's death ends Satan's capacity to "accuse" God's people (12:10), whatever influence this may have had on God's providential care of the covenant community (see Job's story), but Satan is granted authority

---

10. The celestial creatures—sun, moon, stars—may symbolize creation. If so, the importance of God's people (= woman) in giving birth and caring for the messiah is understood here in creational terms, for it is the Lamb that God sends into the world to take away sin and restore all creation to its original purposes.

11. The verb CEB translates as "snatched up" carries the sense of an event that suddenly or abruptly occurs. The devil's surprise at finding himself on earth (Rev 12:13) may indicate that the messiah's mission was cut short, a reflection of the gospel's division of Jesus's mission into two parts: his first advent, ending in his rejection and death, inaugurates God's redemptive plan, while his second advent completes its implementation.

to deceive the world (12:9; cf. Dan 7:25)—that is, to contend that evil is good or that God is not good. Once again, John envisions a clear and sharp divide between the believing and unbelieving communities and the influence the powers and principalities of evil have on each. Drawing upon Paul's vivid imagination, a people's faithfulness to God wraps it in "the full armor of God" so that they can "extinguish the flaming arrows of the evil one" (Eph 6:13-17).

The child's return to heaven, clearly referring to the risen Jesus's exaltation, occasions a territorial war over whether the evil one and its angels should have a place left in heaven (Rev 12:8). The next cast member introduced into John's visionary narrative is the archangel Michael, who represents God's people in heaven's war between good and evil (12:7; cf. Dan 10:13, 21; 12:1). We already know who wins: "now the salvation and power and kingdom of our God, and the authority of his Christ have come" (Rev 12:10). Corresponding to the victory of God's Lamb over sin (12:11), then, Michael defeats the evil dragon and its army.

But there is a price to pay: the dragon's occupation of heaven, where it "accuses [our brothers and sisters] day and night before our God" (Rev 12:10; cf. Job 1–2; Zech 3:1), ends and it gets tossed to earth. Here's the price we pay: The dragon is seriously ticked off knowing he has only a short time to do mischief (12:12), and mischief is what the evil one will do as we will soon see. Clearly, however, the dragon's rage is not a Hollywood motif of power but of failure. Its inability to thwart God's messianic plan of salvation (12:4-5) and corresponding defeat by Michael in heaven seals its fate. The dragon knows it's a loser, and a sore loser at that!

The relationship between Christ's death and the costly loyalty of his faithful followers unafraid to die is clear in the lyrics of this hymn (Rev 12:10-12). What is also made clear is the importance of this community's fearless witness: God's victory is forged by a partnership of the Lamb "and the word of their witness" (12:11); it is this solidarity of trust that exposes the evil one's deception. It is an embodied (not spoken) word of witness, especially lived by the faithful martyrs, exemplified by the slaughtered Lamb, that underwrites the truth of the gospel: "Now the salvation and power and kingdom of our God, and the authority of his Christ have come" (12:10).

The prediction that the earth and sea will be the new headquarters of an awfully angry devil and its mischief elicits both heaven's celebration and also the recognition that horrors are about to be visited upon earth (Rev 12:12). The combination of "earth and sea," which is the street address of the devil's new habitat, anticipates their demise in the coming age (see 21:1) when God's fiercest enemies, devil and death, already defeated by the exalted Son, are then thoroughly destroyed (cf. 20:10-15).

John's vision returns to elaborate the earlier sighting of the woman who had fled to the wilderness where God could care for her over an extended period of time (see Rev 12:6). The devil's immediate reaction, once realizing its sudden defeat and exile to earth, is to target and pursue the woman (i.e., God's people; 12:13). The word CEB translates as "chase" connotes the intention to persecute whoever is chased—a chase scene in which the bad guy pursues the heroine to harm her. As we would expect, however, the woman is protected from "the old snake" at her desert refuge (12:14-17).

The woman's transformation into a giant "eagle" to escape the devil's grasp (Rev 12:14; cf. 12:6) recalls God's description of Israel's exodus from Egypt as a flight "on eagles' wings" (Exod 19:4). Escaping the devil's deceptions (cf. Rev 12:9) by "eagles' wings" is a standard metaphor used of God's rescue operations, whether by miraculous deliverance or by empowering God's people to endure their trials (cf. Isa 40:31). The period of safety extended to the woman is again counted, "a time and times and half a time" (Rev 12:14) or "one thousand two hundred sixty days" (12:6, since one "time" = one year according to John's apocalyptic timetable).[12]

The serpent attempts to drown the church with a flood of deceptions from its mouth (Rev 12:15); they are the verbal attacks that ridicule and seek to marginalize Christian faith (cf. 1 Pet 4:4). One cannot help but think of today's aggressive band of so-called new atheists, who engage in name-calling and political tactics (rather than thoughtful discourse) to discredit the intelligence and morality of God's people. It is creation ("earth") itself that comes to the rescue by swallowing the river of deception that flows from the serpent's mouth. While this image surely recalls the creator's use of nature to force the Pharaoh's hand in rescuing Israel from Egypt, thereby fulfilling a promise made to Sarah and Abraham, perhaps it also suggests that God's protection of the gospel's proclamation against the attacks of God's enemies results indirectly from evidence that a faithful people produces, which falsifies the serpent's deceptions. After all, the dragon's rage is directed not at God but at God's people "who keep God's commandments and hold firmly to the witness of Jesus" (12:17).

One last image in this passage that is easily missed carries forward a message for the global church. The dragon's initial failure to defeat the woman only increases its resolve to take the battle to "the rest of her children" (12:17).

---

12. See Dan 7:25; 12:7, where it times the last days of human history just prior to the in-breaking of God's eternal age.

A tension is provoked by this refrain. On the one hand, we hear the chorus celebrate the devil's defeat in heaven and the securing of God's eternal reign; we also hear its lamentation of coming horrors for God's people on earth. But on the other hand, we also are witnesses of the ineffectiveness of God's enemies to win the ground war. But a ground war is often prolonged; and the woman's children (that's us, people!) are now engaged in the same spiritual and intellectual struggle that shaped our ancestors. The lyric of heaven's chorus, sung loudly, is now the church's battle song: "Now the salvation and power and kingdom of our God, and the authority of his Christ have come" (12:10).

The Church Is Apostolic

The number "twelve" is used throughout the Apocalypse as a symbol for God's people. Wherever the reader finds it, the covenant between God and God's people is envisioned. John's use of the number comes to a climax in his vision of the New Jerusalem come down to earth in Revelation 21. The twelve tribes of God's people (7:5-8), the victorious woman (a trope for God's people) who is introduced wearing a crown of twelve stars (12:1), the 144,000 who stand with the Lamb on Jerusalem's Zion (14:1-5), the city's twelve gates and foundations (21:12-21), and the twelve different crops of fruit produced by the city's "tree of life" (22:2) all use the number to symbolize God's covenant people whose enduring life with God is founded on the ministry of "the Lamb's twelve apostles" (21:14)—an image of the apostolic witness that squares with the teaching of the NT (1 John 1:1-3; Eph 2:20-22).

Gregory K. Beale notes that the city's apostolic foundation shows that the "fulfillment of Israel's promises has finally come in Christ, who, together with the apostolic witness to his fulfilling work, forms the foundation of the new temple, the church, which is the new Israel."[13] Christ's promise to "those who emerge victorious" that he "will make them pillars in the temple of my God, . . . [for] the New Jerusalem that comes down out of heaven from my God" (Rev 3:12) comes to fulfillment on an apostolic foundation. Simply put, John's vision of this eschatological community envisions the nature of an apostolic church.

Along with sightings of new things and nonsightings of former things, John's vision of the New Jerusalem is introduced by an audition: he hears a commanding voice that redirects his attention to "the holy city, New Jerusalem" (Rev 21:2). He observes the city not as a particular place but as a peculiar

---

13. G. K. Beale, *The Book of Revelation*, New International Greek Testament Commentary (Grand Rapids: Eerdmans, 1999), 1070–71.

person beautifully adorned like a bride on her wedding day, walking down the aisle leading from heaven to earth where she and the Lamb will make their home together in a renewed creation (21:2-3; cf. Isa 65:17-19). The old city, Babylon, and the prostitute who personifies its repulsive evils are replaced by this new city, Jerusalem, and the bride who personifies its sanctified goods.

The victorious declaration of Alpha and Omega, "Look! I'm making all things new" (Rev 21:5), envelops a promise to the community who "overcomes" (2:7 NASB). This is one of the Apocalypse's catchwords, designed to attract our attention when John uses it. Recall the Lord's address of the seven congregations in Revelation 2–3 when repeatedly the verbal noun "[one] who overcomes" (NASB) is used to promise salvation to all those who obey "what the Spirit is saying" and overcome evil (2:7, 11, 17, 26; 3:5, 12, 21), even as he overcame evil to broker God's salvation on their behalf (3:21; 5:5; 12:11; 17:14).

Although the prophet nowhere links the testimony of the Spirit to the church's apostolic witness, 1 John 4:1-6 does. Teachers who follow the apostolic message about Jesus "are from God" and speak the truth. Their message functions as the community's rule of faith, so that not only is an individual's membership based upon its embrace but so also is the community's "fellowship . . . with the Father and with his Son, Jesus Christ" (1:3). Conversely, those false prophets whose teaching is funded by the "spirit of error" lead people away from God and therefore away from eternal life that is "with the Father" (4:6; 1:2).

Those who do not belong to this people are classified by a catalogue of evils (Rev 21:8). At the head of this catalogue are the cowardly and faithless—doubtless meant as a warning to those believers tempted to compromise their faith for the evils of Babylon (18:4). To do so is an act of cowardice, when faith is exchanged for the niceties of the "good life" offered by the beast. The courage to resist the comforts of Babylon and follow the Lamb wherever he goes requires deep faith in the apostolic testimony: this Lamb is the risen Lord who has overcome evil for the world's salvation (cf. 3:21; 17:14).

Once before the prophet was invited by "one of seven angels" to observe the judgment of "the great prostitute" (17:1-6) only then to be given a Cook's tour of the city she represents, evil Babylon (17:18). But this is a happier season because a new creation has dawned. This time John is invited again by "one of the seven angels" to observe the Lamb's bride, the church (21:9). Once again a reversal of expectation helps readers draw the connection: the woman John is shown is the city she represents, the New Jerusalem, which he tours "in a Spirit-inspired trance" (21:10).

The expansive contrast between Babylon and Jerusalem could not be drawn more sharply. The holy city's vastness is everywhere observed: its great size, its high walls, its jeweled brilliance, its many gates open in every direction, and its firm foundation, all built with precious materials suitable for the creator's dwelling place. And unlike Babylon, observed as a two-dimensional city, Jerusalem is measured in three dimensions (its length, width, and height are the same). Its gates also number twelve to allow entrance and support for the entirety of God's people (Rev 21:12; cf. 7:9). It's a place of great beauty, a home suitable for the Lamb's bride: God's creations are beautiful things. Streets of pure gold shining like a mirror, bejeweled foundations, and decorated walls envision an apostolic city, which is a place of great beauty.

After taking notes on what he sees, John also makes the surprising observation that "I didn't see a temple in the city" (Rev 21:22). John has in mind the OT prophecy of New Jerusalem's temple (Isa 60; Ezek 40–48; Zech 14), which he interprets as fulfilled not by building a third temple (as some Zionists suppose) but as the living presence of God and the Lamb, which fills the city top to bottom (Rev 21:22; see Isa 60:19-26; Ezek 48:35; Zech 14:20-21). The glory of God supplies the city's electricity (21:23); there is no darkness that requires the gates to close at night for safety (21:24-5). All twelve gates remain open in every direction to welcome the Lamb's faithful people from every nation and from all directions into God's presence (21:26-27).

Precisely because this place is home to a sanctified people and off-limits to the faithless, the people who populate the New Jerusalem form a very different community, one that makes good at long last what the church confesses about itself today: we are one, holy, catholic, and apostolic.

Summary

The church has always placed John's Apocalypse last in its biblical canon. Although there are historical reasons for this, readers may think of this as strategic: the book is placed last to perform the role of scripture's concluding chapter. Its visions, formatted by the prophet into a pastoral letter, tell how the various subplots layered into the biblical story of God's salvation conclude—how a broken world is remade into a new creation, how the reign of evil is unmasked and unmade, how the Lamb's messianic death effects God's purifying judgment, which clears the brush for a ransomed people—an eschatological community of overcomers—and how the Lamb returns to lead this people into the New Jerusalem, where they take up residence to worship the triune God forever.

Scripture's concluding snapshot of God's people is grounded in the prophetic address of the sevenfold church in Revelation 2–3, which sets out various threats—some external (idolatry, cultural expectations) and others internal (false teachers, laxity)—to the church's solidarity with Christ and others. The church's capacity to overcome these threats is predicated on its close and consistent attention to imitate the exalted One who addresses them.

The church's holiness is aptly conceptualized by a vision of the 144,000 disciples standing with the exalted Lamb on Mount Zion, the epicenter of God's sacred universe (Rev 14:1-5). They are those who fearlessly follow the Lamb wherever he goes, even to death at the hands of the unholy trinity (Rev 13). Holiness is presented not so much as a moral perfection but as a radical obedience to God's commandments, as nonparticipation in a corrupt political and economic reign of terror, and as a faithful confession of God's truth—all of which are covenant-keeping practices that bear witness of a community's allegiance to God.

Revelation presents the catholicity of God's people in cosmic idiom. The church gathers communicants from around the world—from "every nation, tribe, people, and language" (7:9)—not only to worship God forever but to worship God in fearless witness (12:11) to the messiah born to "strike down the nations" (19:15) to unmask the spiritual powers of death, those who "destroy the earth" who seek to deceive the nations (Rev 11:18. This international community therefore participates with the risen One to ensure that God's promise to restore order to a broken cosmos is realized.

Finally, the church's apostolic tradition is reimagined as supplying the firm foundation of the walled residence of God's eschatological people (Rev 21:14). The twelvefold crop of the city's tree of life indicates that the community of overcomers, who inherit the promise of eternal life, do so because they have received and trusted the truth of apostolic teaching. Like the city itself, it is a word of great beauty.

A Brief Epilogue

Why the Church?

The Apocalypse concludes a biblical story that envisions God's plan to restore creation. Readers tour its sweeping textual terrain hearing words that recall antecedent moments of scripture's unfolding drama of God's victory over death, as an invitation not only to participate in the victory parade but also to worship the triune God forever after it concludes.

The prophet Ezekiel, from whom John draws much of his language to translate the various visions he receives, uses the image of temple—a place of worship and praise—in imagining Israel as a restored people, whose life of worship realizes the primary activity of God's new creation (Ezek 40–48). The mingling of images from the creation story ("river of life-giving water," "tree of life," the abundant "fruit," and the presence of God) with those of a worshipping community from Ezekiel in Revelation 22:1-5 provides this photo album of "the great day of God the Almighty" with a final snapshot of salvation's endgame (16:14). This is the New Jerusalem's "Central Park," and in the middle of this park is God's throne (now with the victorious Lamb dwelling "in it" (22:3) with God), which orders all of life as an act of unending worship. The source of the river that feeds the never-ending crop of the tree of eternal life is God's throne; the God who is worshipped is the same God who cultivates a people that lives on "forever and always" (22:5).

Even though this snapshot should be viewed with the one that begins scripture in Genesis 1–2 to form the "bookends" of scripture's story, the one promising a life the other says will be fulfilled in Christ, John observes several elements that belong to this new and improved order. Even though the observation that there is "no longer . . . any curse" (Rev 22:3; cf. 21:27; Zech 14:11) may allude to Eden's curse, it probably has an even more general implication that covers everything banned by God, including the prohibition to eat the fruit from the "tree of life." Clearly the fruit of eternal life, banned by God after the fall, is now eaten. Not even in Isaiah's great vision of the new creation was the prospect of eternal life envisioned (see Isa 65)! Of course, all other covenant-breaking practices cursed by God need no longer be banned because there is no longer any evil or agent of evil to prompt a people's disobedience or idolatry. This all is in the past tense.

The prophet also notes that the people "will see [God's] face" (Rev 22:4; cf. Exod 33:20-23; 1 John 3:2-3). The distance maintained between God's people and God underscores the disparity between them: God is holy, God's people not yet. But it also symbolizes the inability of God's people to have a deep level of intimacy with God this side of the end-time. The relational effect of the great day of God is to break down any barrier left that prevents or inhibits personal access to God; to see God is to love God in a profoundly intimate, knowing, fully wakeful way.

Even more striking, however, is the relationship between God and the Lamb. Throughout the Apocalypse, although sharing God's status and worship, the first sightings of the Lamb placed him alongside or in front of God's throne (Rev 5:7), engaged in redemption's activities that are "for God" (5:9). It is God who sits alone on heaven's throne. But now heaven has come to earth, and what is so in heaven is now realized in this new creation. Not only does the Lamb's messianic service result in a people's full participation in the reign of God (22:5; cf. 5:10), but also the Lamb himself now shares equally and fully in the Godhead: the throne come to earth belongs jointly to "God and the Lamb" (22:1), thus "the throne of God and the Lamb will be in it" (22:3). In fact, the two, God and Lamb, are here so closely intertwined that the antecedent of the singular "him/his" used in 22:3-4 refers to both as though one person, a single object of worship and joy. Such is the eschatology of the holy Trinity.

John's vision of the New Jerusalem as an expansive metaphor of God's people is brought to conclusion in the same way it begins (see Rev 19:9-10): the angel who carries divine revelation to the prophet to write down confirms its truth (22:6; cf. 19:9). In this case, the angel confirms the truth of what John sees when heaven opens and he is able to see, in a series of stunning visions, what soon must take place: the return of the messianic warrior to destroy the defeated enemy once and for all time. This is what John called in the prologue, "the words of *this* prophecy" (1:3, emphasis added; cf. 22:7a), which "must soon take place" (1:1; 22:6b); this prophecy is what is written down on the scroll the Lamb retrieves from God (22:7; 5:1-14) that he then opens to begin the last days (Rev 6–11). The angel's words sound the final amen to the final vision of "the great day of God the Almighty," the very last of the last days, which happily concludes in the Eden of the renewed creation (16:14).

Why the church? Because this peculiar fellowship of saints, whose loving communion is with the risen One, has been appointed by the triune God to herald this coming day. Given its sacred vocation, then, every demonstration of the church's oneness, holiness, catholicity, and apostolicity—each eschatological mark enabled and brought to maturity by God's grace—is the concrete means by which God's people testify to the coming victory of God. May God the Father, Son, and Holy Spirit grant us courage and wisdom for this good work.

Bibliography

Allison, Dale C. "The Embodiment of God's Will: Jesus in Matthew." In Gaventa and Hays, *Seeking the Identity of Jesus*, 117–32.

———. "The Historians' Jesus and the Church." In Gaventa and Hays, *Seeking the Identity of Jesus*, 79–95.

Barna, George. *Grow Your Church from the Outside: Understanding the Unchurched and How to Reach Them.* Ventura, CA: Regal Books, 2009.

Barr, James. *The Concept of Biblical Theology: An Old Testament Perspective.* Minneapolis: Fortress, 1999.

Bassler, Jouette M. *1 Timothy, 2 Timothy, Titus.* Abingdon New Testament Commentaries. Nashville: Abingdon, 1996.

Bauckham, Richard. "James and the Gentiles (Acts 15.13-21)." In *History, Literature, and Society in the Book of Acts*, edited by Ben Witherington III, 154–84. New York: Cambridge University Press, 1996.

———. "Revelation." In *The Oxford Bible Commentary*, edited by John Barton and John Muddiman, 1287–1306. New York: Oxford University Press, 2001.

Bauckham, Richard, Daniel R. Driver, Trevor A. Hart, and Nathan MacDonald, eds. *The Epistle to the Hebrews and Christian Theology.* Grand Rapids: Eerdmans, 2009.

Beale, G. K. *The Book of Revelation.* New International Greek Testament Commentary. Grand Rapids: Eerdmans, 1999.

Black, C. Clifton. *The Disciples according to Mark: Markan Redaction in Current Debate.* Journal for the Study of the New Testament: Supplement Series 27. Sheffield, England: JSOT Press, 1989.

Bock, Darrell L. *Luke 9:51-24:53.* Grand Rapids: Baker, 1996.

Booth, Wayne C. *The Rhetoric of Fiction.* 2nd ed. Chicago: University of Chicago Press, 1983.

165

Brodie, Thomas L. *The Gospel according to John: A Literary and Theological Commentary.* New York: Oxford University Press, 1993.

Brueggemann, Walter. *The Bible Makes Sense.* 1st ed. Louisville: Westminster John Knox, 1977.

Burge, Gary M. *The Anointed Community: The Holy Spirit in the Johannine Tradition.* Grand Rapids: Eerdmans, 1987.

Burridge, Richard A. "The Genre of Acts—Revisited." In *Reading Acts Today: Essays in Honour of Loveday C. A. Alexander,* edited by Steve Walton, Thomas E. Phillips, Lloyd Keith Pietersen, and F. Scott Spencer, 3–28. Library of New Testament Studies 427. New York: T&T Clark, 2011.

Charry, Ellen T. *By the Renewing of Your Minds: The Pastoral Function of Christian Doctrine.* New York: Oxford University Press, 1997.

Childs, Brevard S. *Biblical Theology of the Old and New Testaments: Theological Reflection on the Christian Bible.* Minneapolis: Fortress, 2011.

———. *The Church's Guide for Reading Paul: The Canonical Shaping of the Pauline Corpus.* Grand Rapids: Eerdmans, 2008.

———. *The New Testament as Canon: An Introduction.* Philadelphia: Fortress, 1984.

Conzelmann, Hans. *Acts of the Apostles: A Commentary on the Acts of the Apostles.* Edited by Eldon Jay Epp and C. R. Matthews. Translated by James Limburg, A. Thomas Kraabel, and Donald H. Juel. Hermeneia. Minneapolis: Fortress, 1987.

Dupont, Jacques. *The Salvation of the Gentiles: Essays on the Acts of the Apostles.* New York: Paulist, 1979.

Evans, C. F. *Saint Luke.* TPI New Testament Commentaries. London: SCM Press, 1990.

Evans, Craig A. *From Jesus to the Church: The First Christian Generation.* Louisville: Westminster John Knox, 2014.

Fitzmyer, Joseph A. *The Acts of the Apostles.* Anchor Bible. New York: Doubleday, 1998.

Gamble, Harry Y. "The New Testament Canon: Recent Research and the Status Quaestionis." In *The Canon Debate,* edited by Lee Martin McDonald and James A. Sanders, 267–94. Peabody, MA: Hendrickson, 2002.

Gaventa, Beverly Roberts, and Richard B. Hays, eds. *Seeking the Identity of Jesus: A Pilgrimage.* Grand Rapids: Eerdmans, 2008.

Goodspeed, Edgar J. "The Place of Ephesians in the First Pauline Collection," *Anglican Theological Review* 12 (1930): 189–212.

Green, Joel B. *The Gospel of Luke*. New International Commentary on the New Testament. Grand Rapids: Eerdmans, 1997.

———. *The Theology of the Gospel of Luke*. New York: Cambridge University Press, 1995.

Haenchen, Ernst. *The Acts of the Apostles: A Commentary*. Translated by Bernard Noble and Gerald Shinn. Philadelphia: Westminster, 1971.

Hagner, Donald A. "Holiness and Ecclesiology: The Church in Matthew." In *Holiness and Ecclesiology in the New Testament*, edited by Kent E. Brower and Andy Johnson, 40–56. Grand Rapids: Eerdmans, 2007.

Hays, Richard B. "'Here We Have No Lasting City': New Covenantalism in Hebrews." In Bauckham et al., *The Epistle to the Hebrews and Christian Theology*, 151–73.

Irenaeus. *Against Heresies* 3.4.2. In *The Apostolic Fathers, Justin Martyr, and Irenaeus*. Vol. 1 of *The Ante-Nicene Fathers*, edited by Alexander Roberts and James Donaldson. Buffalo, NY: Christian Literature Publishing, 1885.

Jenson, Robert W. *Canon and Creed*. Interpretation: Resources for the Use of Scripture in the Church. Louisville: Westminster John Knox, 2010.

Jervell, Jacob. *The Theology of the Acts of the Apostles*. New Testament Theology. New York: Cambridge University Press, 1996.

Johnson, Luke Timothy. *The Acts of the Apostles*. Sacra Pagina, edited by Daniel J. Harrington. Collegeville, MN: Liturgical Press, 1992.

———. *Prophetic Jesus, Prophetic Church*. Grand Rapids: Eerdmans, 2011.

———. *The Writings of the New Testament: An Interpretation*. 3rd ed. Minneapolis: Fortress, 2010.

Kingsbury, Jack Dean. *Matthew*. Proclamation Commentaries. Philadelphia: Fortress, 1977.

———. "The Figure of Peter in Matthew's Gospel as a Theological Problem." *Journal of Biblical Literature* 98, no. 1 (1979): 67–83.

Lohfink, Gerhard. *Does God Need the Church? Toward a Theology of the People of God*. Collegeville, MN: Liturgical Press, 1999.

Luz, Ulrich. *Matthew 8–20: A Commentary on the Gospel of Matthew*. Hermeneia. Grand Rapids: Fortress, 2001.

———. *Studies in Matthew*. Grand Rapids: Eerdmans, 2005.

Maddox, Robert. *The Purpose of Luke-Acts*. Edinburgh, Scotland: T&T Clark, 1982.

Massaux, Edouard. *The Influence of the Gospel of Saint Matthew on Christian Literature before Saint Irenaeus.* Translated by Norman J. Belval and Suzanne Hecht. Edited by Arthur J. Bellinzoni. 3 vols. New Gospel Studies 5. Macon, GA: Mercer University Press, 1990–93.

Moessner, David P. "Luke's 'Witness of Witnesses': Paul as Definer and Defender of the Tradition of the Apostles - 'from the beginning.'" In *Paul and the Heritage of Israel: Paul's Claim upon Israel's Legacy in Luke and Acts in the Light of the Pauline Letters,* edited by David P. Moessner, Daniel Marguerat, Mikeal C. Parsons, and Michael Wolter, 117–47. Library of New Testament Studies 452. New York: T&T Clark, 2012.

Nanos, Mark D. "*New* or *Re*newed Covenantalism? A Response to Richard Hays." In Bauckham et al., *The Epistle to the Hebrews and Christian Theology,* 183–88.

Nienhuis, David R., and Robert W. Wall. *Reading the Epistles of James, Peter, John, and Jude as Scripture: The Shaping and Shape of a Canonical Collection.* Grand Rapids: Eerdmans, 2013.

Osiek, Carolyn, and David L. Balch. *Families in the New Testament World: Households and House Churches.* The Family, Religion, and Culture. Louisville: Westminster John Knox, 1997.

Przybylski, Benno. *Righteousness in Matthew and His World of Thought.* Society for New Testament Studies Monograph Series 41. New York: Cambridge University Press, 1980.

Rowe, C. Kavin. *World Upside Down: Reading Acts in the Graeco-Roman Age.* New York: Oxford University Press, 2010.

Soards, Marion L. *The Speeches in Acts: Their Content, Context, and Concerns.* Louisville: Westminster John Knox, 1994.

Stanton, Graham N. "The Early Reception of Matthew's Gospel: New Evidence from Papyri?" In *The Gospel of Matthew in Current Study: Studies in Memory of William G. Thompson, S.J.,* edited by David Aune, 42–61. Grand Rapids: Eerdmans, 2001.

Talbert, Charles H. *Literary Patterns, Theological Themes, and the Genre of Luke-Acts.* Missoula, MT: Scholars Press, 1974.

Tannehill, Robert C. *The Acts of the Apostles.* Vol. 2 of *The Narrative Unity of Luke–Acts: A Literary Interpretation.* Minneapolis: Fortress, 1994.

Thompson, Marianne Meye. "Word of God, Messiah of Israel, Savior of the World: Learning the Identity of Jesus from the Gospel of John." In Gaventa and Hays, *Seeking the Identity of Jesus,* 166–79.

168

Wall, Robert W. *1 & 2 Timothy and Titus*. Two Horizons New Testament Commentary. Grand Rapids: Eerdmans, 2012.

———. "The Acts of the Apostles." In *The New Interpreter's Bible*, edited by Leander E. Keck, 10:62–65. Nashville: Abingdon, 2002.

———. "A Canonical Approach to the Unity of Acts and Luke's Gospel." In *Rethinking the Unity and Reception of Luke and Acts*, edited by Andrew F. Gregory and C. Kavin Rowe, 172–91. Columbia: University of South Carolina Press, 2010.

———. "The Canonical View." In *Biblical Hermeneutics: Five Views*, edited by Stanley E. Porter and Beth M. Stovell, 111–30. Downers Grove, IL: InterVarsity, 2012.

———. "Martha and Mary (Luke 10.38-42) in the Context of a Christian Deuteronomy." *Journal for the Study of the New Testament* 35 (1989): 19–35.

———. "Reading the Bible from within Our Traditions: The 'Rule of Faith' in Theological Hermeneutics." In *Between Two Horizons: Spanning New Testament Studies and Systematic Theology*, edited by Joel B. Green and Max Turner, 88–107. Grand Rapids: Eerdmans, 1999.

———. "A Response to Thomas/Alexander, 'and the Signs Are Following' (Mark 16.9-20)." *Journal of Pentecostal Theology* 11, no. 2 (2003): 171–83.

———. *Revelation*. Understanding the Bible Commentary Series. Peabody, MA: Hendrickson, 1991.

Walton, Steve. *Leadership and Lifestyle: The Portrait of Paul in the Miletus Speech and 1 Thessalonians*. Society for New Testament Studies Monograph Series 108. New York: Cambridge University Press, 2000.

Watson, Francis. *Gospel Writing: A Canonical Perspective*. Grand Rapids: Eerdmans, 2013.

———. "*Veritas Christi*: How to Get from the Jesus of History to the Christ of Faith without Losing One's Way." In Gaventa and Hays, *Seeking the Identity of Jesus*, 96–115.

Webster, John. *Holiness*. Grand Rapids: Eerdmans, 2003.

Winter, Bruce, and Andrew D. Clarke, eds. *The Book of Acts in Its First Century Setting*. Vol. 1 of *The Book of Acts in Its Ancient Literary Setting*. Grand Rapids: Eerdmans, 1993.

Wolterstorff, Nicholas. *Art in Action: Toward a Christian Aesthetic*. Grand Rapids: Eerdmans, 1980.

Index of Scriptures

Index of Scriptures

Index of Modern Authors

Index of Subjects

Index of Subjects

repentance and, 37, 51
  of sin, 43–44, 51, 60
fourfold Gospel, 28–70
  and Acts, 34, 70, 72–73
  apostolicity and, 61–69
  canonical approach to, 29,
    31, 33
  catholicity and, 55–61
  holiness and, 43–55
  Jesus in, 28–34
  oneness and, 34–42
  order of, 20
  freedom, 7–8
  friendship, 67, 75–76
  fruit, good, 45, 46

Galatians, 63
Galilee, 35, 39
Genesis, 6–7
Gentiles
  concerns regarding, 83–86
  Jews and, 86, 91, 118,
    119, 122
  and kings, 91
  mission to, 78, 79
God
  church as home of, 5, 131
  church as partner of, 5–6
  church as witness of, 6–8
  as Father of Jesus, 5, 33, 54, 57
  humankind in image of, 7
  Lamb and, 52, 149–52,
    155n10, 156, 163–64
  and need for church, 4–8, 42
  one and only true, 42
  rejection of, 3
  and will disclosed in Torah,
    44n19
God's kingdom
  benefits of, 50n26
  definition of, 88
  mission to establish, 4
  righteousness of, 44, 46
  understanding of, 33
  grace, 7, 47. See also divine grace
Great Commission, 44, 56, 58, 59

hagiasō (consecration, act of), 42
hagioi (holy ones, saints), 112,
    132, 139
hagnizō (purify), 133
halakhah (particular situations),
    36–37, 83, 84n6
Hebrew Bible, 20, 22
Hebrews, 121–23
Herod, 79
holiness, 14–16

Acts and, 82–86
  Apocalypse and, 147–52
  CE and, 132–35
  code, 50, 59, 84
  fourfold Gospel and, 43–55
  John and, 52–55
  Luke and, 49–52
  Mark and, 47–48
  Matthew and, 43–47
  participatory, 16
  Paul and, 84–85
  Pauline Letters and, 112–13,
    118–20
  Peter and, 83–85
  three elements of living in,
    45–46
holy nation, 14, 124
holy ones (hagioi), 112, 132, 139
Holy Spirit, 15, 25, 53
holy Trinity, 143, 144n3, 152, 163
holy war, 151
home, church as God's, 5, 131
household
  church as, 108–10, 133
  family, 17, 105, 108–9, 116,
    118, 123–24
  Pauline Letters and, 105,
    108–10, 116–21, 123–24,
    130, 139

idolatry, 18, 147
Irenaeus, 30–31, 72, 93, 102, 126
Isaiah
  Judah and, 154
  vision and prophecy of, 39,
    89, 163
  on year of Lord's favor, 76
Israel
  election of, 7
  and exodus from Egypt, 157
  intentions for, 49
  lack of mention of, 9, 22
  and "Law and Prophets," 46
  mission to, 56, 78
  OT and, 16, 21–22, 32, 128
  people of, 55, 58, 64, 91
  restoration of, 66, 77, 85,
    88–90, 122, 162

James
  Acts and, 84–85, 92–93,
    101, 125
  ending of, 136
  execution of, 79
  at Jerusalem Council, 104
Jeremiah, 65, 122
Jerusalem

decree of, 85, 103
  departure from, 65
  as holy city, 151, 158–60
  journey to, 58
  mission in, 76
  temple of, 86, 160
Jerusalem Council, 79, 80, 83,
    84, 104
Jesus. See Christ
  birth of, 154–55
  body and blood of, 54, 65,
    106–7, 109
  as bright morning star, 147
  death of, 47, 52, 61, 68,
    155–56
  departure of, 41
  farewell address of, 66
  in fourfold Gospel, 28–34
  as God's Son, 5, 33, 54, 57
  identity of, 35–37, 38, 52,
    53, 54
  magi's adoration of, 55
  and ministry among poor, 76
  and ministry in Galilee, 35, 39
  mission of, 5, 19, 32, 40
  Peter's exchange with, 60, 62
  rejection of, 39, 52, 55, 136
  and relationship with disciples,
    12, 28, 34–35, 38–39,
    41, 69
  risen compared to historical, 19
  and the Sea of Tiberias
    appearance, 69
  and sermon on greatness, 37
  story of historical, 33
  titles for, 52
Jews and Judaism
  circumcision and, 80, 83
  conflict with, 95
  contest between various, 43
  division of, 39, 87
  feasts of, 54
  Gentiles and, 86, 91, 118,
    119, 122
  identity of, 80
  legacy of, 21
  parting of ways with, 87n7
  practices of, 75, 76, 83–86
  saving of, 55
  Second Temple period of, 50
Jezebel, 147, 151
Joel, prophecy of, 72, 75, 79,
    85, 91
Johannine corpus, 31n7, 141
John. See Apocalypse
  apostolicity and, 5, 67–69
  catholicity and, 60–61

183

CPSIA information can be obtained at www.ICGtesting.com
Printed in the USA
LVOW11s0829300115

424913LV00003B/4/P